TO KILL HITLER

To Kill Hitler

The Officers' Plot
July 1944

CONSTANTINE
FITZGIBBON

SPA BOOKS

ISBN: 0–907590–48–9

Publishing History: This work was first published in 1956 under the title of *THE SHIRT OF NESSUS*. It was published in the United States first as *20 JULY* and then later (abridged) as *OFFICERS' PLOT TO KILL HITLER*. This edition reproduces the original work, complete and unabridged.

Published by SPA BOOKS LTD
              PO Box 47
              Stevenage
              Herts, UK
              SG2 8UH

Printed in Great Britain by The Bath Press

For
Nandl and Ilse
friends of many years

CONTENTS

ILLUSTRATIONS

INTRODUCTION

IN this book I have attempted, as best I can, to tell the story of July 20th, 1944, and of the events which led up to that day, in terms which I hope will interest British readers. There has been a great deal published on this subject in German, comparatively little in English. Owing to wartime propaganda, both German and British, many people still believe that what occurred was a sort of palace revolution, carried out by a small clique of reactionary Prussian officers interested in preserving the German Army against the next war. I hope that I may succeed in laying this ghostly fiction.

I am not a historian. My excuse for trespassing in fields not my own is that the events here described are perhaps not sufficiently remote, nor all the facts sufficiently revealed, to permit a strictly historical approach to what is still very much a contemporary event. I have relied almost entirely on published German documents, memoirs, articles and books, though a few persons have been kind enough to tell me of incidents hitherto unknown to me, while others, who were involved in the tragedy, have read my manuscript and have enabled me to correct any errors which they have detected. I acknowledge their help, and also the printed sources on which I have drawn.

There is therefore very little in this book that will be new to the expert. In consequence I have dispensed with footnotes, nor do I always give my source references, since for the reader who is not himself a historian the paraphernalia of research is sometimes more of a hindrance than a help.

My purpose in writing this book has been a simple one. I hope that it may be possible to interest people in what was, in some ways, the most remarkable incident of our generation.

Those are large words, but I use them deliberately. Our century has seen many horrors, and may well see many more. Perhaps the greatest horror of all, for it is the most fundamental, has been the individual's negation of responsibility in favour of the party, the movement, the ideology. In past ages this would have been accurately described as the selling of souls. Its results are plain to see. In the name of the people, few of whom are criminals, abominable crimes and follies have been and are being committed by other, often honourable, men, acting, as they believe, in the interests of a class or race or doctrine. The human element is subtracted, and with it the Divine, so that evil is left to flourish and propagate and devour. We have seen these ideologies, mistaking as they must the part for the whole, turn and rend our society, and almost destroy our values and our heritage of civilization, in their illusory gratification of temporary emotions and desires. The climax, so far as the Western World goes, came in Germany.

And it was in Germany that the group of men of whom I write, acting as men, as individuals who had examined their conscience, decided that since life was not intended to be lived in terms of comfort, torture, robbery, hatred and fear, they, as individuals, were prepared to risk their lives in an attempt to change the world about them. They were many, but it is of the few who were most directly concerned that I write in the pages which follow. They failed, and they are almost all dead, yet if their courage is remembered and understood, it will perhaps not have been in vain. Courage is a rare commodity, and should not be squandered through neglect.

POSTSCRIPT

I wrote this book some fifteen years ago. A little material relevant to the subject has since then come to light. There are one or two very minor errors of fact, as for example that the O.K.H. staff was lodged a couple of miles away from the O.K.W. For these and other such facts, which by reason of the printer's timetable I have not been able to incorporate into this new edition I would like to express my gratitude to General a. d. Warlimont who did me the kindness of reading the book and indeed who was himself in the bunker when the bomb went off. Secondly, I would like to express my gratitude to Graefin von der Schulenburg who has also recently re-read this book and who had no suggestions for alterations. I myself feel that I underestimated the vitally important role that her husband played in the attempt to save Germany's honour. Finally I would like to thank my close friend, Fr. von dem Bussche for all his help and encouragement over many years.

CHAPTER I

THE facts are remarkably well established. We know, as well as ever we are likely to, what happened on that particular Thursday morning, July 20th, 1944, at Hitler's headquarters among the birches and beeches and gloomy pines of East Prussia. The motives are, of course, much harder to disentangle, and the atmosphere is gone. But the facts are there.

Colonel Claus Count Schenk von Stauffenberg had got up very early in his house at Wannsee, a residential suburb on the western outskirts of Berlin. The staff car was coming for him at six o'clock. Dressing took him somewhat longer than it does most men, since he possessed only one hand, the left, and only three fingers of that, namely the thumb, index and middle fingers. This was the result of wounds sustained in Tunisia fifteen months before; at the same time he had lost his left eye and had suffered severe leg wounds. These latter had healed, and he could walk normally. He had taught himself painstakingly to write with his left hand and, with the help of his teeth, to dress himself. Indeed, he always insisted on doing this and laughingly refused all offers of help.

A little after six he got into the staff car, telling the driver to go first of all to the house of his adjutant, Lieutenant Werner von Haeften. Haeften was a remarkably handsome man of thirty-five, that is to say only two years younger than Stauffenberg, but unlike his chief and close personal friend he was not a professional soldier, which explains his comparatively low rank. Before the war he had been a Berlin businessman. In 1943, while commanding an infantry platoon on the Eastern Front, he too had been seriously wounded—his pelvis had been shattered—

which accounted for his seconding to the headquarters of the Reserve Army (the *Ersatzheer*) of which Colonel von Stauffenberg later became Chief of Staff. Now he jumped in, and the car drove on through Berlin to Rangsdorf airfield, three-quarters of an hour or so away. Werner von Haeften's brother Bernd accompanied them as far as the airport.

It was a fine and sunny morning. No doubt the three officers sat in silence; at least they did not discuss their proposed deed in the presence of the staff driver. Stauffenberg was at all times most careful not to inculpate men who, by reason of their position, could not join him of their own free will. This was not solely for reasons of security on Stauffenberg's part: indeed, as will be seen, the boldness with which, when he felt it necessary, he disclosed his plans to officers who were strangers to him was startling. On the other hand his soldier-servant, who was devoted to him and with whom his relationship was particularly close on account of Stauffenberg's physical infirmities, knew nothing of what his master was really up to. Certainly his batman would not have betrayed him. It is equally certain that Stauffenberg's reticence saved that man's life. Had he known anything at all he would later have been shot.

So they drove through Berlin in the early morning. There had been no raid the night before: Bomber Command had been over the Rhineland and Westphalia, cutting German communications with the Normandy front while simultaneously attacking German industry. But there had been plenty of large-scale raids on Berlin in the recent past. The staff car drove past many heaps of rubble and the sightless façades of bombed houses. Stauffenberg, looking out of the car window, his one hand on the brief-case beside him, must have thought that if he were to succeed today there would be no more air-raids, Berlin would not be utterly smashed. In the brief-case lay his weapon, his bomb, his *machine infernale*. In Werner von Haeften's brief-case there was a second bomb.

The bomb was of English origin and of very simple construction. It consisted of a slab of plastic high explosive. This was a putty-like substance which could be moulded into various shapes. It was designed primarily for acts of sabotage. The saboteur could wrap a slab of this plastic around, say, a girder in a bridge or attach it to an important piece of machinery in a factory. Its explosive powers were very great, but since it had no metal shell there was no fragmentation and its effects were purely those of blast. The British had supplied quite a lot of hexite to Germany's enemies in Poland, France and, to a much lesser extent, in Germany itself. The normal means of delivery was by air. The fuses which the R.A.F. also supplied were equally simple to use, being stuck into the plastic explosive by the agent. Fabian von Schlabrendorff, whose name will recur in this book, has described them as particularly ingenious, and goes on to say: 'There are three different settings: one detonated after ten minutes, the second after half an hour, and a third type after two hours. The fuse would thus be chosen according to the time at which the explosion was desired, and in burning made no noise of any kind. By simply nipping the neck of the fuse, a small glass globule was broken releasing a corrosive fluid. This acid bit into a wire which held back a spring and the striker. The wire once destroyed, the striker would decompress and detonate a cap that would explode the bomb.' The fuse that was stuck into the plastic explosive inside Stauffenberg's brief-case was of the ten-minute variety.

The bomb, however, was not a present from the British to Stauffenberg. The German Counter-Intelligence Service, the *Abwehr,* had collected a considerable quantity of these plastic slabs in the normal course of their anti-sabotage activities. The *Abwehr* contained many active anti-Nazis and was, indeed, for several years the practical centre of the German resistance move-ment. One of these *Abwehr* officers was Colonel Freiherr von Freytag-Loringhoven who had been involved in plans to assassi-nate Hitler since at least as early as 1942. Until late in 1943 he was chief *Abwehr* officer at Army Group Centre, after which he was transferred to central *Abwehr* headquarters as head of the military sub-section of *Abwehr* Section II, the section responsible for sabotage and special duties. In both posts he was thus in a position to obtain samples of this particular explosive and of these fuses, though of course not in unlimited quantities nor too frequently if he did not wish to attract attention. It was the only type of bomb available to the conspirators which combined in itself three essential characteristics: high explosive content, comparatively small bulk and malleability to enable disguise, and above all a silent, smokeless fuse.

Freytag-Loringhoven had supplied those explosives to friends and fellow-conspirators at Army Group Centre, on the Russian front. This headquarters was the most actively anti-Nazi of the military headquarters in the field, largely owing to the Army Group First General Staff Officer, Henning von Tresckow, who had made it his business to surround himself with men whose ideas corresponded to his own. He and his friends had in 1943 made more than one attempt to kill Hitler, but by the summer of that year it became apparent that Hitler would not again visit the headquarters of Army Group Centre, or indeed any other head-quarters if he could possibly avoid it. Therefore it was decided to hide the remaining stock of valuable explosives until a man be found who could and would carry a bomb into Hitler's presence and blow him up in his own almost impenetrable inner sanctum.

The stock of high explosives was therefore handed to a group of officers—Stieff, Klamroth, Kuhn and Hagen—who worked at the Army High Command (the O.K.H.) in the Organizational Department, of which General Stieff was the head. For some time Stieff kept them in his trunk, under his bed, at the O.K.H. headquarters in East Prussia. In late 1943, however, he went on leave. Fearing that his batman might examine the contents of his trunk during his absence, he suggested to Kuhn and Hagen that they bury the explosive in a patch of scrub between the barrack huts. This was done, but two members of the Army Secret Field Police, watching from afar, saw them at it. When the officers, whom they failed to identify, had gone, the policemen dug the parcel up again. But fortunately the *Abwehr* officer charged with investigating the business was himself a member of the conspiracy. He managed to prevent the Gestapo being called in. He also played on the vanity of the Army Chief of Staff, Colonel-General Zeitzler, and persuaded him that the bomb had been planted by a British agent who intended to return and blow up Zeitzler. In fact he thoroughly confused the whole investigation, which petered out when, a few weeks later, the O.K.H. followed Hitler to Berchtesgaden. During those weeks the Secret Field Police had constantly watched the patch of scrub, awaiting the return of the mythical Englishman. Luckily they did not do any more digging, or they would have discovered the draft plan for seizing power in East Prussia which Kuhn and Hagen had also buried nearby. During the years of the conspiracy there were many such nerve-racking moments, of which this was far from being the most acute. The strain under which these men lived for months and even years on end without cracking is one of the most astonishing aspects of the whole story.

Hagen was sent to Army Group Centre with the task of procuring the necessary ingredients for a new bomb, but there only German explosives and fuses were available. Therefore application had to be made once again to Freytag-Loringhoven who was able, not without difficulty, to obtain a new supply, apparently approximately four pounds together with at least two fuses. This was taken by Hagen to his chief, General Stieff, whose office was now—this was the spring of 1944—at Berchtesgaden. Stieff put it in his safe where it remained for some months, an uncomfortable little parcel to have behind one's desk. When at last Stauffenberg acquired access to Hitler and it was decided that he would perform the deed, the explosives were taken to him in Berlin. By now, July 20th, Stauffenberg was intimately acquainted with his explosive brief-case, for during the last ten days he had twice taken it to a Führer conference and been compelled to carry it away again.

It contained one kilogram of the explosive—more would have made the brief-case, in which were also numerous papers, suspiciously bulky, and even now it was so heavy that Stauffenberg dare not permit any stranger to carry it. Kuhn, an engineer officer, had decided that such a charge was absolutely certain to fulfil its purpose. It was inconceivable, even in the open air, that anyone within two or three yards of the explosion could survive. In an enclosed space, of course, the effect of the blast would be much greater. Kuhn had no doubt that the bomb would be effective. Like everybody else connected with the conspiracy he was well aware that his life, and more than his life, was at stake: he therefore certainly would not have expressed such an opinion without most careful thought. Furthermore, Tresckow and Schlabrendorff had carried out experiments with such bombs a year before, which confirmed this. Furthermore again, the conspirators had at their disposal the technical advice of the *Abwehr*, which provided additional confirmation. However, Stauffenberg had with him this second brief-case, Haeften's, containing an equal quantity of explosive. On the occasion of his two previous attempts he had also got his adjutant—then Klausing, since Haeften had been ill—to carry a spare bomb.

This is a minor mystery. Stauffenberg could hardly have lugged two heavy brief-cases into the conference hall: physically he was almost incapable of doing so: it would have aroused considerable suspicion: and, besides, he was assured that it was unnecessary. Perhaps he had hoped that his adjutant, Klausing or Haeften as the case might be, would be permitted to enter the conference room with him, though he must have known that this was most unlikely. Or, which seems a more probable explanation, he had feared lest the fuse fail—as it had failed once before when Schlabrendorff and Tresckow had completed a perfect plan for Hitler's assassination. Should this have happened, maybe he hoped that he would be able to re-enter the conference room with the second brief-case unnoticed by the guards. In any event, the second bomb was not taken into the room. Had it been, had two kilograms of the explosive been simultaneously detonated, there can be no question of doubt that everybody about that conference table would have been killed.

Such, then, was the bomb that lay beside him on the seat of the staff car as he and Haeften drove through Berlin to Rangsdorf. In his pocket was a little tool, which has been described as resembling a sugar tongs but which was, in fact, a pair of pliers. Berthold von Stauffenberg had encased the jaws of this instrument in rubber in order that they might grip more firmly. Claus needed this to break the capsule in the fuse. And it was the very fact of his needing it which made him in many ways the ideal man for planting the bomb. In view of his appalling wounds, it was almost impossible for him to do any man physical damage. He could not fire a revolver; he could not, alone, pull a fuse: it was therefore unlikely that Hitler's guards would suspect him of any intention to assassinate their master, since they must think him incapable of such a deed. But he had his little pair of tongs. He had practised over and over again. He could, if unobserved, open the brief-case and squeeze the capsule in a matter of seconds.

At Rangsdorf the aeroplane was waiting. It was now about

seven o'clock. The plane into which Stauffenberg and Haeften climbed was the military property of General Eduard Wagner, the Quartermaster-General of the German Army. General Wagner had been a convinced anti-Nazi since 1938, when he had been closely connected with Colonel-General Beck's first attempts to destroy the National Socialist government. By 1944 he was the most senior officer still on active service to be directly involved in the conspiracy. He had known Stauffenberg professionally for some considerable time. Indeed, when Stauffenberg was in hospital during the previous summer, Wagner had visited him there and had proposed that on recovery Stauffenberg be assigned to his office, a suggestion which had not appealed to the young colonel: the field of activities of the Quartermaster-General was too remote from the actual conduct of the war for him. During the months of detailed preparation which preceded the *coup d'état*, Wagner had worked closely with Stauffenberg and the others in building up throughout the German army a widespread network of officers prepared to seize control when the moment came. For this purpose, in a country where every telephone wire was likely to be tapped, every letter opened and therefore all arrangements had to be made by personal interview, his private aeroplane had proved invaluable. Now, since Stauffenberg was ostensibly going to East Prussia on official business, Wagner could lend it to him quite openly. It is highly appropriate that this should have been the plane which carried the bomb. The plane also bore two additional passengers, General Stieff—who had for so long guarded the explosives—and his adjutant.

It was a long flight, three or four hours depending on the wind, over the flat lands of northern Germany, the Prussian plain. Of Stauffenberg's two last flights with the bomb, on July 11th and July 15th, the first had been to Berchtesgaden, which is about the same distance from Berlin as Rastenburg. Stauffenberg had, it is believed, made one previous flight, with a bomb, to Rastenburg, back in December of 1943. On this occasion Hitler had cancelled the conference at the very last minute, when Stauffenberg was actually in the ante-room. Thus neither Rastenburg nor the bomb were new to Stauffenberg. What was new was his realization that this was the last chance.

Hitler's choice of headquarters, at least during the second half of the war, was erratic and emotional. He alternated between his home, at Berchtesgaden, and what he no doubt regarded as 'the field', enormously elaborate and expensive camps near Smolensk or Giessen or in East Prussia. Until nearly the end he avoided Berlin, his country's capital and communications centre. Apparently the sight of bombed buildings upset him. Also, it seems, the pressures of personality and of history distracted him: he preferred to be alone with his dreams of Ghengiz Khan and Frederick the Great. And so the whole vast apparatus of his immediate control was carted about Germany in a more or less haphazard manner. The reason for his return to Rastenburg, six days before July 20th, is characteristic.

Rastenburg had at this time almost nothing to recommend it. It was remote, uncomfortable, intensely depressing—Jodl described it as a cross between a concentration camp and a monastery—and far too close to the front. Already during the previous winter the 'Wolf's Lair', as it was bombastically called, had proved an inadequate installation and Hitler had ordered that it be enlarged and rebuilt. He had thereupon retired to Berchtesgaden, installing his large staff in cramped quarters at a somewhat lower altitude than himself. On June 23rd, before the rebuilding of the 'Wolf's Lair' was completed, the Russians launched their massive attack in the East, and almost immediately broke through Army Group Centre on a huge front. By the middle of July they were on the East Prussian border only a hundred miles or so from Rastenburg: the Chief of the General Staff, Zeitzler, had had a nervous breakdown and was in disgrace and out of action: Hitler was giving those violent and disastrous orders to hold at all points which were partially responsible for the failure of the German army to win a single major defensive battle on the Eastern Front after Stalingrad. Officers in the field who disobeyed or even argued were removed, degraded and sometimes shot. In the West Hitler's commanders, Rommel and Rundstedt, frankly informed their Commander-in-Chief that the war was lost. His fury and frenzy were beyond control, his control or anybody else's. At this point he learned, accidentally it appears, that the appropriate department of the staff having decided quite correctly that Rastenburg was no longer a suitable supreme headquarters, had begun to move its elaborate signals network to Zossen, near Berlin. This was the last straw: his very own staff officers were attempting to make him retreat, when he had laid down that there must be no retreat. With chaotic, screaming illogicality he ordered that his whole elaborate headquarters be moved immediately from Berchtesgaden back to Rastenburg. Mussolini, who was to meet him on the 20th, was casually informed that he must travel a further seven hundred miles. The enormous caravanserai set off.

Guderian, who took over as Chief of the Army General Staff, describes conditions as he found them there on July 21st. It is apparent that the events of the previous day were not primarily responsible for this state of affairs: 'I made my way to the office block assigned to the Chief of the Army General Staff, which was to be my place of work from now on. I found the office block empty. There was nobody to meet me. After looking through various rooms I eventually came upon a private soldier by the name of Riehl, sound asleep. I sent this splendid fellow off to find me an officer. . . . I then attempted to telephone the army groups in order to find out the situation at the front. There were three telephones in the Chief of Staff's office, and no way of telling what purpose each one served. I picked up the nearest one. A female voice answered. When I said my name she screamed and hung up on me. It took some time before I managed to calm down the switchboard operators sufficiently to secure the connection I wanted.'

Such, then, was the headquarters to which Stauffenberg was flying. But in one respect at least, its security arrangements, it was most efficiently and elaborately administered. These arrangements were in the hands of the S.S.

The aeroplane landed a little after ten o'clock. The camp commandant had sent a staff car which was waiting to take Stauffenberg and the others the odd ten miles to the 'Wolf's Lair'. Before leaving the airfield Haeften told the pilot that from twelve o'clock on he must be ready to take off at once. The drive lasted about a half-hour, the reason for its slowness being that there were no less than three separate check points before the innermost enclosure—*Sperrkreis I*—was reached. The first was at the gate through the main perimeter, a large circle of mine-fields and pillboxes, which lay some two miles from the second defensive ring: this was likewise mined and was also provided with an electrified barbed-wire entanglement. At both these points all cars were checked and the guards at the other points informed by telephone who was arriving or leaving. Eight hundred and eighty yards beyond the second checkpoint was the third, the so-called Officers' Guard. Here was the car park and the true camp began. Two hundred yards farther on was the small and most closely guarded compound of all, *Sperrkreis I*. This was encircled with a stout wire-mesh fence seven and a half feet high which was constantly patrolled day and night by S.S. guards and secret service men. It contained three buildings only, the *Lagebaracke*, 'Situation Hut' or map-room, Hitler's rein-forced living quarters, the *Führerbunker I*, and the large wooden kennel provided for his Alsatian bitch, Blondi, which he had been given by Bormann to cheer him up after Stalingrad and on which his limited powers of affection were centred. No member of the staff had a pass to *Sperrkreis I*, and even the most senior officers had on each visit to be provided either with a written pass or checked in by S.S.Oberführer Rattenhuber: if they were un-known to Rattenhuber, an enormous trigger-man, they were frequently, perhaps usually, searched for lethal weapons. How-ever, except for the officers attending the daily midday confer-ences, few persons ever had occasion to enter this holy-of-holies, where Hitler lived underground between bare concrete walls and heard little save his own endless monologues addressed to secretaries and Party yes-men. These daily military confer-ences—which were really a reading of reports by the senior officers and the pronouncing of orders by Hitler—were held in a reinforced bunker outside *Sperrkreis I*, on the not infrequent occasions when enemy aircraft were within bombing range.

When Stauffenberg's car reached the Officers' Guard post, the party separated. Stieff and his aide-de-camp made their way to their office. Stauffenberg and Haeften reported to the camp commandant and then, with the latter's adjutant, Captain von Moellendorf, walked across to the 'teahouse' for breakfast. After breakfast Stauffenberg left the two junior officers and visited General Fellgiebel with whom he had a short and important con-versation. General Fellgiebel was Chief Signals Officer of the German army. Though not, of course, directly in command of the signal corps installations at Rastenburg, his power over the men who did control them was considerable. He had a key part to play in the events planned for this day and was fully aware of what was expected of him.

The plan, in its bare essentials, was simple, as one would expect of any plan drawn up by such highly experienced staff officers. Once Hitler was dead Fellgiebel would neutralize the surviving Nazis of his entourage by cutting Rastenburg's communications with the outside world. Meanwhile in Berlin the conspirators would first gain control of the capital and then make use of the army's extensive signals network to issue the orders of the new government throughout Germany and occupied Europe. In Vienna, Paris, Prague and Oslo, at the headquarters of the army groups and of the district commands within Germany, men were awaiting the orders that had already been typed, and in some cases signed, in Berlin.

Fellgiebel too was ready, but it must be realized that he could not physically destroy the massive and multifarious signal installations. All he could do was to order his men to pass on nothing and this, of course, he could only do for so long as his men accepted his authority. Now he presumably told Stauffenberg that all was prepared and that for at least an hour or two Rastenburg would be isolated.

After leaving Fellgiebel, Stauffenberg called on General Buhle. Buhle represented the army on Hitler's supreme staff and so far as he was a political man he was a Nazi. He enjoyed Hitler's confidence—he was a colourless individual—and indeed it was Hitler's intention to appoint him Chief of the Army General Staff in succession to the unfortunate Zeitzler. He was deprived of, or perhaps spared, this problematical distinction by being wounded that very day when Stauffenberg's bomb exploded. Stauffenberg's visit to him was connected with official business.

The reason that Stauffenberg was at Rastenburg that morning was that he had to report on the setting up of new German infantry divisions. The Reserve Army was responsible, among other matters, for training and establishments. The detailed work connected with the latter was handled by the Chief of Staff of the Reserve Army, Stauffenberg, rather than by its commander, Colonel-General Fromm.   At this time, the summer of 1944, total mobilization was belatedly being enforced in the Reich, many new divisions were being formed, and this explains Stauffenberg's frequent visits to Führer conferences.   Incidentally, it also illuminates two aspects of Hitler's direction of the war.   First of all, it is hard to imagine any other Head of State wishing to see the Chief of Staff of the Reserve Army three times within nine days for the purpose of hearing about what was a comparatively minor matter.   These visits involved over twenty-four hours' travel for the officer in question in that short period. When it is considered how many senior officers were similarly forced to waste their time, one sees how Hitler's growing habit of meddling in petty details of military administration and tactics hampered the work of his soldiers.   Secondly, the very fact of setting up these new formations, which appeared in battle a few months later as *Volksgrenadier* or People's Grenadier divisions, is evidence of Hitler's wasteful methods.   At this time almost all the infantry divisions on the Eastern and Italian fronts were well below strength.   The logical course was to reinforce them with fresh recruits.   But Hitler preferred to set up new divisions.   As a result of this the cadres of the old divisions were largely wasted, administrative and supply problems were increased, and tradition, that invaluable quality of *esprit de corps*, sacrificed.   Stauffenberg and his fellow staff-officers were aware of this, and equally aware of Hitler's reasons.   In the first place, by this time, he actively disliked the traditions of the German army.   He wished those traditions and that army to be ultimately liquidated and replaced by a Nazi army.   The creation of People's Grenadier divisions—the name is significant—was a step in this direction: the refusal to reinforce regiments which proudly claimed direct descent from the old guards or infantry regiments of Imperial days is another—the future *élite* was to be the S.S. But there was a second and perhaps more personal reason. Hitler had risen to power on propaganda, that is to say on lies. Throughout his ignominious career he believed in the power of lies.   To have an army which in fact is two hundred divisions strong and so to number it that it appears to consist of three, four or even five hundred divisions is the lie in practice.   Hitler, by this wasteful and Potemkin-like act of deceit, perhaps hoped to fool his enemies, certainly wished and managed to fool himself. He could not of course fool his staff officers, who thus once again saw their country's dwindling military resources being squandered for the sake of a megalomaniac's ego. In the administrative field, this constant formation of new divisions was a very minor equivalent of Stalingrad or Tunisia in the strategic control of Hitler's war.

When Stauffenberg was discussing the People's Grenadier divisions with Buhle, he perhaps had to open his brief-case and consult one or two of the documents in it. It is said that the bomb was wrapped in a shirt. General von Thadden, the officer commanding the East Prussian military area, was also present in Buhle's office and with him Stauffenberg exchanged a few words concerning the contribution that the Reserve Army could make to the defence of that province against the impending Russian invasion. At a little after twelve Stauffenberg and Buhle walked across to Keitel's office. Stauffenberg hung up his cap and belt in an ante-room.

Keitel has since been subjected to the full glare of the principal Nuremberg trial. He emerged from it as a man in whom limited ambition had replaced soldierly honour and even human dignity. By constant kowtowing to Hitler over a period of ten years he achieved the rank of field-marshal and the reputation of a lackey. No order was too base for Keitel to pass on, always without protest; no loyalty too sacred for him to jettison it in the interests of the fount of power from which he derived his promotions, his medals and his income. He had no talent as a strategist and exerted no influence on the course of operations. But he did manage to administer the Armed Forces Supreme Command to Hitler's satisfaction. To compare him to a footman because of the rather feeble pun that was current upon his name (*Lakaitel*) is slightly to underestimate his functions: he was rather a sort of uniformed *maître d'hôtel*. His florid appearance and manner, which was obsequious to his seniors and hectoring to his juniors, would have well become the head waiter in an expensive and squalid night-club.

Stauffenberg gave Keitel a brief résumé of what he proposed to say at the forthcoming conference. Keitel told him that he must limit his remarks to the absolute minimum, since the conference would be one of short duration. Mussolini was expected at the nearby railway station at three o'clock. For this reason, too, only two dozen officers would be present. The conference would be held in the map-room inside *Sperrkreis I.* A few more remarks were exchanged, while Keitel glanced repeatedly at his watch, and just before 12.30 the four officers—Keitel, his adjutant, Buhle and Stauffenberg—left the office for the *Lagebaracke.*

On the way out Stauffenberg excused himself for a moment, remarking that he must pick up his cap and belt. He was gone for longer than seemed necessary and Keitel, standing outside in the sunshine and worrying lest they be late, re-entered the building and shouted at him from the entrance hall to hurry. Stauffenberg emerged almost immediately. As they walked across to the barrier around Hitler's quarters, Keitel offered to carry Stauffenberg's brief-case, but the latter smilingly declined this offer and a similar one from Keitel's adjutant.

While alone in the ante-room he had broken the capsule with his tongs. Nothing now could prevent the bomb exploding in ten minutes' time. Talking freely and without showing any evidence of strain, Stauffenberg accompanied Keitel past the guards and into the *Lagebaracke.* They were a few minutes late, the conference had begun, and for some three minutes the acid had been eating away at the wire which retained the firing pin.

The *Lagebaracke* has been described as a flimsy wooden building and the reason that the bomb failed to kill all those present has been blamed on this. However, it is not so. Nor is it true to say that it was an unfortunate chance that the conference was held here on this particular day. The *Lagebaracke* was specifically intended for these conferences: only when there was the risk of an air-raid did they take place in a sealed bunker. In this respect the story of 'divine providence' as put out by Hitler and his followers is a fabrication.

The *Lagebaracke* had originally been a large single-storey wooden building, of standard military design, equipped with the usual number of doors and windows which were also mass-produced. This type of hutment—anybody who has ever visited a military camp anywhere in the world has seen similar edifices—was known in the German army as a 'Speer Hut'. But during the previous winter, among the improvements carried out at Rastenburg while Hitler and his headquarters were away, almost all the wooden barracks had been reinforced with a concrete shell some eighteen inches thick encasing walls and roof alike. This concrete was sufficient to provide protection against incendiary and small fragmentation bombs. (At the same time the *bunkers* were also strengthened: their walls and roofs are said to have been of concrete no less than eighteen feet thick.) There was no alteration made to the windows and doors of the Speer barracks.

The actual conference hall inside the *Lagebaracke* was at the far end of the building and was oblong in shape, the shorter wall being some fifteen feet in length, the longer between thirty and thirty-five. The three outside walls had ten windows in all, while in the fourth there was a large double door which opened onto an entrance hall some eight yards long off which, on the one side, were a cloakroom and lavatories and, on the other, a room used by the telephonists. July 20th was a hot and indeed a sultry day: all the windows of the conference hall were open wide, and this undoubtedly did affect the intensity of the bomb blast.

The room was sparsely furnished. In the middle was a single, large table, eighteen feet long and five feet wide. In the centre of the long side of this table was Hitler's chair, in which he sat with his back to the door. The table was of heavy oak and instead of legs it was supported by two solid oaken planks or socles which ran almost the width of the table near either end. In front of Hitler's place the maps which he would wish to consult were laid in readiness, together with his magnifying glass. He was by this time extremely short-sighted, and since he regarded spectacles as unbecoming to a dictator he required this aid when examining small print. In a corner of the room behind and to the right of Hitler was the stenographer's table; another stenographer, Berger, was seated at the big table opposite and to the right of Hitler. The inside walls of the room were covered with white strawboard, as was the ceiling.

On the way through the entrance hall to the conference room Stauffenberg stopped and spoke to the sergeant-major in charge of the small telephone exchange. He said that he was expecting a call from his Berlin office and that it would contain matter which he needed for his report to Hitler: he was to be summoned the moment the call came through. Then he and Keitel went on into the conference hall.

They were, as Keitel had feared, late. Lieutenant General Heusinger, chief of operations and deputy Chief of Staff of the Army High Command, was reporting on the situation on the Russian front. He was standing immediately to the right of Hitler. (With the exception of the stenographers everyone was standing: a man leaning over a table will have the table-top against his thighs.) On Heusinger's right was the Air Force Chief of Staff, General Korten, and next to him Heusinger's chief staff officer, Colonel Brandt. Brandt was opposite one of the oaken supports of the big table. The remaining twenty-odd men present were, apart from Hitler's adjutants, senior officers of the army, navy, airforce and Waffen-S.S. There were no politicians in the room.

Hitler turned round and nodded as Keitel and Stauffenberg came in, returning their salute. Keitel interrupted Heusinger's report to explain why Stauffenberg was present and what he would be talking about. Hitler said that first he would like to finish hearing the report from the front. Keitel then moved across to his normal place on Hitler's left. Stauffenberg stepped up to the table, between Brandt and Korten, and placed his brief-case under the table, leaning it against the inside of the heavy oaken support. This was at approximately 12.37. Heusinger went on talking.

Stauffenberg slipped out. Brandt, moving closer to see the map more easily, kicked the brief-case. It was in his way, and leaning down he moved it to the far side of the oaken support: this support was thus between the bomb and Hitler. Keitel, in his role of master of ceremonies, was not particularly interested in what Heusinger had to say and glanced about to make sure that the next speaker, Stauffenberg, was ready. Not seeing him and recalling what Stauffenberg had said about a telephone call, he stepped outside and was told by the signals warrant officer that Stauffenberg had hurried out. Indeed at this moment Stauffenberg, who had already left *Sperrkreis I*, was standing, with Fellgiebel, outside the latter's office, smoking a cigarette, his eyes fixed on the *Lagebaracke*. A few yards away Stauffenberg's staff car was waiting, with Haeften already inside.

Keitel, presumably not knowing quite what to do, re-entered

the conference hall. Almost immediately, at 12.42, the bomb exploded.

Stauffenberg and Fellgiebel saw the explosion. It was, Stauffenberg later said, equivalent to a direct hit by a 150-milli-metre shell. The windows were blown out, the roof partially collapsed, there was the sound of men screaming. He was certain that nobody who had been inside that hut could live. Stauffenberg nodded to Fellgiebel who turned away into his office building: he would now inform the other members of the conspiracy, in Berlin, who would set the prepared machinery of insurrection in motion, while he cut off the 'Wolf's Lair' from the rest of the world. Stauffenberg, too, had scarcely begun his day's work; he threw away his cigarette, got into the staff car and drove off. It had begun.

CHAPTER II

IF it was difficult to enter the 'Wolf's Lair', it is readily imagined
how much harder it would be to leave it, particularly when the
dust of an explosion in Hitler's own quarters had not yet subsided.   Standing operational procedure here, as indeed at any
other such headquarters, demanded the immediate sealing of all
exits and entrances by the security forces.

This Stauffenberg discovered at once.   His car was held up
before it had travelled more than a few yards by the sentries of
the Officer's Guard, the innermost of the three rings.   Stauffenberg did not attempt to argue with the soldiers; he jumped out
and finding the officer on duty in the guardroom, asked that he be
permitted to telephone.   After a brief conversation he hung up,
saying:

'It's all right, I'm allowed through.'

This seems to have satisfied the junior officer, for the barrier
was swung back.   An entry was made in the guardroom log:

12.44 Colonel Stauffenberg passed through.

At the next gate the warrant officer in charge was more of a
stickler.   Here the orders for the alert had already been carried
out: the guards had been doubled, the *chevaux de frise* placed across
the road, and nobody at all was allowed in or out.   Stauffenberg
demanded that he be connected by telephone with the camp
commandant's adjutant.   This the warrant officer could not
refuse.   Stauffenberg said:

'Colonel Stauffenberg speaking.   I am at the East Gate.
You will remember that we breakfasted together this morning,
Captain.   On account of the explosion the guard won't let me
through the East Gate.   But I'm in a hurry.   Colonel-General
Fromm is waiting for me at the airstrip.'

This last statement was untrue: as will be seen, Colonel-General Fromm was in Berlin.

Stauffenberg replaced the receiver and said:

'You heard, Sergeant-Major. I'm allowed through.'

The warrant officer, however, was not satisfied, and insisted that he be given a direct order. He therefore rang through to Captain Moellendorf himself. Rittmeister von Moellendorf replied:

'He may pass.'

The *chevaux de frise* were drawn back and the car went through. Presumably the conscientious warrant officer telephoned to the guard post at the outermost ring, for here there was no delay.

The driver of the staff car has reported that Stauffenberg repeatedly urged him on to greater speed. Meanwhile, in the back, Haeften was dismantling the bomb in his brief-case, and tossing its component parts out of the window. The package of hexite was later discovered by the security forces. The staff car must indeed have travelled at a tremendous rate for it reached the airstrip a few minutes after one o'clock.

Stauffenberg's gamble had come off: nobody at the camp had yet thought to inform the airstrip authorities of what had happened and no special security measures had been imposed there. The pilot was ready, the engine of the aeroplane was turning over. Stauffenberg and Haeften hurried on board and the plane took off at once for Berlin. For the next three hours, perhaps the most vital hours of all, Stauffenberg was out of touch and incapable of action, for the plane had no wireless. He could only rely on his friends and accomplices carrying out their pre-arranged parts. During this long period of enforced and doubtless painful inactivity while the plane headed west and Germany slipped by with such apparent slowness down below, perhaps we might glance at Stauffenberg's past life and at the chain of events which was reaching its culmination on this day.

There are four or five scenes from his happy childhood which, fortuitously, have reached us. Of these two are connected with acting.

On one occasion he and his elder brother—Berthold, with whom he was linked by an affection unusual among brothers in its permanence and intensity—acted scenes from *Julius Caesar* in the drawing-room of his parents' home. Their father was Chamberlain at the pleasant little court of the King of Württemberg, in Stuttgart, and their home was in the old Renaissance palace. One of the scenes that the boys had chosen was that in which Lucius, Brutus' page, plays music to soothe his sleepless master's jangled nerves on the night before the battle. Berthold, Claus's senior by two years, was Brutus. *It must be by his death. . . . The abuse of greatness is when it disjoins remorse from power . . . think him as a serpent's egg which, hatched, would, as his kind, grow mischievous, and kill him. . . .* But Hitler was then an obscure political agitator whose name the boys had perhaps not even heard. The passage they acted on that domestic evening long ago was probably, almost certainly, chosen because it gave Claus the opportunity to play his 'cello, an instrument he deeply loved. (As a schoolboy he thought at one time of devoting his life to music.) In this same play, which the boys acted together in that cultured and aristocratic home, Berthold-Brutus said to Claus-Lucius: *I trouble thee too much, but thou art willing.* To which the boy replied: *It is my duty, sir.* Brutus said: *I should not urge thy duty past thy might; I know young bloods look for a time of rest.* And the boy answered, as the man might have answered nearly a quarter of a century later: *I have slept, my lord, already.*

And then we have another scene, this time from a school production of Schiller's *Wilhelm Tell,* a play which was to be banned by the Nazis and was neither read nor acted in the German schools for half a generation. A schoolmate recalls that Claus von Stauffenberg played Stauffacher, and spoke these words: 'No, there is a limit to a tyrant's might! When the oppressed can find no justice here below, when the burden becomes intolerable, then he will summon the courage to reach up to the heavens themselves and there grasp those eternal rights which are as unchangeable and indestructible as the stars in the sky. . . . We must defend the highest virtues against all and every power.'

Of course these incidents, particularly the second, are dusty accidents. In thousands of German schools, thousands of little boys quoted Stauffacher's lines each term; none other, in the nightmarish years ahead, reached up to stars in the sky with such easy courage. But then not many had been taught the values of literature by such a poet as Stefan George, the close friend and adviser of the Stauffenberg boys.

These two dramatic echoes, the voice of Shakespeare and that of Schiller sounding across the yet unfurnished stage, must not be overemphasized. Claus von Stauffenberg was not raised, like some nineteenth-century Russian or Serb, to be a tyrannicide. His childhood was a gay and cheerful time, his home a happy one, his years at school successful, for he was a brilliant boy.

The family of Stauffenberg—the castle from which they derived their name has long vanished—was a Swabian one which in the past had produced a Prince-Bishop of Constance as well as a Prince-Bishop of Bamberg. There are no famous soldiers of that name. But this is more than compensated for by Claus's maternal ancestry. His mother was born Countess Üxküll-Gyllenband; the Üxkülls were of Baltic extraction, coming from those provinces which, together with the Prussian east, were for centuries the embattled outpost of European civilization and were therefore destined to be the cradle of the German army. For several generations, however, her family too had resided in Swabia. Through her Claus von Stauffenberg was descended from Gneisenau, the architect of victory in the campaigns of 1814-1815, Blücher's Chief of Staff at Waterloo, and one of the most brilliant soldiers Germany has produced. Through his mother Stauffenberg was also related to the family of Yorck and thus to the almost equally celebrated General Yorck von Wartenburg who at Tauroggen in 1812 disobeyed orders, detached Prussia from its disastrous French alliance and opened the victorious War of Liberation against Napoleon. Claus von Stauffenberg was proud of his descent from Gneisenau, the co-founder of the German General Staff and colleague of Clausewitz, a man whose talents as an organizer and a diplomatist equalled his great gifts as a strategist and tactician.

Claus Philipp Count Schenk von Stauffenberg was born in 1907 and baptized a Roman Catholic. He took his religion seriously but easily, and among his friends there were to be several priests of his own age. His ability for making, and keeping, friends was one of his outstanding characteristics. He was open in manner, gay and frank.

When he was seventeen years old it was suggested to him that

33

he take charge of the local youth movement. Somebody told him that he could save 'the idea of the youth movement', but such was not Stauffenberg's style. He replied that he was not interested in ideas but only in human beings. Surely this is a remarkable statement for a boy of seventeen to make at any time, but all the more so in 'twenties Germany when the idolatry of the word had reached quite staggering proportions. He had, at a very early age, sensed the poison latent in all ideology, and this is perhaps what makes him so outstanding a figure in a century where human identity has been so blithely thrown away in favour of political machines and Gadarene movements: when he acted, he did so not as the member of a group or party or class but as a human being, as a healthy living man. His enemies, the masters of the Third Reich, were sick, deformed, insane creatures, the proper embodiments of a system whose only enduring monuments are the gas-chamber and the mass grave, paranoiac sadists such as Hitler, crazy, blood-drenched idealists such as Himmler, drunkards like Ley, megalomaniac dope-addicts like Goering, satyromaniacs like Heydrich and Goebbels, homosexuals like Roehm, hysterical buffoons like Ribbentrop. They were men, in that they walked on two feet, but more than that they were the embodiment of an idea, the idea which lurks in every revolutionary ideology that jealousy is a virtue, sickness the normal state of man, evil the reality and chaos the rightful order of the universe. Stauffenberg was a man *tout court*.

For instance, there was his laugh. A friend, who had not seen him for years, when travelling by train, recognized him through the closed door of a sleeping car on hearing that 'wonderful' laugh. Lieutenant von Hagen, when on trial, mentioned how Stauffenberg had laughed as he gave him the parcel of explosives, and added that Stauffenberg always laughed when he talked. Gaiety, health, intelligence, love of the arts, love of horses, physical beauty—he was an extremely handsome man—the tall young cavalry officer was nearly the exact opposite of that frigid, screaming, sexless egomaniac, 'the postman of chaos', as Stauffenberg's cousin, Hofacker, once described Hitler.

After abandoning music as a profession, he thought at one time of becoming an architect. But in 1926 he joined the army instead, as an officer candidate or ensign in the 17th, Bamberg,

Cavalry Regiment with which he had family connections. At that period of his life he was not very strong and he had to train quite intensively in order to pass his medical examination: the physical standard demanded of future officers in the 100,000-man army, where there were always far more applicants than commissions, was a very high one. A little over two years later he took his officer's examination, which he passed first among the candidates for commissions in his arm of the service. His next seven years were spent living the agreeable life of a junior cavalry officer in peacetime. He was a first-class horseman; at the Hanover Cavalry School he rode with the officers who were to form the team which won the 1936 Olympic games; he bought a filly from a farmer and trained her himself in *passage* and the other skills of the *haute école,* eventually winning a prize with her. But unlike most cavalry officers his interests ranged far beyond horses and military matters, though he took the latter seriously enough.

As the depression swept Germany, unemployment rose and revolution threatened from right and left alike. Like a large part of his class, in 1933, Claus von Stauffenberg regarded the Nazi victory as the least of three evils, for the alternatives seemed to be Communism or a continuation of the unworthy and inefficient Weimar republic. But unlike Fritz von der Schulenburg, who was destined also to play a major part in the events of July Twentieth, he was never a Nazi, nor even a Nazi sympathizer. As a soldier he was a-political. As a man with a Catholic, monarchist background he inevitably disapproved of Nazis methods and of their debased ideals.

The influence of Stefan George on young Stauffenberg's thought was also considerable. George's difficult poems are scarcely read outside Germany, and his point of view has, in consequence, been much misunderstood. His hatred of vulgarity was not a political emotion. His belief in order, which all artists must share, was irrelevant to the obvious political issues of the age. He loved loyalty, which he demanded and received from the circle about him. He dreamed of deeper and wider loyalties, but he was well aware of the evil seductiveness that false leaders can exert, and some of his finest poems deal with this terrible theme. He had nothing but contempt for the ostentatious braggadocio of Kaiser William II and his entourage. But he spoke of leadership, and therefore the Nazis attempted to claim him as their poet. His reply was to leave Germany as soon as they attained to power. He retired to Switzerland, refusing all the honours which they were prepared to offer him, and he died there a few months later.

Allowing for the difference of background, his point of view was not dissimilar from that of his contemporary, Yeats. In particular his poem, *The Anti-Christ,* which Claus von Stauffenberg frequently quoted during the last months of his life as an indictment of Hitler, finds a strangely exact echo in the Irish poet's *The Second Coming.* George told the young men about him that they were an *élite*, an aristocracy of talent, a group of modern καλοκαγαθοί. He expected them to behave as such, and when they fell below the high standard which he demanded of them, they lost his friendship at once. The Stauffenberg brothers retained it: indeed he nominated Berthold von Stauffenberg his heir.

Nevertheless, in 1933 a Nazi government did not seem, to Claus von Stauffenberg, the worst possible solution to Germany's complex problems. In this delusion, if delusion it be, he was not alone: German philosophers as diverse as Spengler and Karl Barth, foreign statesmen as varied as Churchill and Baldwin shared it with him. As a young officer he was, of course, glad to observe the increased respect which was now paid to the army.

In 1936 he was sent to the War Academy in Berlin, on an intensive two years course for candidates for the General Staff. It will be recalled that the existence of a German general staff had been forbidden by the terms of the Treaty of Versailles, a curious clause since the German army was allowed to exist and of course a staff is an essential component of any army. It continued to function, thinly camouflaged as the *Truppenamt,* until the military clauses of the Versailles treaty were denounced in 1935, when it resumed its true name. In this same year, the hundred and twenty-fifth anniversary of its first foundation, the War Academy was re-opened, with a speech by the Chief of the General Staff, General Beck. On this occasion Beck remarked: 'We need officers with sufficiently strong character and nerves to act according to the dictates of their reason.' The course which Stauffenberg attended was the second to be held : among the other officers present was Mertz von Quirnheim, whose character and nerves will be seen to have been equally strong, who became a close friend of Stauffenberg's, and who was to die with him on July 20th, 1944.

The years which Stauffenberg spent at the War Academy were those in which Seeckt's *Reichswehr* was transformed into Hitler's *Wehrmacht*. The rate of expansion was fantastic and, from the point of view of many senior officers, disastrous to the quality of the army: each infantry company was subdivided to provide five new companies, the twenty-one infantry regiments of the *Reichswehr* became one hundred and five : whereas in 1932 there had been forty-four generals on the active list, by 1939 there were four hundred. Nor was this all. During this same period Guderian and others began to create the armoured divisions, which with the advent of the *Luftwaffe* involved a major recasting of operational and tactical theory. This was carried out largely in opposition to the views of General Beck, the chief of staff. Beck's dislike of these innovations was not entirely military : he was fully aware of the changing nature of warfare. But he regarded it as folly to create a huge mechanized army without first securing the oil supplies which must be that army's life-blood. And, from a political point of view, he had even greater reasons for hesitation. Though firmly convinced that Germany must have an army strong enough to ensure her against attack by any combination of her enemies, he did not believe that it was safe or right to forge an offensive instrument for Hitler's use. Furthermore, the devotion of resources and man-power to the offensive arms must be at the expense of those defensive forces he was anxious to create.

This, in the broadest terms, was the atmosphere which Stauffenberg entered when he left his horses—the cavalry was in any case being mechanized—and began to train as a staff officer. Beck and his friends were fighting a losing battle to keep the army uncontaminated by Nazi infiltration. So far as the General Staff was concerned he was largely successful, but at a cost. He kept the General Staff small : in 1938, when Stauffenberg joined it, it counted only one hundred and eighty-seven officers.

Beck did his best to keep it homogeneous, and at this same date fifty of those officers were of noble blood as compared with an average of 10 per cent throughout the army as a whole. There was, in fact, to be no liquidation of quality. The price that had to be paid was that the General Staff officers were tremendously overworked. No longer could their staff appointments alternate with field commands, as in theory they were supposed to do, since there were not enough officers available for the staff jobs. The result of this was that many staff officers would spend years working in one particular branch, would become in fact skilled technicians in the field, say, of rail transport or mechanization, and would lose touch not only with the non-military world, but even with the army as a whole. When Hitler, who always hated the General Staff, sneered at it as an 'Intellectuals' Club' he was not talking complete nonsense.

But so long as Beck was there it maintained its traditions, and the spirit of Moltke, the great ascetic soldier-aesthete, reigned over it. Beck could not, however, create an instrument as powerful as the old Great General Staff had been. The principle of co-responsibility, by which a formation's chief of staff shared the responsibility with its commander, was anathema to the Nazis whose pyramidal leadership-principle was opposed in theory to any division of power. The General Staff in the Third Reich was never, until 1944, in the limelight. Moltke, Waldersee and Schlieffen had been great public figures: the Nazis saw to it that Beck remained almost unknown, and indeed from 1934 until his dismissal in 1938 Hitler only granted Beck one brief private interview.

Such then was the General Staff in which Stauffenberg took his place in 1938, a small group of brilliant men, overworked, led by a general deeply opposed to his government, grappling with the endless problems of creating a huge, new army equipped with new weapons and being trained in new tactics. From its one hundred and eighty-seven members must come, it seemed, the generals of tomorrow even as today's generals had served almost to a man in Hindenburg's and Seeckt's staffs of yesterday. Yet those men were out of touch with the spirit of the Germany they served and, increasingly, with the army of which they provided the kernel. It was not a happy state of affairs, and it is surely remarkable that they managed to do their work as well as they did.   That many of them became, in fact, mere skilled technicians is not surprising.   Stauffenberg, however, did not.

Already at the War Academy, Professor Elze, author of the classic work on Clausewitz and one of Ludendorff's sharpest critics, had noticed him and had described him as the man who might infuse a new spirit into the General Staff and overcome the one-sidedly military attitude of that organization.   Even as, when a boy, he had been recognized as the leader of any group in which he found himself, so now his contemporaries regarded him, without envy or hyperbole, as a probable future Chief of Staff.   General Koestring, a man not given to gush, spoke of him as 'the one German general staff officer with the qualities of genius, a worthy successor to Field-Marshals Moltke and Schlieffen.'

It is typical of him that he never seemed to work.   He always had time for everybody and everything.   Yet while only a student of the War Academy, he wrote a prize-winning paper entitled *Defence against Enemy Parachute Troops in the Home Area* which was still regarded as the basic study of this subject during the war, several years later.   He became an expert on mechanized and armoured warfare.   He passed the difficult Interpreter's Examination in English, which secured him a brief visit to England.   He read a great deal of history.   When at the end of the course the students visited the Rhineland to study the crossing of that river, Stauffenberg delivered an address on the history of the area, and on its destiny to become the main artery of Europe when the nation states shall at last have faded away.   A man who then heard him says that he spoke of the past, not in retrospect, but as one who had been there, who had himself participated in the unrolling of history.   He made the past as vivid as the present, which the past illuminates and explains.   His manner of speech on such occasions was, we are told, unusual: it was light and easy, clear yet never superficial, profound without being obscure.   Freiherr von Thüngen says this about him: 'The speed with which he worked was tremendous, his powers of concentration were like steel, he was as fresh late at night as in the early morning.   His nerves and his health, which he certainly never coddled, were enviable.'

On leaving the War Academy, in the summer of 1938, Captain von Stauffenberg was assigned to the 1st Light Division, which was at that time commanded by General Hoepner, as second general staff officer, or Ib, the officer responsible for logistical matters. He was with this division during the period of the Munich crisis, which also saw the departure of Beck. Hoepner's division, a mechanized cavalry division which later became the 6th Panzer, was cast for a most spectacular role in September of 1938, but one which it never had the opportunity to play.

Had war broken out over Czechoslovakia, it was the intention of General Beck and of the Army Group commander, General Witzleben, to arrest Hitler with the other Nazi leaders and put an end to the madness. The unit which was to have covered the Berlin operation was Hoepner's division, a fact of which Hoepner was of course aware. Did Stauffenberg know of this? It seems probable: in any event the atmosphere at Hoepner's headquarters can hardly have been a pro-Nazi one. And during this year, 1938, he was much preoccupied with the plans for an uprising once formulated by his ancestor, Gneisenau.

Certainly within a few months of Munich he was carrying on some very dangerous conversations. His division was at Wuppertal in the Rhineland, where he was visited by Fritz Count von der Schulenburg, and by his uncle, Nikolaus Count von Üxküll. They were both deeply shocked by the Jewish pogrom of November and by the icy menace of war. They told him that he must act to put an end to the shameful government and to prevent war: or, if he could not now act, he must secure as rapidly as possible a position from which he could. And they suggested that he be appointed adjutant to Brauchitsch, the Commander-in-Chief of the army. It is revealing that they should have approached the thirty-one-year-old captain of cavalry. Schulenburg was the deputy police president of Berlin, a former Nazi of the Strasser group who had reacted violently, and he had been involved in Beck's plans of the previous summer. His circle of acquaintances was very wide, and yet he turned to Stauffenberg.

But Stauffenberg refused to take any active steps. His reasons, as explained to another visitor during this same period, were that the army would not come out against Hitler. This friend, also horrified by the persecution of the Jews, had asked him whether there was no hope of military intervention: surely the generals at least must realize that more even than the fate of the Jews was now at stake? Stauffenberg replied that the new German army was the German masses in uniform and would behave as such. As for the senior generals, they had broken faith twice, once with their Emperor in 1918 and once with their traditions in 1934. Who, he said, could expect any deed of principle from men with such a past? Presumably the idea of tyrannicide had not yet seriously occurred to Stauffenberg.

And so the winter passed and the cataclysm drew nearer. Another friend who visited Stauffenberg in the spring of 1939 quotes him as saying: 'The fool is going to make war.' Stauffenberg went on to speak of the disastrous loss of life in 1914–1918, and to express his doubts whether Germany could continue to exist after two such blood-lettings in a single generation. In this mood did he go to war in September, still on the staff of the 6th Panzer Division.

But he enjoyed soldiering, as he enjoyed most aspects of living. Erwin Topf, who served in the same division, describes a conference at which supply problems were to be discussed.

> Stauffenberg, tall, slender and vivacious, a man of outstanding personal charm, received us with genuine, radiant amiability. He saw to it that everyone was given a glass of wine, a cigar or tobacco for his pipe. He told us the latest news, asked questions, digressed on subjects which seemed to have little bearing on our conference, retailed to us all the latest anecdotes current in our division from the reconnaissance battalion to the field bakery, jumped from subject to subject, interrupting each conversation in order to talk to and cross-question the latest arrival. Thus the time passed and none of our problems was solved until suddenly, quite informally and without any assumption of authority, he began to speak: 'Well now, in my opinion what we should do is this . . .' And with his left hand in his trouser pocket, his right holding his wine-glass, he walked thoughtfully up and down the room, stopping now here, now there, picking up the maps, issuing the supply orders in complete detail. . . .

During the French campaign he was still with the 6th Panzer. The speed of its advance—as part of Reinhardt's corps it fought its way from the German frontier to the outskirts of Dunkirk in eleven days—depended on the supply problems being well handled. And there can be no doubt that Stauffenberg found the spectacular victories of those hot, May days exciting and enjoyable. But he was not deceived by the appearance or even by the reality of victory. The conquest of France, he remarked at the time, would be pointless if it were not to result in friendship between that country and Germany. He was not intoxicated by the easy success of German arms: unlike many soldiers, he did not now believe that Germany could conquer the world. Furthermore, he was enough of a historian to remember that by a just and tactful peace after Sadowa, Prussia had made Austria her ally, whereas the injustices of the two Versailles treaties had led only to further hatred and new wars.

A victory, in Stauffenberg's opinion as expressed during the summer of 1940, was senseless unless something constructive were built upon it. The truly great soldiers have also always been great law-givers. But Hitler, of course, was no Charlemagne or Justinian, nor even a Napoleon. General Halder has reported a conversation which took place in his Paris office during the summer of that year, when Hitler was planning a huge triumphal parade down the Champs Élysées. Among the younger staff officers present, Stauffenberg and his friend Mertz von Quirnheim both spoke at some length. They drew a horrifying picture of a conqueror so lacking in sentiment and a sense of proportion that he must thereby become his country's doom. They went so far, even then at the apex of victory, as to say that if Hitler were incapable of mastering his lust for nihilistic power and his passion for cruel display, then he should be removed or, if necessary, killed. Generals Stülpnagel, Fellgiebel, Wagner and Colonel Tresckow were also present at this highly treasonable discussion, according to Halder. So much for the legend that Stauffenberg and his friends only turned against Hitler when the German army faced imminent defeat. What made him Hitler's enemy was the fact that Hitler abused the enormous faith which the German people had placed in him and misused the great power that had thereby been given him.

In the first days of June, before the battle of Dunkirk had begun, Stauffenberg was transferred from the 6th Panzer Division

to the Army High Command, the O.K.H.   Here he was assigned
to the Organizational Department, being put in charge of the
office entitled 'Peacetime Army'.   His job was long-range
planning, to decide what the future organization, weapons and
equipment of the German Army should be.   This naturally
involved a continual study of tactical and technical developments
at the front and he thus had occasion frequently to visit the
fighting troops.   A secondary duty which came his way from
time to time was to act as guide to foreign military missions, an
employment for which his tact and charm made him particularly
well-suited.

He remained with the O.K.H. for two and a half years until
February of 1943.   This headquarters was located at various
times in Belgium, at Fontainebleau, at Zossen near Berlin, in
East Prussia, at Vinnitsa in the Ukraine.   Meanwhile Stauffen-
berg's duties took him all over occupied Europe from Finland to
Greece, from the Crimea to the Channel coast.

During this period we have another picture of him at work,
again from the pen of Freiherr von Thüngen, whom Eberhard
Zeller quotes.   Thüngen, who had served in the 17th Cavalry
Regiment with Stauffenberg, was now also employed at the
O.K.H.

> I never opened Claus's door without finding him on the telephone.
> In front of him would be piles of papers, his left hand holding the
> telephone, in his right a pencil with which he annotated the docu-
> ments before him.   He would be speaking forcibly, laughing a lot
> (as he always did) or swearing (which he was also not slow to do)
> or giving orders or instructions.   At the same time he would be
> writing, either his big sprawling signature or brief, remarkably
> precise notes.   By his side would be the clerk who would take
> advantage of any pause in the general activity to snatch the annotated
> files, draft letters or memos (on which Stauffenberg never forgot to
> put the necessary, tedious bye-products of senior staff work: letter
> heading, addressee, subject matter).   Claus was one of those men
> who could do several tasks simultaneously with full concentration
> on each.   He was astonishingly competent at dealing with the flood
> of paper which passes over a staff officer's desk, being able to separate
> the significant from the irrelevant at a glance.   He expressed him-
> self most clearly, and his sharp comments, which always hit the nail
> exactly on the head, not infrequently embarrassed the man with

whom he was talking.   His natural good manners, the incomparable grace with which he addressed his elders, the ease and openness of his style towards his contemporaries, these were the external manifestations of Claus's great personality and they won him other men's respect and trust quite effortlessly.   What in most men is the external expression of personality—clothes—meant nothing to Claus: he was too preoccupied with major matters to give them a thought.

Another friend describes a summer's afternoon in Greece. Stauffenberg was able to take a few hours off, and they motored out to the seashore.   They found a sandy bay, but it was full of German soldiers, Alpine troops who had fought in Norway and in Greece, now swimming and playing handball, sunburned, naked young men.   For some time Stauffenberg stood there, silently looking down at them, and the soldiers saw the General Staff officer watching.   Then, with a wave of his hand, he turned away and he and his friend swam from another, deserted cove.

Again we see him in the Ukraine in 1942, visiting camps in which anti-communist formations of volunteers were being created from among Soviet Union nationals. Major von Stauffenberg, as he then was, was largely responsible for setting up these fighting units, and indeed he and his friend, Lt.-Col. Roenne, at that time head of the O.K.H. Intelligence Section 'Foreign Armies East', had inaugurated this policy without, it seems, Hitler's approval or even his knowledge.   Their primary motive was to counter the wicked and foolish programme of oppression with which Bormann, Koch and Rosenberg had befouled Germany's reputation in the occupied Eastern territories. These potentates used Russian man-power as coolie labour: the only alternative, in their brutish minds, being extermination. Stauffenberg arranged that homogeneous fighting units be set up, commanded by men of their own race, and he hoped thus to create a compact, well-trained and self-confident anti-communist Russian army.   He did not, of course, treat these soldiers as 'racial inferiors'.   And he was deservedly popular with them in consequence.   We have a description of him listening to a Cossack male choir: on another occasion a group of Russian soldiers danced in his honour before their camp fires.

Walter Goerlitz, in his *History of the German General Staff,* has suggested that there was a secondary motive on the part of the O.K.H. in setting up these voluntary units. The volunteers were objectors to the totalitarian methods of Stalinism. The responsible staff officers of the O.K.H. were objectors to the totalitarianism of Hitlerite Germany. It seems most unlikely that Roenne and Stauffenberg should have contemplated the overthrow of the German government, or even of local government, by means of Russian troops. On the other hand, were there to be a *putsch* in Germany, with perhaps a period of chaos in the occupied territories, it would clearly be to the advantage of the new government to have a body of trained Russian troops who could ensure a modicum of order in the East. Such an army, too, might provide the basis for a sensible settlement in the East if—as still seemed possible in 1942—the Germans were to conquer Russia. If there were by then an anti-Nazi German government, this army would be of great help in re-creating Russo-German friendship: if the Nazis were still in power, it would be a useful card to play against the murderous policy of the gauleiters.

(These anti-communist volunteers—later on others were simply conscripted from the prison camps into the German army—had a sad fate. Most of them were taken prisoner by the Western Allies in 1944 and 1945. The Russian authorities demanded that they be handed over. The Americans did so, well aware of what was in store for their prisoners, and the trees in the forests on the Russian side of the zonal border were soon laden with the bodies of hanged men. The British were frequently more humane and many of their Soviet prisoners were officially declared to be 'Poles'. These can often be met with working in the English countryside today, tragic, silent, lonely figures who will never see their homes or families again.)

Soon the Stalingrad battle was to rule out any possibility of German victory, and at this time we know for sure that Stauffenberg was actively plotting for Hitler's overthrow. The occasion was to be the so-called 'Field-Marshals' Strike'.

The idea of the senior army officers acting as a group had long appealed to such men as Beck and the ex-ambassador, Hassell. Stauffenberg's opinion of the generals has already been given, and it was largely justified. But now, with the Sixth Army surrounded and ordered by Hitler to commit suicide, there seemed once again a chance of rousing the marshals from their political lethargy. The plan was this. Paulus, the Sixth Army commander, should disobey orders and break out of the Russian encirclement, westwards. This would be the signal for the Field-Marshals in the East, Küchler, Kluge and Manstein, to make a concerted approach to Hitler, demanding his immediate withdrawal from the military direction of the war. Should this démarche succeed, and it was difficult then to see how even Hitler could successfully resist a concerted demand by his Field-Marshals, political results were sure to follow. Should Hitler refuse, then the Field-Marshals would find themselves in a position which compelled them to act.

It was, in fact, a golden opportunity and its exploitation depended on two men, Manstein who commanded the southern army group and was at that time Germany's most successful and distinguished soldier, and Paulus. Kluge, in command of Army Group Centre, was already morally more or less under the thumb of his first operations officer, Tresckow, one of the most implacable and determined anti-Nazi officers. Küchler, who had Army Group North, was a less important figure. But neither Paulus nor Manstein would act, though the former seems to have considered doing so quite seriously, and had Manstein agreed, Paulus would probably have done so too.

Stauffenberg went to see Manstein on behalf of the conspirators and outlined the plan to him. This was in December of 1942. Manstein's reply to the young major's arguments was curious. He said that he sympathized with the motives behind the proposed action, that it was a sensible plan, but that he could not act against Hitler or even threaten him without superior orders. After all he, Manstein, was a soldier and as such he acted only on orders from above. But above him were only five men, or rather one man who held five positions: Hitler was by then Commander-in-Chief of the Army, Commander-in-Chief of the Armed Forces, War Minister, Chancellor and President. Therefore what Manstein in fact said was that he could only act against Hitler on Hitler's orders.

Was this irony? Possibly. But still, if someone were to give

Manstein orders . . . The train of thought is obvious. Only the Field-Marshals could remove Hitler without first killing him. This they refused to do. But if Hitler were no longer there, then the Field-Marshals would accept orders from his successor. No doubt Stauffenberg pondered this on the long, disappointed flight back to the Army High Command.

Meanwhile, with the failure of the Field-Marshals' Strike, the atmosphere of the O.K.H. had become utterly depressed and depressing. Tresckow, at Army Group Centre, had by now decided that he would do his best to kill Hitler as soon as possible and by any means. Stauffenberg, who was not aware of these plans, felt that he could no longer bear the endless disillusions of life at the O.K.H. He asked that he be sent to the front. He was appointed chief operations officer, Ia, of the 10th Panzer Division, and early in February he was in Tunisia.

He arrived during the last stages of the battle of the Kasserine Gap, in which his division was heavily engaged. It remained constantly in action until the end of the Tunisian campaign, but by then Stauffenberg was back in Germany.

For on April 7th the car in which he was travelling was shot up by low-flying aircraft and he received those wounds which left him with only three fingers and one eye. Indeed for some time he did not know whether he would see again at all, and not until the bandages about his head were removed in Carthage hospital could he be sure that he was not henceforth totally blind.

He was brought by sea and rail to Munich where he was on the danger list for several weeks. Professor Sauerbruch, the celebrated surgeon, whose son was a friend of Stauffenberg's, arranged that the case be treated by Dr. Lebsche. These weeks of immobility and pain in Munich hospital were Stauffenberg's period of decision. For the first time in his life he now had ample opportunity to examine his conscience and to decide what to do with that life which had been so remarkably spared.

And soon enough he began to recover. A multitude of friends came to see him—others sent presents from almost every corner of Europe—and his visitors noticed in him a new determination, what one of them has described as a radiance of purpose and an inner energy surpassing even what he had revealed before being wounded. In late April he was already writing to General

47

Olbricht, the head of the Army General Office, that he expected to be fit again within three months. By early May he was learning how to write with the three fingers of his bandaged left hand. Later that summer, when Lebsche suggested making him an artificial arm, Stauffenberg declined: this would have involved several more weeks of hospitalization, and he knew that he could not spare the time. For he had decided what must be done, and he knew that he himself must do it.

His wife, the Countess Nina, who was the mother of his four little children, has said that once when she visited him in hospital he remarked to her, almost casually:

'You know, I feel I must do something now, to save Germany. We General Staff officers must all accept our share of the responsibility.'

He knew the dangers to which he was exposing not only himself but also his family. But he had made up his mind. Henceforth his life was to be devoted to a single purpose, the salvation of his country. When at last his broken body was free of surgical dressings, he put upon it the shirt of Nessus which once on can never be removed.

CHAPTER III

THE phrase is Tresckow's, pronounced early in the morning of July 21st, 1944, a few hours before Tresckow, knowing that the plot had failed and fearful lest under torture he betray his friends, took his own life:

'God once promised to spare Sodom should there be found ten just men in the city. He will, I trust, spare Germany because of what we have done, and not destroy her. None of us can complain of his lot. Whoever joined the resistance movement put on the shirt of Nessus. The worth of a man is certain only if he is prepared to sacrifice his life for his convictions.'

Tresckow's photograph shows us a serious but far from humourless face, a high, broad forehead, deep-set and penetrating eyes, a firm, Roman nose above a strong mouth and chin. It is the face of a man who is sure of himself and of his standards, a relaxed and yet a thoughtful man. Bernd von Kleist, who knew him well for a quarter of a century, has ascribed these qualities to his friend: God-fearing, loyal, moral, modest, respectful of tradition, possessing a strong sense of duty. These were the virtues which the Prussian military aristocracy admired. They also, of course, respected brains and courage.

Tresckow sprang from the heart of that tradition. The men of his family had been soldiers since the Middle Ages. An ancestor had won military glory in the Seven Years' War and from then on there was almost always a General von Tresckow in the Prussian and Imperial German army list. He had also married into that same tradition: Tresckow's father-in-law, General von Falkenhayn, had been Chief of the Great General Staff during part of the First World War.

Henning von Tresckow, born at Magdeburg in 1901, was

49

commissioned in the 1st Regiment of Foot Guards and served as a platoon commander on the Western Front in 1918. During the years of revolution and smothered civil war he was with the *Reichswehr*, but in the early twenties he resigned his commission and became for a few years a very successful stockbroker and banker. Like the Anglo-Irish, whom in some ways they closely resemble, the Prussian landowning and military families had lost a great deal of money as a result of the decline in agricultural prosperity during the late nineteenth and early twentieth centuries. In many families the alternatives were to make money in business or to lose their estates. Henning von Tresckow made money and saved his home, Wartenberg.

Having done so, he rejoined his old regiment, now the 9th Infantry, being specially recommended by Hindenburg himself. In 1932 he was selected for training as a General Staff officer and during the last three years of peace he served with the O.K.H. He was one of Beck's men, whose ideas and ideals he shared. The events of 1938 turned him from a non-political soldier into a convinced and determined anti-Nazi. He was one of the officers at the O.K.H. responsible for the elaborate staff planning which might well have led to the overthrow of the Nazi régime had there been no Munich pact.

He served on the staff of an infantry division during the Polish campaign, with Rundstedt's army group during the French campaign, and in the early summer of 1941 was appointed first staff officer of the army group which Field-Marshal von Bock was to command in Russia. Thanks to Tresckow, the headquarters of Army Group Centre became one of the most important and active centres of anti-Nazi activity in the German army.

Shortly before the opening of the Russian campaign Keitel issued Hitler's notorious 'Commissar Order', according to which captured commissars were to be shot. Another order, simultaneously issued, gave an even clearer idea of how the war in Russia was to be waged: this stated that in the event of crimes being committed by a German soldier against Russian nationals, the soldier was not to be court-martialled automatically, but only at the discretion of his unit commander. Tresckow immediately realized the full implications of these two criminal orders, and went at once to see Field-Marshal von Bock. On the way there he remarked to his friend Freiherr von Gersdorff, the intelligence officer who was accompanying him:

'Gersdorff, remember this moment. If we fail to convince the Field-Marshal that he must act, that he must fly to Hitler's headquarters at once and that he must insist on resigning his command unless those orders are cancelled, then we shall have lost the war and the German army its honour.'

To Bock, who was Tresckow's brother-in-law, he said, using the familiar second person singular:

'You must get in touch with the other army group commanders immediately. The best thing would be for you to go with them and together present Hitler with an ultimatum.'

Bock answered that this could lead only to his dismissal. Tresckow, 'his eyes blazing' according to Gersdorff, replied:

'At least then you will have made an honourable exit from the stage of history.'

But of course it came to nothing. Bock sent a written protest and did no more than try to arrange that the beastliness within his army group be kept to a minimum. Throughout the next eighteen months Tresckow was constantly attempting to persuade Bock and his successor, Kluge, that they must act. But though both Field-Marshals disapproved of the Nazis and their methods, neither was prepared to take the initiative. Tresckow therefore decided, some time during the summer of 1942, that he and his friends must kill Hitler. The conspirators in Berlin, of whom Generals Oster, the deputy chief of the *Abwehr*, and Olbricht, of the Home Army, were the most important, were fully involved. There were several attempts on Hitler's life for which Tresckow was primarily responsible.

Fabian von Schlabrendorff, who was closely connected with these attempts, has described them in his book *Officers Against Hitler*:

All the threads of the conspiracy were gathered in the hands of Oster, who in the meantime had been promoted to the rank of General. It was he who reported all matters of importance to the head of the movement, General Beck, and who received in return Beck's instructions. It was his task also, conjointly with General Olbricht, chief of the *Heeresamt* on the staff of the commander of the home army, to prepare all measures to capture Berlin and other important German cities. Olbricht and Oster were the two men who conceived and worked out the first serious plans for seizing power at home. They then looked round for some man in the army who would be in the right position to provide the 'flash' by assassinating Hitler. This man they took to be Henning von Tresckow.

Oster and Tresckow never met or talked to each other. It was one of my responsibilities to act as link between them and to keep this contact unbroken. Only one who lived in Germany during the war can appreciate what extreme precautions had to be observed to prevent a premature discovery of our plans by the Gestapo. All intercourse not strictly necessary was avoided, and even between intimates the names of persons connected with the plot were never mentioned. The anxiety that the Gestapo might be spying upon and shadowing us, was a paralysing weight, accompanying us by day and robbing us of our sleep at night. To shake it off required considerable strength of will.

At the last meeting between Olbricht and Tresckow, towards the end of 1942, Olbricht asked for eight more weeks to perfect the plans for seizing power in Berlin, Cologne, Munich and Vienna. At the expiration of this period, that is by the end of February, 1943, I was charged by Tresckow to have another talk with Olbricht; and it was then that he spoke the memorable words: 'We are ready; it is time for the flash.'

To elucidate all details and avoid any possible friction in the sequence of events, one more meeting was imperative between our circle at the eastern front and our confederates in Berlin. This time the talks did not, as before, take place in Berlin, but in Smolensk at the headquarters of the Central Army Group on the Russian front. For that purpose, Admiral Canaris organized a service flight from Berlin to Smolensk. He arrived at our headquarters accompanied by many officers of his staff. To cover his real intentions, he had summoned a large meeting of intelligence officers.

The decisive talk, however, took place far from the bustle, in a modest room used by the officer in charge of the war diary. Here at a late hour of the night Tresckow, Dohnanyi and I met, and Tresckow informed Dohnanyi of our intention to attempt the assassination of Hitler in the near future. He made sure of the state of preparations in Berlin, and we explored and co-ordinated ways and means of communication, agreeing on a code that only those immediately concerned could understand. Then we separated.

In the meantime Tresckow had redoubled his efforts with the

Commander of our Army Group, Field-Marshal von Kluge, to win him over to the idea of doing away with Hitler. It seemed essential that Kluge, as Commander-in-Chief, should support the insurrection from the outset, as thus he might exercise decisive pressure upon hesitant commanding generals at the front, as well as upon those of the home army.

At the same time, Tresckow was busy preparing 'Operation Flash'. This required that Hitler should leave his headquarters in East Prussia for a visit to the staff of our army group, which was then quartered in a forest camp near Smolensk. We wanted to lure Hitler to unfamiliar surroundings, where we would have the advantage over him. To induce Hitler to pay such a visit was a most difficult undertaking, as he lived in an atmosphere of deep suspicion and refused to leave his heavily guarded headquarters except in answer to impulses of his own.

For this purpose Tresckow made use of a long-standing acquaintance with Hitler's chief aide-de-camp, General Schmundt. He suggested to him that he should persuade Hitler to visit our headquarters. Schmundt was a firm believer in Hitler, but he was not intelligent enough to perceive that Tresckow's request was a trap.

So it came about that Hitler announced his intention to visit Kluge in Smolensk early in March, 1943. But Hitler ran true to form and cancelled his visit shortly before the fixed date. The visit, in fact, had been arranged and postponed several times before Hitler at last arrived by air, on the 13th of March, 1943. Had the Field-Marshal then been ready to take action the tyrant would have been destroyed. With Kluge's consent, the assassination of Hitler would have been easier, particularly as Lieutenant-Colonel Freiherr von Boeselager, the commander of a cavalry regiment stationed at the headquarters of our army group, was in the plot. The officers of this regiment had been carefully selected for our purpose, and Boeselager combined in his person soldierly efficiency with boundless audacity.

But Kluge, although he recognized the right course, had not the strength of will to follow it. He kept raising objections, saying that neither the German people nor the German soldier would understand such an act at that time and that we ought to wait until unfavourable military developments made the elimination of Hitler an evident necessity.

Kluge's attitude made it impossible for us to use for our revolt the channels of the military command, which the Central Army Group provided. For this reason, Tresckow and I decided to take matters into our own hands. We hoped that, once the deed was done, Kluge would accept a *fait accompli* and follow his fundamentally sound convictions. To make it easier for him and for the Army Group Command, Tresckow and I planned the following course: We would not shoot Hitler, but would eliminate him during a flight by smuggling a delayed-action bomb into his aeroplane. The appearance of an air accident would avoid the political disadvantages of a murder; for in those days Hitler still had many adherents who, in the event of his assassination, would have put up a forceful resistance to our revolt.

Tresckow had procured the material necessary to carry out the attempt some months before through Colonel Freiherr von Gersdorff, who was second staff officer of our army group, as gay a comrade as he was an accomplished and courageous soldier. His military position enabled him to obtain explosives without causing suspicion. At that time Gersdorff had not yet been informed of our plans, but we felt enough confidence in him to have no misgivings about asking him to provide the explosives that we needed.

The explosive supplied was of the same sort, with the same fuse, as that which Stauffenberg used the next year at Rastenburg. Schlabrendorff describes the lengthy and detailed study which he and Tresckow made of this explosive and these fuses, calculating the power of the former and the effect on the latter of the extremely low temperatures prevalent in Russia which delayed the action of the acid upon the wire.

Having successfully concluded our experiments, we undertook the more immediate preparations. To make doubly sure, we took not one but two explosive bodies and made one parcel of them which by its shape seemed to contain two ordinary bottles. We had to do the packing in such a way that it was possible, without damaging the covering, to set the fuse in motion by hand. On the 13th of March I took this parcel and locked it in a steel chest accessible only to myself.

Meanwhile Kluge and Tresckow drove to Smolensk airfield and waited for Hitler to arrive. He appeared with his usual large escort, including his doctor and his cook. In the meantime I had rung up Captain Ludwig Gehre, our contact man, in Berlin and had given him the code word that signalled the imminence of the attempt. He transmitted the code word to General Oster, who passed it on to General Olbricht. It was these two men who had made the final preparations for the seizure of power in Germany.

The meeting with Hitler took place in Field-Marshal Kluge's personal quarters. As he entered the office, Hitler laid down the peculiar military-style cap he always wore. I had always been curious about this cap. Now, with no one watching, I impulsively reached to pick it up and have a look. I was startled to find it heavy as a cannon ball. On examination, I saw why. Our dauntless dictator, who professed to be beloved by all Germans, had his cap lined with fully three and a half pounds of protective plate.

Tresckow, as well as the commanders of the armies forming the Central Army Group, were present at the meeting. It might have been possible to introduce the time bomb into the conference room. But by striking here we would have killed not only Hitler, but also Field-Marshal von Kluge and the army commanders. Thus we would have destroyed the military apparatus which we planned to use for our revolt once Hitler had been killed. After the conference there was a dinner in the officers' mess. The same consideration applied here: the bomb would have eliminated not only Hitler but men whom we needed badly for carrying through our plans.

As was his custom, Hitler touched only food specially prepared by the cook he had brought with him, and it had to be tasted before his eyes by his physician, Professor Morell. The proceedings reminded me of an oriental despot.

Hitler at table was a revolting sight. His left hand he kept poised upon his thigh, while with his right hand he shovelled his food, a diet of all sorts of vegetables, into his mouth. But he did so without lifting his hand to his mouth, keeping his right arm flat on the table and bringing his mouth down to his food. Between bites he consumed different non-alcoholic drinks set by his plate. Beforehand, the officers had been notified that there was to be no smoking after the meal.

During lunch Tresckow approached Colonel Brandt, one of Hitler's staff officers, and asked him whether he would oblige him by taking back to headquarters a small parcel containing two bottles of brandy for one of Tresckow's friends, General Helmuth Stieff. Colonel Brandt agreed.

After lunch, Hitler accompanied by Kluge and Tresckow, returned by car to his aircraft, while I took the time bomb and drove with it in another car to the airfield. Hitler and his escort had used two big aeroplanes for their trip. Hitler sat in one with the persons belonging to his immediate entourage, while in the other the rest of his escort were accommodated. The two aeroplanes were accompanied by several fighter aircraft.

Having arrived at the airfield, I waited until Hitler had dismissed the assembled officers of the Central Army Group, and when I saw that he was boarding the plane I started the fuse of the bomb. The detonator was set, as it were, in the neck of the bottles and the parcel had been so wrapped that I could get hold of it through a small chink in the paper. To make sure that the pressure on the fuse would be strong enough I kept a key hidden in my hand, and with it I dinted the fuse. The bomb was timed to explode within half an hour. At a sign from Tresckow, I handed the parcel to Colonel Brandt, the officer of Hitler's staff who had promised to take it with him to supreme headquarters. It required some self-control to remain calm at that moment. Shortly afterwards Brandt stepped into Hitler's plane, and both aircraft with their fighter escort started in the direction of East Prussia. Hitler seemed to be doomed!

In tense excitement we returned to headquarters. I immediately rang up Gehre in Berlin and gave him the next code word, which meant that the fuse had been started. It was known to us that Hitler's plane had a special security arrangement: it was divided into several sealed-off cabins. That of Hitler was armour-plated and had a contrivance for descent by parachute. We had calculated, however, that the explosive charge in the bombs was sufficient to blow up the whole plane, including the armoured compartment. Even if that should not happen, such damage would be done that the armoured compartment was bound to crash with the rest.

The explosion could be expected to happen shortly before Hitler's plane would reach Minsk in White Russia. We supposed that the first news of the accident would be sent in a radio message from one of the accompanying fighters. Our excitement during the period of expectation was acute; but nothing happened.

After more than two hours of waiting, the shattering news arrived that Hitler had landed safely on Rastenburg airfield in East Prussia, and had reached his headquarters. There was no longer any doubt that the attempt which we had so carefully prepared had been in vain.

We did not know the cause of our failure. I immediately rang up Gehre in Berlin and passed to him the code word that the attempt had miscarried. Then Tresckow and I consulted as to what action to take next. We were deeply shaken. It was serious enough that the attempt had not succeeded, but even worse would be the discovery of the bomb, which would unfailingly lead to our detection and the death of a large number of our confederates.

After considerable reflection Tresckow resolved to ring up Colonel Brandt, at Hitler's headquarters, and ask him whether the parcel for General Stieff had already been delivered or whether it was still with him. Colonel Brandt replied that the parcel was still in his keeping. This gave us hope that the bomb had not been discovered. We had to prevent its being delivered to General Stieff, all the more so as he was not one of our number. So Tresckow asked Colonel Brandt not to deliver the parcel, but to keep it for a day, adding that there had been some mistake. I would call on him the following day to exchange the parcel, as I had anyway to go on official business to supreme headquarters in East Prussia.

On some military pretext, I flew to headquarters with the regular courier plane. I called on Colonel Brandt and exchanged a parcel containing this time two genuine bottles of brandy for the one containing the bomb.

I can still recall my concern when Brandt, unaware of what he held, smilingly handed me the parcel and gave it a jerk that made me fear a belated action. Feigning a composure that I did not at all feel, I took the parcel, immediately got into a car and drove to the neighbouring railway junction of Korschen.

From Korschen a sleeper train left for Berlin in the evening. I got into a reserved compartment, locked the door, and with a razor blade opened the packet. Having stripped the cover I could see that both explosive charges were unaltered. With care I dismantled the bomb and took out the detonator. When I examined it, I found to my great surprise what had happened. The fuse had worked; the glass globule had broken; the corrosive fluid had consumed the retainer wire; the striker had operated; but—the detonator cap had not reacted.

I felt both disappointment and relief, disappointment that a singular misfortune had frustrated our attempt; relief, because I could hope that we had managed to avoid discovery of our conspiracy.

This was Tresckow's second attempt. The first had been on the occasion of an earlier visit by the dictator to Army Group Centre, when Tresckow had tried to insert a bomb in the side-pocket of the car which was to carry Hitler from the airfield to headquarters. The car, however, had been too closely supervised for Tresckow to be able even to approach it. Meanwhile owing to the influence which Tresckow exercised over the unfortunate Schmundt, Hitler's adjutant and head of the Personnel Department of the O.K.H.—Schmundt was eventually killed by Stauffenberg's bomb—he had arranged that Colonel Schultze-Büttger be appointed Manstein's first staff officer at Army Group

South.   This arrangement was made because Hitler was about to visit that army group, and Schultze-Büttger was prepared to kill him.   Once again it came to nothing.

The next attempt, which also took place in March 1943, a few days after the 'brandy bottles', was carried out by Colonel von Gersdorff himself.   He survived the war, and has described what happened in these words, which are quoted by Dr. Pechel:

Army Group Centre had arranged an exhibition of war pictures, models, et cetera in the Berlin *Zeughaus* or Arsenal.   A few days before, General Schmundt had informed us that it was Hitler's intention to open this exhibition as part of the celebrations of Heroes' Memorial Day.   Since Goering and Himmler, as heads of the Luftwaffe and of the S.S., were to be present at these celebrations, this was a chance which would never recur.   The exhibition having been organized by my department, it was particularly suitable that I be sent to Berlin.   In reply to Tresckow's question I said that I was prepared to undertake the assassination attempt.   At the last moment Field-Marshal von Kluge, who was not as yet fully informed of our intentions, expressed a desire that his wife attend the opening of the exhibition: what is more, at this juncture we had no ten-minute fuses available.   The first difficulty was solved by Tresckow who talked the Field-Marshal out of sending his wife; the second was dealt with by Schlabrendorff who, following in a second plane, delivered the fuses to me in the Hotel Eden, in Berlin.   I had flown with Field-Marshal Model, who was to represent Field-Marshal von Kluge.   In Berlin I was informed by General Schmundt of Hitler's programme.   After making a speech in the glass-roofed courtyard of the *Zeughaus* he proposed to spend about half an hour examining the exhibits in the company of a small group which would include Goering, Keitel, Himmler, Dönitz and their adjutants: then he would take the salute at the traditional march past of the 'Honour Battalion'.   At first Schmundt did not wish me to be present; it required all my powers of persuasion to make him change his mind, in which effort I was supported by the unwitting Field-Marshal Model.   Schmundt imparted to us, as a top secret, that the time officially announced for the ceremony and the inspection would be altered by several hours immediately before it was due to begin.   When he told us what the true time would be, he certainly did not dream that he was thus helping a would-be assassin.   Such a procedure is, incidentally, significant of the security measures which were deemed necessary to protect the head of the state.

I examined the condition of the *Zeughaus* and was convinced that the assassination could only be carried out during the walk through the exhibition. In the courtyard the arrangements had not yet been completed. The orator's podium stood alone and bare, so that there was no chance of secreting a bomb here, let alone of touching off its fuse. The most vital factor was that the tour of the exhibition should last *at least twenty minutes,* since the temperature of the un-heated halls was only a few degrees above freezing point and I must therefore assume that the (ten minute) fuse would take between fifteen and twenty minutes to work. Another consideration was the great height of the halls which would limit the blast effect. Tresckow had told me that I was to avail myself of any favourable opportunity which offered a 100% chance of success. In the event that an attempt were definitely to be made, he planned to send a preliminary warning to all those who were in the plot: I was therefore to meet Schlabrendorff on the preceding evening at the Hotel Eden and tell him what the prospects were. I told him that I was determined to do it, during the tour of the exhibition, but that the conditions which I have mentioned above must exist. Whether the warning was sent out or not, I do not know.

The next day I carried in each of my overcoat pockets a bomb with a ten-minute fuse. I intended to stay as close to Hitler as I could, so that he at least would be blown to pieces by the explosion. When Hitler, with Goering, Dönitz, Himmler, Field-Marshal von Bock and three or four adjutants entered the exhibition halls, Schmundt came across to me and said that only eight or ten minutes were to be spent on inspecting the exhibits. So the possibility of carrying out the assassination no longer existed, since even if the temperature had been normal the fuse needed at least ten minutes. This last minute change of schedule, which was typical of Hitler's subtle security methods, had once again saved him his life.

Tresckow who was listening to the broadcast of the ceremonies on his radio in Smolensk, a stop-watch in his hand, knew that the plan could not be carried out when, only eight minutes after Hitler had entered the exhibition hall, the announcer reported that he had left the *Zeughaus*.

These were the two attempts made by the group of men about Tresckow which came nearest to success. Other plans were dis-cussed. These included a mass shooting of Hitler by a group of staff officers: an attack on his headquarters by the cavalry regi-ment commanded by Boeselager: a *coup de main* by this same regiment when Hitler was visiting Army Group Centre. But none of these got beyond the discussion stage. Meanwhile many critics have wondered why one of the conspirators did not at some point or other simply draw his revolver and shoot Hitler dead.

Psychologically it is, of course, extremely difficult to shoot a man in cold blood. Boeselager, for instance, categorically refused to do so, though quite prepared to lead a military operation which would result in Hitler's death. There were, however, several other officers who were not so squeamish. But here at least three major difficulties arose. First of all, none of these officers ever had regular access to Hitler; though some of them saw him occasionally. Secondly, it was by no means easy for any officer to carry a revolver into Hitler's presence. Had an officer concealed a small pistol in, say, his trouser pocket, he might have managed to have a single shot at Hitler, but it would only have been one. Hitler's bodyguard of S.S. men, led by the formidable Rattenhuber, were very wide awake indeed and extremely quick on the draw. Since the conspirators could not risk a failure which probably would have exposed the whole conspiracy, everything would have depended on this single bullet, fired very rapidly in conditions of great tension. Few men are sufficiently expert with a revolver to guarantee hitting a man-size target even at comparatively short range without first taking aim. The chances of killing Hitler, even if he were hit, were not good, since it was known that he usually wore a bullet-proof waistcoat. No, the chances of killing so well guarded and suspicious a man were not as many nor as easy as some of the subsequent critics have implied. The conspirators decided at quite an early stage that the bomb was the only possible weapon offering any reasonable hope of success.

After the failure of the two attempts in March of 1943, it became apparent to the conspirators that the bomb would probably have to be carried into Hitler's own headquarters, which from then on he only very seldom left. Meanwhile, in the same spring of 1943, the whole German resistance movement suffered a blow which might well have shattered it. This was the dismissal of General Oster and the virtual break-up of the *Abwehr*.

The role of the *Abwehr*, the German intelligence and counter-intelligence service, in the years from 1933 to 1943 is extremely important and very complicated. Its head, Admiral Canaris, was a consummate master at covering up his tracks and confusing his opponents, to the extent that even today a man like Dr. Paul Leverkühn, who worked with him closely, has maintained in his book, *German Military Intelligence,* that Canaris was never involved in the conspiracy nor ever wittingly allowed his organization to be used by the conspirators in their attempts to establish contact with the Allies. On the other hand, men, equally well or better informed, have also asserted exactly the contrary. The truth would seem to be that Canaris, engaged in a duel of wits with the British, American and Russian intelligence services and simultaneously fighting the Nazi Party intelligence service, the *Sicherheitsdienst,* gave at least his benevolent protection to men within his own organization who were actively engaged in plans to overthrow the government and to ensure a victory for the Western Allies. Of these Hans Oster was the leader, concerning whose activities and beliefs there can be no doubt whatsoever.

Oster was older than either Stauffenberg or Tresckow, having been born in 1888. His father was a Lutheran clergyman, of Alsatian extraction but with a living in Saxony, and he himself went to school in Dresden, later joining a Saxon artillery regiment. He served throughout the First World War, being highly decorated for gallantry before his transfer to the General Staff in 1917. Like Stauffenberg, he had as a boy shown a great love of music, and he, too, had played the 'cello, that thoughtful instrument. Another passion that he shared with the younger man was for horses. It is indeed curious how many of these officers were exceptionally keen horsemen, particularly when one remembers that Hitler nourished a pathological hatred of those animals. For Hitler horses were simply another symbol of the landed gentry which, as a product of the Vienna slums, he envied and would destroy, and he forbade the keeping of horses by his entourage. General Fellgiebel, the signals officer with whom Stauffenberg spoke at Rastenburg on the morning of July 20th, successfully defied this order throughout most of the war, listing his hunter as a draught-horse: no doubt Hitler would not have recognized the deception, had he seen the animal.

After the First World War, Oster continued as a staff officer in the *Reichswehr.* He was in Dresden during the revolutionary period and observed the Communist riots. He was present when an infuriated mob seized the Saxon Minister for War, himself a working-class man, and drowned him in the River Elbe. It was a scene he never forgot. By inclination and upbringing he was a monarchist: by reason and sympathy he inclined towards socialism. During the years of the great depression he pinned his hopes on the much misunderstood General Schleicher, who would have ordered the *Reichswehr* to suppress both Nazism and Communism alike before using the authority of the army to bring about those essential changes to the German economy and German society which Weimar democracy had proved incapable of carrying out. Meanwhile Oster was a personal friend of Goerdeler, the conservative Mayor of Leipzig, and of Kaiser, the Christian trade unionist leader.

When he joined the *Abwehr*, Colonel von Bredow, one of Schleicher's closest collaborators and like Schleicher a convinced anti-Nazi, was its head. Bredow, with Schleicher, was murdered by S.S. men on June 30th, 1934. From then on Oster's activities were devoted to a single aim, the overthrow of the National-Socialist government.

For this purpose the *Abwehr* provided in many ways the ideal cover, so long as Canaris, who took over its command in 1935, was prepared to resist encroachment by the Nazi secret service. Not only did it possess its own network of agents and means of communication within Germany, which was of vital importance in the fight against the totalitarian methods of a police state where every letter was liable to interception and every telephone conversation might be tapped: it was also able to send men abroad, both before and during war, while its technical branch could provide explosives, false papers and all the other gadgets needed by spies, saboteurs and conspirators alike. The *Abwehr* central office was constantly in touch with all the senior military head-quarters: since it was, administratively, directly under the Supreme Command of the Armed Forces—it was an inter-service organiza-tion—it was almost beyond supervision: and as by the nature of its true work it was automatically shrouded in mystery, nobody was surprised to see some very odd and unexpected people going in and out of Oster's office.

It will be recalled that early in 1938 a false charge of homosexuality was levelled against the Commander-in-Chief of the Army, Colonel-General von Fritsch, with the purpose of removing an officer who was insufficiently malleable for Hitler's taste and of weakening the army's position *vis-à-vis* the Party. Oster made it his business to discover the sordid truth behind this slanderous attack on an honourable man and, having done so, laid the result of his findings before General Beck, the Chief of the General Staff. This was a revelation to Beck and to various other senior officers, removing once and for all what few illusions they may still have cherished about the type of men now governing Germany. Oster's action in the Fritsch affair was thus of importance in preparing the ground for the proposed Beck-Goerdeler-Witzleben-Hoepner *putsch* which was foiled by the Munich pact, plans in which, of course, Oster was fully involved. He kept a dossier of Nazi crimes and made it his business to see that few senior officers could plead ignorance of what was happening in Dachau and Buchenwald and, later, in Poland and the other occupied territories. During those years, by means of his contacts with the police, he was repeatedly able to warn men that their arrest was imminent and to provide them with papers which would enable them to disappear.

The part he played in the dealings of the German resistance with the Western Allies was even more spectacular. With his knowledge, the leaders of the German resistance sent Freiherr von Schlabrendorff to London, with the mission—which he accomplished—of informing Winston Churchill and Lord Lloyd of Hitler's plans to invade Poland. Oster was so certain that Nazi Germany must not be allowed to win the war that he deliberately revealed the plan for the occupation of Norway to the Norwegian government. He told the Dutch military attaché, Major now General Sas, of the proposed operations in the West, giving the exact date on which Holland and Belgium would be invaded. So complete was the information, that the Dutch intelligence service—and apparently the British one too—decided that it must be a plant: at least no action was taken. Through Dr. Josef Müller, the *Abwehr* man in the Vatican, Oster and his friends were in almost standing contact with the British during the first two years of the war. He arranged other contacts via Madrid, Berne and Stockholm, which will be described later.

But it must now be stated that these contacts were sadly and singularly unproductive. The responsibility for this lay partly with the German conspirators and partly with the Western Allies, in particular Britain. The German pre-war opposition had not in general created a good impression in London even among men who at no time favoured appeasement of the Nazis. For one thing, it did not present a tidy and homogeneous front: it did not, in fact, resemble a political party. Then certain self-styled members of the German opposition, such as Schacht, were believed or known to be carrying reinsurance in Berlin. After Munich many Germans, who sincerely loathed Hitler and his ways, lost all faith in the Western statesmen and peoples who had so apparently preferred dishonour to danger. Some of these men now decided that there was no choice save to make the best of the tyranny at home, and the strength of the opposition declined. It was reinforced by disgust at the anti-semitic atrocities which followed Munich, but the new recruits did not look to the seemingly decadent democracies for help, as had their seniors. In the period preceding the war spokesmen for the opposition sometimes claimed far more backing in Germany than actually existed. For example, in 1938 Goerdeler stated that Brauchitsch was an anti-Nazi and implied that he could speak for the Commander-in-Chief of the Army. When Brauchitsch heard this, and learned that Hitler had also been informed, he was not unnaturally furious that his name should be used in so casual and dangerous a fashion, and promptly denied the statement. Incidents of this sort made a very painful impression abroad and served to strengthen the hand of those who, like Lord Vansittart, maintained that there was in fact no opposition worth mentioning inside Germany. In brief, the voices of the German opposition, as heard in London, struck a cacophonous note.

The voices of the *émigrés* were far better attuned. These men and women, almost always unfortunate and in most cases admirable, counted among their numbers a very high proportion of persons with left-wing views. The Communists were the most vocal, the most disciplined and therefore the most clearly heard. If the influence of the Beck-Goerdeler opposition group within Germany was slight during 1939, that of the *émigrés* was for all intents and purposes nil. On the other hand the in-

Claus Count Schenk von Stauffenberg.
Sculpture by Frank Mehnert,
1929

(Foto-Werkstatte Ingeborg Limmer)

Field Marshal Hans von Kluge
(Paul Popper Ltd.)

Major-General Henning von
Tresckow

fluence that these left-wing representatives of Weimar Germany exerted in London and later in Washington was considerable. Inevitably perhaps, they still tended to see the struggle within Germany in the discredited terms of right versus left, with Hitler, the army, the churches and the civil service lumped incongruously together as the 'right', while the Socialists, Communists and Trade Unionists formed the virtuous 'left'. In order to fit their antiquated and doctrinaire version of history, the overthrow of the Nazis could only be engineered by this 'left'. And since the really active opposition derived from what they called the 'right', they distrusted it. They, and their fellows in the West who viewed the world through the same blinkers, persuaded the Allies to treat the German opposition with the greatest caution.

In the early months of the war, the Chamberlain government was prepared, in a half-hearted sort of way, to talk to the men who represented civilized and Christian values within Germany, but of course opinion against all Germans, as Germans, was hardening. Once France had been defeated, almost all these tenuous links were deliberately cut by London. The story of these abortive contacts is clearly and admirably related by John Wheeler-Bennett in his book, *The Nemesis of Power*. Henceforth the Foreign Office, now headed by Anthony Eden, seems to have been interested in such contacts only for purposes of espionage.

In 1942 the German opposition, and particularly the *Abwehr* group, made renewed and sincere attempts to re-establish touch with, and gain support from, Britain and the United States. The United States government sent Allen Dulles to Switzerland, and, to judge by his book, proceeded to ignore the information he sent home. British diplomacy had meanwhile apparently become paralysed by a most remarkable fear of the Soviets. The Foreign Office had reason to believe that at least one of its links with the German opposition was being tapped by the Russians. It also knew that the Russians were attempting, in 1942 and 1943, to negotiate a separate peace with Germany. The Foreign Office therefore feared to encourage the pro-Western and anti-totalitarian opposition within Germany lest this reach Stalin's ears and be used as a pretext for a new Nazi-Communist pact. The logic is odd, and only comprehensible in terms of the atmosphere of the day. Even at that time, though, did the British diplomats really believe that Stalin was influenced in making major decisions by such trivial considerations as these? Perhaps when the Foreign Office files are at last made available, a generation or so hence, British policy in this matter will seem less frivolous than it does at present.

By the spring of 1943 Oster had apparently given up hope of obtaining any help, or even a clear statement of post-war aims, from London or Washington. Western diplomacy was already imprisoned, in its dealings with the enemy, within the strait-jacket of the unconditional surrender slogan that had so delighted Stalin. Other Germans, as will be shown, refused to believe that Britain and America could really be so blind to Russia's obvious intentions, and continued in their attempts to gain support from the West. They failed, as will later be seen. Meanwhile, let us return to the development of the anti-Nazi conspiracy within Germany, during the early stages of the war.

At home in Germany, while the *Abwehr* provided a good cover for the conspiracy and the Beck-Goerdeler team an excellent nucleus for a post-Nazi government, one vital element for the success of the plan was lacking, namely a force strong enough to transform the will of the conspirators into reality. There was only one quarter from which this force could come and that was the army. Ideally, what was needed was a body of soldiers strong enough to overcome the S.S. and other armed Nazi troops so that the danger of civil war, abhorrent to all, would be im-mediately smothered. Oster and Beck therefore set about look-ing for such a private army.

In 1938 they had had one, in Witzleben's army group. In 1939, during the Polish campaign, they again thought to have one in the army which Hammerstein commanded on the lower Rhine: had Hitler come within Hammerstein's reach there can be little doubt that he would have been arrested and probably shot. Then Hammerstein was retired. The next plan, worked out during the winter of 1939–40, involved the use of reliable divi-sions which were to be halted in and about Berlin, while in transit from Poland to the West. A special section of the General Staff, under Colonel Groscurth, was formed to work out the details and General Olbricht, now at the headquarters of the

Home Army, was among those involved. But this plan again came to nothing, largely owing to the refusal of any senior general with command powers to accept the responsibility for issuing the necessary orders. An exception was General Hoepner. Professor Gerhard Ritter, in *Goerdeler und die Deutsche Widerstandsbewegung,* quotes a private letter to himself from Halder. Halder states that in March of 1940 Hoepner, then commanding a Panzer Corps at Düsseldorf, announced his willingness to carry out a *coup,* and if need be assassinate the dictator, provided he could be assured of Brauchitsch's and Halder's support. It may be assumed that Halder could not speak for the Commander-in-Chief of the Army.

During the good years for the German army, from the summer of 1940 to the winter of 1941–42, Beck and Oster had no greater success in convincing any of the generals who was in a position to act that he should do so. (And Hammerstein expressed his contempt for those generals to Dr. Pechel in the phrase: 'Dr. Pechel, these men have turned me, an old soldier, into an anti-militarist.') With the opening of the Russian war, an entirely new state of affairs arose. The bulk of the German army was now fully engaged, and the conspirators would not have ordered it to face about, even had they been able to do so, for it was no part of their plan that Germany should be conquered by Russia and a brown dictatorship replaced by a red one. Therefore they now looked to those divisions which were stationed in France— from 1941 on there were almost no divisions stationed in the Reich proper. The commander in France was Field-Marshal von Witzleben, and in January of 1942 he agreed to use his army group against the government. The time chosen for the invasion of Germany by a German army was to be the summer of 1942, when the second German offensive in the East should have started and the Eastern armies be therefore not available for immediate counter-action should their commanders obey the orders which Hitler's headquarters would presumably issue. Unfortunately before this happened Witzleben was retired, and Rundstedt, who succeeded him, was not prepared at any time to play the part of a General Monk.

So now only one source of military strength remained available to Oster and his friends, the *Ersatzheer* or Home Army, a disparate collection of training schools, demonstration units, depot troops and guard battalions. This army was an army in name only, not in any way comparable to the armies beyond the frontiers, lacking in homogeneity and generally neither equipped, trained nor organized as a fighting force. It consisted of small groups of men scattered throughout Germany and administered by the twenty *Wehrkreise* or Area Commands. It was in many places outnumbered by troops of the Waffen-S.S. Among this diverse collection of rear area troops there were always a few first-class fighting units, usually of battalion strength, but these were at all times liable for transfer to the front. It was not, in fact, much of a weapon in the hands of the conspirators, even if they succeeded in gaining control of it. And it was commanded by General Fromm, who though certainly not a convinced Nazi, was very far from being the sort of man who would risk his neck.

Nevertheless the very fact that it was scattered across Germany made the Home Army a desirable weapon for the conspirators since they could hope, with its help, to gain control of some if not all of the more important centres of population. Its command network was the only alternative to those of the government and of the party. Therefore once the possibility of using the occupying army in France had vanished, Oster, Goerdeler and Beck concentrated on winning the *Ersatzheer*. They had there an invaluable ally in General Olbricht, who was head of the General Army Office and, after Fromm, the most senior officer at the headquarters of the Home Army. But Olbricht again was only a staff officer and, unlike Fromm, had no command powers over troops.

Olbricht, who had commanded a division during the Polish campaign, was a Saxon and a deeply religious man. He was, it seems, a quiet, pleasant, efficient and extremely discreet one, slight of build and in appearance more like a man of letters or a scientist than a soldier. During the summer of 1942 he had several meetings with Goerdeler. At one of these at least Tresckow was present, and Olbricht then promised to build up, within the Home Army, an organization capable of seizing control of Berlin and of the great provincial cities the moment that Hitler had been killed. It will be recalled that late in 1942

Olbricht had asked Tresckow for eight more weeks in which to perfect his plans.

During this period he was still struggling to win over Fromm, even as Tresckow was trying with Kluge and had tried with Bock. But neither Olbricht nor any of the other men whom Olbricht introduced to Fromm could persuade the latter to commit himself. The most that they could get out of him was a half-promise that in the event of Hitler being out of the way, he would be prepared to deal with the men who would then take over. This attitude, so similar to Manstein's when approached by Stauffenberg a few months later, was the best that Olbricht could manage. Had the bomb gone off in the aeroplane, or had Hitler spent a further twelve minutes inspecting the exhibition at the *Zeughaus,* Olbricht was ready.

But these two failures were only the prelude to a further major set-back and disaster. Early in 1942 a man named Beppo Römer had been arrested. Römer, who was on the fringe of the military conspiracy, was a former *Freikorps* leader who had long been attempting to assassinate Hitler; he had done two spells in Dachau. At this time he was attempting to establish relations with the remnants of the German Communist Party, fell into the hands of a blackmailer and was betrayed. He talked under torture; one hundred and twenty persons lost their lives in consequence. The Gestapo's investigations continued, though at a curious dilatory pace which would perhaps indicate obstruction in high places, and gradually it became clear that certain threads led towards the centre of the *Abwehr* itself. However the men who knew most, Halem and Mumm von Schwarzenstein, kept silent despite torture, and for the moment the group within the *Abwehr* was safe. It was only a respite.

Oster's closest collaborator was Hans von Dohnanyi, a lawyer who had worked in the Ministry of Justice from 1929 to 1938 and who had availed himself of the knowledge there acquired to give Oster the material on which much of his dossier of Nazi crimes was based. Oster took him into the *Abwehr* at the beginning of the war. Later the Gestapo was to describe Dohnanyi as the 'originator and spiritual leader of the movement to remove the Führer'. Certainly he was deep in every conspiracy from the very beginning, including that of 1938, that of

Army Group Centre and the many attempts to contact the Allies. So, too, were his life-long friends, Claus and Dietrich Bonhoeffer (who were also his brothers-in-law), Justus Delbrück and Ernst von Harnack. Dietrich Bonhoeffer was the eminent theologian who visited Stockholm and asked Dr. Bell, the Bishop of Chichester, to arrange a link between the conspirators and the British government. (Bonhoeffer had been pastor of the German Lutheran Church in London before the war.) Though Dr. Bell was able to give the Foreign Secretary full plans and names, Mr. Anthony Eden showed no interest in the matter. Bonhoeffer's attitude was as uncompromising as Dohnanyi's and Oster's. In 1941, in Geneva, he had said at a secret church meeting: 'I pray for the defeat of my nation. Only in defeat can we atone for the terrible crimes we have committed against the world.' The reasoning which had brought this brilliant man to such a conclusion, was largely shared by the other members of the group within the *Abwehr*.

Early in 1943 the Gestapo came upon a breach of the currency regulations. Dohnanyi was ostensibly responsible—the funds were to be used by members of the conspiracy and by fugitives abroad—and he was arrested in April, as were Dietrich Bonhoeffer and Josef Müller who from his *Abwehr* post within the Vatican had also attempted to establish a solid contact with the British. It was touch and go that Oster was not himself arrested. However he was able, for the time being, to hide all incriminating papers which he could not destroy, and since neither Dohnanyi nor Bonhoeffer nor Müller talked, he was simply dismissed. He retired to a suburb of Leipzig, where he was under constant Gestapo supervision and therefore unapproachable to the conspirators. In December of that year he was placed on the inactive list. By then Canaris, too, was under grave suspicion, his battle against Himmler and Kaltenbrunner (the head of the *Sicherheitsdienst*) had been lost, and the *Abwehr* was being incorporated into the S.D.

And so the brain centre and driving force of the German military resistance movement was neutralized. Tresckow, who curiously enough had never met Oster, immediately realized the full implications of his dismissal and the arrest of the others. He applied for two months' sick-leave, pleading nervous exhaustion.

It was granted him; instead of resting he went straight to Berlin to see what could be saved from the wreck, and what steps should now be taken. He had many and long conversations with the various leaders there. What was needed was a man of drive, courage and personality to replace Oster at the centre of the movement. It was decided, at what exact point is not clear but it must have been early in the summer, that Stauffenberg was the man and the Home Army the place.

Olbricht, who had learned to know Stauffenberg well during the previous year, asked that he be appointed his Chief of Staff. Stauffenberg, in his hospital bed, agreed, fully aware of what he was taking on. Henceforth he was to be the guiding hand in the attempt to save Germany's honour. Meanwhile Tresckow, his sick-leave over, had been appointed commander of a regiment on the Eastern front. The great battles that raged from the Baltic to the Black Sea during that summer and autumn of Russian victory, must have seemed almost a rest-cure after the life of tension that he had been leading.

CHAPTER IV

STAUFFENBERG, though his appointment as chief of staff to General Olbricht at the General Army Office became effective only on November 1st, 1943, had already been working in that office since late September, learning the routine and taking over from his predecessor. The General Army Office was one of three major departments subordinate to the Home Army commander, the other two being the Army Weapons Office and the Army Administration Office. The General Army Office was the most important of the three, its principal function being the supply of trained replacements to the German armies in the field, both in the form of new units and formations and of trained drafts to regiments and battalions that already existed. Its offices were in the Bendlerstrasse, in the old Defence Ministry, a great grey building which contained many other military organizations including part of the O.K.H. The Bendlerstrasse, as this office block was called, was an administrative headquarters, the strategic conduct of the war being carried out wherever Hitler might choose to be. Of the great number of officers who worked in the Bendlerstrasse, a high proportion of whom were unfit for active service, the majority were unknown to Stauffenberg personally and even fewer knew the real reason for his presence there.

Even his ostensible job was not an easy one. The tremendous casualties which the German army had suffered and was suffering on the Russian and Italian fronts far exceeded the ever-diminishing flow of replacements. Nor were those replacements being used logically. There was fierce inter-service rivalry to obtain recruits, with Goering, Dönitz and Himmler all hotly competing for the best human material. The Waffen-S.S., now no longer a voluntary organization, and the Navy received the pick of the new man-power. In the dwindling air force, the ground establishment remained enormous and Goering, instead of relinquishing these men to the army, persuaded Hitler that he be allowed to set up his own divisions, two of which were armoured, half a dozen parachutist who were in fact *élite* infantry, and nearly a score of inferior infantry divisions. These, of course, also needed replacements. Thus Olbricht and Stauffenberg, in order to do their duty by the army, were engaged in constant bureaucratic battle with other headquarters.

Nor was that the end of their troubles. The German armaments industry, prodigious though its capacity might be, could not keep up with the wastage at the fronts. It, too, was not logically organized and controlled to anything like the same extent as were the equivalent industries in Britain or the United States. There was a perpetual shortage of arms and equipment for the troops and units in training.

It is thus apparent that Stauffenberg's new job, which he carried out with extreme competence, was anything but a sinecure. Guderian, who was not in the conspiracy, and who as Inspector of Armoured Troops drew his replacements through Stauffenberg, thought most highly of him. Indeed during these winter months when Himmler once asked Guderian who could be chosen to replace Zeitzler as Chief of the General Staff, Guderian proposed the young colonel, describing him as 'the best horse in the stable'. Hitler himself was aware of Stauffenberg's brilliance. When shown Stauffenberg's draft plan for Operation Valkyrie, he is said to have remarked, in his usual gracious manner: 'At last a staff officer with brains!' He was quite right: it was far more subtle a plan than Hitler realized.

The orders for Operation Valkyrie were designed to supply the conspirators with that body of armed troops without which they could not hope to carry out their *coup d'état*. The idea seems to have been Olbricht's and Tresckow's who in the late autumn of 1942 had already discussed plans for seizing control of Berlin, Vienna, Munich and Cologne as soon as Hitler was killed: the circumstances were created by Canaris: the execution was Stauffenberg's.

Canaris pointed out to Hitler the danger to internal security which was constituted by the presence in Germany of several million foreign workers. In fact he must have known that from a military point of view this unarmed and unorganized mass of labourers was no danger whatsoever. But Hitler, who himself had been raised to power by the dumb and tidal mob, quite naturally ascribed an unnatural force to that stratum of society. Canaris easily persuaded him that in view of the deteriorating situation at the front, plans must be drawn up to deal with a possible revolt by these foreigners. Such an operation was given the code name *Valkyrie*. He went on to persuade Hitler that *Valkyrie* must be the responsibility of the Home Army. The appropriate staff office for drawing up the órders to be carried out in the event of *Valkyrie* was the General Army Office. Thus did Stauffenberg find himself in the position of authority—at least for planning—which Olbricht and the others had intended that he hold. To those who were outside the conspiracy, it seemed particularly suitable that the officer who had drawn up the pre-war plan for dealing with enemy parachutists should now be entrusted with a similar study. However, command over the troops of the Home Army in the event of *Valkyrie* remained, as before, in the hands of the commander, Colonel-General Fromm.

Tresckow was once again on leave in Berlin in September of 1943 and he and Stauffenberg, who was also still on convalescent-leave, set about drawing up the orders of which there were two sets, one open and the other sealed, 'only to be opened on the issue of code word *Valkyrie*'. For many years now the conspirators within the General Staff had been drafting ambivalent orders, and they had become masters at preparing plans which, while apparently designed for one set of circumstances, were in fact intended for quite another. To anybody not in the know, *Valkyrie* was exactly what it purported to be, a plan for moving the active units of the Home Army into the great centres of population, and particularly into Berlin, to crush a rebellion by the foreign workers. In truth it was designed to deal with the situation which would arise after the assassination of Hitler. In this crisis time would be the essential factor.

During the first two hours after Hitler's death, the conspirators must seize control of the means of communication, or, where this could not be done, the major signals centres must be made inoperative. This meant the neutralization of the signals office at Hitler's headquarters, for which Fellgiebel was responsible, and the capture of the great Berlin broadcasting station for which troops would be needed. During the next four hours, that is to say as soon as Berlin was secured, the code word *Valkyrie* would be issued for all the rest of Germany. The conspirators and their friends must now ensure that their orders would be obeyed by the various headquarters of the Home Army and by the administrative headquarters and the Army Groups across the frontiers. Within twenty-four hours the revolution must be over, the S.S. either disarmed or incorporated in the army, and the new government firmly established.

The point of crisis was Berlin, the time H-hour to H plus 2, and the primary objective the broadcasting station. (The conspirators knew Malaparte's *Technique du Coup d'État,* a book long banned in Germany. In a modern country stunned by a sudden rebellion the men who control the means of mass communication have already won the major battle.) Furthermore, since the conspiracy would have its headquarters and its signal centre in the Bendlerstrasse, there must be troops to guard that centre from counter-attack by the S.S. and possibly by units of Goering's air force, particularly the anti-aircraft troops. Finally there were considerable bodies of S.S. troops in and about Berlin who must be made harmless with all speed. In all these operations the conspirators could rely on the support of at least a part, and perhaps the whole, of the Berlin police force: its chief, Count Helldorf, was fully involved in the conspiracy. In the arrests which must immediately take place, the presence of police officers would give the appearance of legality. But the power could only be supplied by the troops.

In Berlin itself there were few troops available, the most important being the Guard Battalion of the *Grossdeutschland Division,* an *élite* unit with tanks. There was also the Artillerymen's School and the Armourers' School as well as two battalions of low grade, home-guard-type infantry. Within fifty miles of Berlin, the maximum radius for effective intervention, there were four army training areas which could supply combat troops from their instructional and demonstration units and perhaps from the troops in training: the infantry school at Döberitz, the school for armoured troops at Wunsdorf, the artillery school at Jüterbog, and the school for mobile troops, formerly the cavalry school, at Krampnitz. There was an armoured reconnaissance battalion as well as a motor-cycle battalion at Krampnitz which, if warned in time, should be able to reach central Berlin very quickly. One part of the plan for Operation *Valkyrie*, perhaps the most important, was the marching orders for these units which necessitated detailed staff work and arrangements for their armament and equipment. In some cases it was possible to arrange that these troops be equipped and ready to march ahead of time. In others, arms could only be issued after the publication of the code word. Since, in some cases, several hours must elapse between the issue of marching orders and the arrival of the troops in the centre of the city, it was considered desirable that these orders be sent out to certain units before Hitler was actually assassinated. They would thus be available to arrest any leading Nazis—such as Goebbels, who was usually in Berlin—and seize control the moment Hitler was dead. The conspirators had no doubt that once the dictator was gone, the troops would obey their officers, and the officers their generals. Nor did they anticipate very serious resistance from the S.S. with Hitler dead.

The next part of Operation *Valkyrie*—as Stauffenberg and Tresckow saw it—was concerned with gaining control of the Home Army. This was a question of personal relations. The programme was that at each major headquarters, from the *Wehrkreise* or District Commands downwards, one senior officer at least should be involved, if not the commander then his chief of staff, and if neither of these, then the first operations officer. All these men were known personally to one or other of the conspirators (who included, among the planners, Generals Lindemann, the general of artillery with the O.K.H., and Wagner, the Quartermaster-General) and in many cases it was not necessary to tell them what was afoot: they could be relied on to obey orders from the Bendlerstrasse once the 'flash' had been fired. Others were known to be Nazis, and they must be removed and alternative commanders, who were to be held ready, immediately appointed in their place. In doubtful cases

Stauffenberg had no hesitation in bluntly stating what he proposed to do and in using all the powers of his personality to convince the men in question that they must act with the army. He did this repeatedly, quite frankly and fearlessly, and it is an indication of his personal magnetism and of the respect which he enjoyed that no man thus approached betrayed him during ten long months: the solidarity of the army and particularly of the General Staff also, of course, contributed to this practical loyalty.

In Berlin itself there were three key positions, held by three generals. Fromm, at the Home Army, was a problematical figure. It was decided that if he would not co-operate he would be immediately replaced by Colonel-General Hoepner, the brilliant tank general who had been cashiered by Hitler for disobeying orders when commanding a Panzer Army outside Moscow in 1941. Kortzfleisch, the commander of *Wehrkreis III* in which Berlin was located, was a known Nazi. His chief of staff, General von Rost, was not. He would arrest Kortzfleisch, who would be succeeded by General von Thüngen. The commandant of Berlin, General von Hase, was an elderly man and an honourable one. The conspirators had no doubt that they could rely on him, nor were they to be disappointed. Similar arrangements, so far as was possible, were made at the other headquarters throughout Germany and abroad, those in Paris and Brussels being particularly thorough.

In addition to the group of orders which could be prepared 'openly'—that is to say with the collaboration of staff officers not in the plot—there were others of quite different purport. Since, once the flash had been given, utmost speed would be required, it was necessary that everything should be made ready beforehand. This involved a considerable number of papers, including signals prepared for signature by Fromm, ordering the arrest of individuals and the disarming of Nazi units, proclamations to be read over the wireless by Beck, the proposed new Head of State, orders to the Army Groups drawn up and already signed by Witzleben, who was to be the new Commander-in-Chief, and much else as well. The text of the orders that were issued on July 20th and of the prepared announcements which could not, in fact, be made are given in Appendix II, page 252. The drafting and safe-guarding of these incriminating papers was again the responsibility of Stauffenberg, though of course the text of the political ones was decided in consultation with the appropriate leaders. Two secretaries in the Bendlerstrasse worked late at night typing the several copies that would be needed when the moment came. These brave women were absolutely reliable, since one was Fräulein von Oven, who had been secretary to General Hammerstein-Equord and later to General von Fritsch, while the other was the wife of Henning von Tresckow himself. As these most dangerous documents were finished, they were locked away in a special safe in General Olbricht's office. Some were already signed: all that was needed, before handing them to the signal clerks, was the addition of the date stamp and of the hour.

By the middle of October, when Tresckow returned to the Eastern Front, all was ready. The conspirators immediately set about making arrangements for the murder of Hitler. For it must not be imagined that they now waited until July of the following year: all through the winter of 1943–44 they were trying to kill the dictator. On several occasions they came very near to success.

The problem was the same for Stauffenberg as it had been for Tresckow: Hitler's inaccessibility. He himself, in his capacity of chief of staff to the General Army Office, did not see Hitler. Indeed only one of the active conspirators, Stieff, was regularly present at Hitler's conferences—the only time when there was the slightest chance of getting at him. Stieff was then head of the Organization Department of the O.K.H., and it seems that he agreed, with the help of Hagen and Kuhn, to smuggle a bomb into the noon meeting on October 12th or 14th. The facts are not quite clear but it appears that after examining the conference-room with its elaborate security arrangements—a regulation was now in force by which officers' brief-cases were liable to search by S.S. guards—he decided that he could not do it on his own. Furthermore he seems to have had doubts about his courage and his conscience was not easy. And here one is face to face with the problem of the German officers' attitude towards Hitler in all its tragic complication.

Hitler disliked, and even despised, the great majority of the men who had conquered Europe for him. In general they returned his dislike and loathed his methods and mentality, though many, such as Brauchitsch and Kluge, were subject to the undoubted hypnotic powers which he could and did exercise on individuals as on the masses. Nevertheless, that was not the main cause for his hold over his officers. He was the Chief of the State, the heir, no matter how debased and vile, of the German Emperor, of the King of Prussia, of those feudal monarchs whom generations of German soldiers had served loyally and unquestioningly unto death. Here we are in a world of symbols and abstractions which to all mankind are of a power that is incalculable. To the older generation of officers, brought up in the Empire, emperor and country were symbolically almost one and the same: they swore an oath to their emperor, and that was the pledge of their loyalty to their country. The fact that another segment of German society had destroyed this bond in 1918 was to them a matter of shame and a cause of loathing. Yet the tradition of loyalty had remained. Seeckt had defended the Germany of Weimar and buttressed a system of government which he openly despised and could easily have overthrown. Schleicher, too, never seriously considered breaking his oath to his President in the name of his ideals. For the great majority of German officers, to whom politics was an obscure and rather sordid occupation, treason was simply unthinkable, as it would be to the majority of officers in any army or navy. Throughout his life, and in many cases throughout generations of his ancestors, an officer is trained in the mystique of obedience. In the case of Hitler, that unscrupulous man had reinforced this mystique by demanding, and getting, a personal oath of loyalty to himself as Führer and Reichs Chancellor. *I swear by God this sacred oath that I shall render unconditional obedience to the Führer of the German Reich and People, Supreme Commander of the German Armed Forces, Adolf Hitler, and that as a brave soldier I shall be at all times prepared to give my life for this oath.*

One of the conspirators was the retired General von Rabenau, Seeckt's friend and biographer. In that biography, published early in the war, he had discussed the question of a *coup d'état* by the Reichswehr which had been mooted in 1923. He dismissed the possibility of this proposed action with the remark that a Prussian general would never, in any circumstances, break his oath. Within five years he was to find himself doing precisely what he had believed to be impossible. Halder, who had been a member of the conspiracy since 1938, though seldom a particularly active one, summed up the dilemma in these words, when under cross-examination at Nuremberg after the war:

> May I make a personal remark? I am the last masculine member of a family who for three hundred years were soldiers. What the duty of a soldier is I know. I know too that in the dictionary of a German soldier the terms 'treason' and 'plot against the state' do not exist. I was in the awful dilemma of one who had the duty of a soldier and also a duty which I considered higher. Innumerable of my old comrades were in the same dilemma. I chose the solution for the duties I esteem higher. The majority of my comrades esteemed the duty to the flag higher and more essential. You may be assured that this is the worst dilemma that a soldier may be faced with. That is what I wanted to explain.

No, an officer is not easily brought to break his oath. Before he can bring himself to take so terrible a step—in this case one which would entail murder as well—he must, if he be an honourable man, invoke a higher loyalty. In our century loyalty to humanity as a whole is only a vague concept. It is therefore not surprising to find that the majority of the officers prepared to overthrow Hitler were devout Christians. In the long and agonizing struggle which preceded their decision to break with all their training, they could only appeal in conscience to the highest court of all.

Stieff's decision that he could not act was a serious blow to the conspirators. Stauffenberg visited Hitler's headquarters and after examining the circumstances there decided that an alternative method would have to be devised. The plan he now chose was a harrowing one, for it involved the certain and deliberate suicide of the assassin. The man whom they found, and who was prepared to lose his life for the honour of his country and the cause of human decency, is still alive to tell the tale. His name is Axel von dem Bussche, and his task was to demonstrate a new type of uniform to Hitler.

The standard German uniform had proved ill suited to the Russian climate and a new model, together with a new type of infantryman's pack, had been designed. These were now almost completed, and Hitler had expressed a desire to see them. Stieff would accompany the 'model' to a demonstration in the 'Wolf's Lair' at which Goering and Himmler were also expected to be present, since their private armies would be similarly re-attired. This promised to be a unique opportunity for blowing up the junta: Himmler and Goering had been on very bad terms ever since Stalingrad and almost never met. The chance of killing three such birds with one bomb was unlikely to recur.

The plan now was that a volunteer should fill the new pack with high explosives and blow himself up with the others. Fritz von der Schulenburg said that he knew an officer who would agree to do this, and Axel von dem Bussche was summoned from the Eastern Front. Schulenburg had learned to know this twenty-four-year-old captain when they were both serving in the 9th Infantry Regiment, the old 1st Foot Guards in which Tresckow had also once served, during the Polish campaign. Von dem Bussche had then been an admirer of Hitler's, but the treatment meted out to the conquered Poles and later to the Russians had nauseated him to the extent that he now regarded only three courses as open to an honourable German: death in action, desertion, or an act of rebellion. He has described how he came to the conclusion that it was his duty to break his oath and to attempt, regardless of his own life, to destroy Hitler. He was sent for to act as the model for the new uniform.

He arrived in Berlin in October and had a long conversation with Stauffenberg. The latter told him what the plan was in the coolest and most factual terms. Both these men took it for granted that circumstances can arise in which a nation's best sons must be prepared to sacrifice their lives for their people; such circumstances existed now. They talked for several hours, and Bussche has described 'the bright glow of steady composure' which emanated from the older man and the self-assured and noble manner of this one-eyed colonel who, as another man has remarked, seemed more like a poet than a soldier. Stauffenberg, says Bussche, was the sort of leader young Germany had long hungered for.

The details of the assassination were worked out with Stieff, and it was decided that each of them would carry a bomb into the room where Hitler and the others would view the equipment. Bussche requested that his pack be filled with a German explosive which could be operated instantaneously, though the fuse would hiss for a fraction of a second. This was obtained. Meanwhile the demonstration was postponed more than once, and Bussche was summoned from the front, where he was commanding an infantry company, on several occasions. Finally, in late November, all was ready and from November 23rd to 25th Bussche was in East Prussia, awaiting the arrival of the equipment. He has said: 'Those sunny days of late autumn among the forests and lakes were illuminated with that brilliant clarity which soldiers learn to know in the hour before the attack.'

And then, in a heavy air-raid on Berlin, the model equipment was destroyed. There was apparently no spare set and it would be weeks before a new lot was ready, the leather parts, that is to say the pack itself, being particularly difficult to replace. The demonstration was postponed until Christmas and Bussche returned to the front. He was back in late December and once again prepared himself for the ordeal. But on Christmas Eve Hitler suddenly decided to go to his home on the Obersalzberg. The demonstration was postponed until late January. Bussche's divisional commander insisted that he return to the front at once, where a few days later he was seriously wounded. He lost a leg. For months he was in bed. After July 20th he was arrested in hospital and this one-legged captain was subjected to all the cruelties of which the Nazi régime was capable.

Meanwhile in January of 1944 Schulenburg found another young man who was willing and able to play Bussche's part. This was Ewald Heinrich von Kleist, also twenty-four years old, also an infantry officer, the son of a conservative Pomeranian land-owner who was an old friend of Schlabrendorff's and Goerdeler's and who had twice been arrested in 1933 for his outspoken criticism of Nazi atrocities: in the 1938 crisis he had come to London as the emissary of the German opposition, and in interviews with Chamberlain, Vansittart, Lord Lloyd and Churchill had disclosed the plans of the German military leaders to overthrow the Nazis in the event of war with Czechoslovakia, and had urged the British government to hold fast. His mission had failed: now it was the son's turn to act.

On January 28th young Kleist arrived in Berlin and had a six-hour conversation with Stauffenberg, during part of which Schulenburg was present. As with Bussche, Stauffenberg spoke factually and without any attempt to prevail upon Kleist. He simply told him what the position was. In view of the recent conference at Teheran it was clear that major Allied operations against Germany were imminent. If the German resistance wished to save Germany's name, it must be done now or else it would be too late. As members of Germany's ruling class, it was up to them to act. There would soon be an opportunity, but it would almost certainly cost Kleist his life. Did Kleist feel that he had the courage and determination to do what was required?

Kleist spent the next Sunday on his father's estate in Pomerania. He discussed with him what his answer should be. Old Kleist-Schmenzin told him that it was his duty, on such an occasion as this, to act, regardless of the consequences.

The demonstration was now fixed for February 11th, and Himmler was to be present as well as Hitler. And then, at the last minute, both the demonstration and the assassination were cancelled, according to Kleist because Stieff had discovered that Himmler would not be there after all. Both father and son were arrested after July 20th. The son survived, but the father was executed. His last words to the judge who sentenced him were: 'It will be easier for me to submit to the death penalty than for you to inflict it.'

The next and apparently final attempt to make use of the new equipment is an obscure incident, the authenticity of which Eberhard Zeller doubts. It was carried out by a certain Johann Hofmann who, in a sworn statement given in December of 1945, and quoted by Dr. Pechel, states:

> My father was Colonel Josef Hofmann who worked at the head-quarters of the Reich Chancellery, which was stationed finally at Zossen. My father was in close contact with those military circles which had long been planning the removal of Hitler. He did not inform me in detail of his plans and relationships.
> On February 11th, 1944, he said to me—I was a signals officer in the Reich Chancellery at the time—that I was to demonstrate a new combat pack to Hitler. A certain Lieutenant Hans Schneider

would also be doing this. My father specified that the new combat pack was to be shown on February 20th at 11 o'clock in the morning. When first informing me of this, that was all my father said.

On February 18th he expressed himself to me as follows: 'Dear boy, I have something to tell you, it is a heavy task that you must undertake; there is a bomb in the combat pack'. I replied: 'Nevertheless, I am prepared to carry out the demonstration, since it is important for the future of us all.' He told me no further details.

On February 20th the demonstration of the combat pack did not take place at 11 o'clock, as planned, but two hours earlier. However the bomb was timed to explode at 11.05. When the demonstration of the pack was completed, we handed it in. It was placed in the courtyard of the Chancellery. We ourselves left. My father then told me that the bomb had exploded at 11.05 o'clock. He did not tell me anything else.

After the assassination attempt of July 20th, my father and I were arrested on July 26th . . .

He goes on to say that his father was condemned to death, as was he but that his own sentence was subsequently commuted and he was sent to a Penal Battalion, being taken prisoner by the Russians in May of 1945. If the story is untrue, as Zeller implies, it is probably a garbled version of what happened to the Kleists.

During these long months of tension and frustration, while the British and American bombers methodically smashed the cities of Germany and the Wehrmacht was thrown back to the pre-war Russian frontier, Stauffenberg had to bear more and more of the burden of conspiracy. Beck had been sick through most of 1943 and though by the end of the year he had recovered his health, he was now an old man, though there was certainly no diminution in his intellectual powers. Witzleben, too, was an old man and had also been very sick. He was quite recovered, but was to a certain extent out of touch, living a retired life in his home outside Berlin. Goerdeler, the third of the older triumvirate, was neither tired nor sick; indeed his activity was phenomenal, constantly on the move, drafting plans, interviewing all and sundry, listing shadow governments, writing letters. He has been described as the driving force of the German resistance, but his rashness worried and finally annoyed Stauffenberg, whose sense of reality was far more acute than that of the politician. Nor did Goerdeler's vision of the future tally with his own. The ex-

Mayor of Leipzig, a rigid conservative, was lacking in those qualities of imagination which Stauffenberg and his contemporaries prized: for them a return to the principles of Weimar, of statistical, centralized democracy, no matter how reinforced and purified, was inadequate as a goal. Nor was he interested in Goerdeler's ideas concerning a monarchical restoration. Indeed he regarded a future Beck-Witzleben-Goerdeler government as purely a caretaker government whose first domestic task was to arrange free elections with all speed. What future he envisaged for Germany after those elections is by no means clear. Goerdeler, when in prison after July 20th, described him as 'a political crank' with a confused policy for the future to be based on left-wing socialists and communists. This can be largely discounted as Goerdelerese. The socialist leaders, Maass and Leuschner, described Stauffenberg's position during the winter of 1943–44 as quite different from this. They said that his views were 'reactionary'. The basis for this accusation seems to have been his remark that he saw no reason why families should not be allowed to keep their inherited estates, particularly since the nobility had, in the past, rendered great services to the state. In fact both these comments on his politics were those of older men, brought up in a world divided between left and right, a world which had ceased to exist. For friendship and intellectual nourishment, Stauffenberg looked elsewhere, to men of his own generation.

Closest to him was his brother Berthold, now an adviser on international law to the Ministry of Marine. Berthold was a very different type of man from Claus, quiet, introspective and gentle, widely travelled, speaking Russian and Italian as well as French and English, a scholarly lawyer and a humanist. Throughout the war he had regarded it as his duty to use his position for the good of others. It was, for example, largely his doing that American ships were allowed through the German blockade to carry food to the starving Greeks. But his primary interests were artistic. His knowledge of literature was both wide and deep: during this winter of 1943–44 he was engaged in translating the *Odyssey* into German. He was well enough acquainted with the world to realize that National-Socialism was more than a purely German phenomenon and that the evil forces which it had loosed were the result of more than local circumstances. And thus he could view the world in which he lived and the actions in which his brother was engaged with a considerable detachment, as from a higher eminence. The company of this cool, sensitive and brilliant man must have been a great help to Claus.

Stauffenberg, during this period was seeing a considerable amount of his cousin, Peter Yorck von Wartenburg, who had been a member of that group of men now in dissolution, loosely called the Kreisau Circle, of which Helmuth von Moltke had been the central figure and whose house had given the group its name. Of these men, Helmuth von Moltke, Peter Yorck von Wartenburg, Adam von Trott zu Solz, Carlo Mierendorff, Theodor Haubach, Theodor Steltzer, Dr. Eugen Gerstenmaier, Father Delp and the others, I shall have more to say in the next chapter. For the moment, let it be remarked that they were, as a group, the intellectual force which epitomized the opposition to Hitler and Nazism. They realized that this was a time for intensive thought, thought about the future even more than about the past. Had they lived they would have had a great part to play in twentieth-century Europe.

Another friend of Stauffenberg's who has been frequently mentioned was Fritz von der Schulenburg, a man given more to action than reflection and who had placed his talents and abilities unreservedly at the service of the younger officer. Through him Stauffenberg met Julius Leber, a remarkable character and an astonishingly brave man, whom Stauffenberg would have preferred to Goerdeler as Chancellor of the new Germany.

Leber was born in 1898, the son of an Alsatian peasant, and was brought up in great poverty. He worked his way through the higher school grades and through the Universities of Freiburg and Strassburg, studying social economy and history and living from part-time jobs which included journalism. He volunteered for the German army in 1914 and was later commissioned and much decorated for gallantry. In 1920 he fought against Kapp, after which he left the army. The following year he became editor of the *Lübecker Volksbote* and from then on was preoccupied with socialist politics in Northern Germany, being a member of the Reichstag from 1924 to 1933. He was one of the

Social-Democrats who were equally opposed to the totalitarianism of the right and of the left. The Nazis, recognizing in Leber an enemy of great stature and incorruptible conviction, arrested him in the spring of 1933.

In Sachsenhausen Concentration Camp they did their best to break his spirit. For one whole year he was kept in solitary confinement in a darkened cell, without a single stick of furniture: even when the temperature was many degrees below freezing point, he had no bed, nor straw, nor blanket, nothing save the naked earth on which to lie. The other tortures to which he was subjected can be left to the reader's imagination. But they failed to break him and, surprisingly enough, in May of 1937 he was released from prison. It was his habit, in later years, to describe his torturers as 'those poor devils'.

As soon as he was free he immediately set about establishing contact with what remained of the German working-class movement. It was little enough. By their surrender in '33 most of the heads of the Socialist and Communist parties and of the enormous trade union movement, had forfeited their claims to leadership. Then came the massive persecutions, the huge waves of arrest, which pulverized those once great organizations finally. (Between 1933 and 1939 about a million persons had served prison or concentration camp terms. In that last year a third of a million were still in gaol. Of these the great majority had committed no offence save that of holding left-wing views.) By 1937 the old left wing was utterly smashed. What Leber found was a condition in which a great number of very small groups of anti-Nazi working men, former socialists or communists or trade unionists, was scattered throughout the length and breadth of Germany, mostly inactive, with no central leadership and indeed almost no contact between groups. Numerically this left-wing opposition was strong, politically it was entirely impotent.

But there were one or two men, almost all of whom had, like Leber, been recently released from the concentration camps, who now began attempting to create at least the basis for future political action. The chief of these was Carlo Mierendorff who, like Leber, had been one of the younger Socialist deputies in the Reichstag and who succeeded, before his death in an R.A.F. raid in December of 1943, in building a network, thin but nevertheless strong, of anti-Nazi workers throughout the greater part of Germany. Others were Wilhelm Leuschner, the former deputy chairman of the General Trade Union League, who now worked closely with Jacob Kaiser, the former head of the Christian Trade Unions, and Haubach, who had been among the creators of the Socialist organization called the *Reichsbanner*. There were others, men who knowing all the horrors that the Nazis inflicted on their enemies were yet prepared to fight in the factories and under the very eyes of the Gestapo.

They were not fighting for the old Weimar Parties. Leber, indeed, had long ago seen the futility of those great impersonal machines. He had realized that the old socialist idea of conquest solely by numbers had produced only that lethargy of the individual which led inevitably to surrender and defeat. He had learned the lesson, which still seems to be only dimly comprehended in Europe, that men must be valued, not counted. He saw that politics like everything else in which man is involved here on earth, is a matter of human relations, of personality. But he was a politician who had never lost his faith in democracy. As early as 1924 he had proposed that the Communist Party be banned in Germany, and by now he had thrown the Marxist dialectic overboard as well.

In 1933, when first under arrest, he wrote a long and searching paper on the reasons for the failure of democracy in Germany. Not only was the electoral system all wrong, with its multiplication of parties and splinter parties, and its endless reshuffling of meaningless coalitions—depriving the parties of the true responsibility of office, and producing a state of affairs in which the country was governed by party bureaucrats making deals behind the scenes rather than by the people's representatives—but there was also a fundamental misunderstanding in Germany of the duties and functions of the electorate and of its deputies. At this moment, when so many German democrats were in despair, he set about examining the errors of the past which must be avoided in the future. That there would be a future, he never doubted.

'Democracy,' he wrote, 'requires in every man who would have a place in the business of the state a consciousness of responsibility as well as self-discipline. Uncurbed and irresponsible attitudes and criticisms are incompatible with that external order which assures every man his personal freedom of opinion to a high degree. Strong authority on the part of the state must here engrave boundaries to popular thought, but in such a manner as to leave each citizen the sensation of maximum personal freedom.' So blunt a statement sounds very foreign to Anglo-Saxon ears, for we accept the authority of the state and perhaps believe our sensation of maximum freedom to be the reality. In Germany authority had, when he wrote this passage, been replaced by terror born of anarchy, and freedom was a word which had become sullied by misuse. Leber's views must, in fact, be seen within the framework of his time, the age of Weimar and of the temporary failure of the Social-Democrat Party to whom, primarily, he spoke.

He was, indeed, looking for a new, positive concept to oppose the nihilism of the Nazi *Weltanschauung*. In the epilogue to the selection from his writings and speeches, entitled *Ein Mann geht seinen Weg,* his friends say that in the years preceding 1944 he admitted that he had so far failed to find one. The largely abstract programme of the Kreisau Circle, which will be discussed in the next chapter, interested but did not convince him. He remained a practical, practising politician, the heir of the old Social-Democrats: he represented the working class, and he intended to go on doing so and, if possible, to obtain power as such: he was quite uninterested in Goerdeler's out-moded bourgeois theories of *laissez-faire*. Indeed perhaps the concept which he sought, and believed that he had failed to find, is to be discerned in that very failure. A politician whose interests are primarily practical does not accept abstract and detailed doctrines on which to stretch and distort facts and situations, but adjusts his larger, primarily moral, attitude to those facts and situations as they develop. In the years before his death Leber's entire energies were devoted to one, primary task, the elimination of Hitler and the destruction of the Nazi tyranny. Beyond that, he has both much and little to say. That is why, from the far side of the grave, Leber's voice seems so persuasive, though his views on such matters as constitutional reform, national economy and the rest are elusive. He was the political artist, he possessed the paints,

89

but he never obtained the canvas which only office can give. But if, unlike Goerdeler or the men of Kreisau, he lacked a hard and fast doctrine, he certainly did not lack opinions.

In the first place, he proposed that the system of proportional representation, by which the electorate eventually and inevitably votes for a party or a slogan rather than for a man, be abolished. A state, whether it be an aristocracy, a democracy or a bureaucracy, in which power is divorced from the people who are the source of power, will always degenerate into tyranny. He believed that the people's representatives should in fact be the representatives of people rather than the nominees of parties. Secondly he believed that the men chosen by the people to govern them, should do so; that they should not be constantly pre-occupied with the ephemeral advantages to be gained by offering the electorate what it wanted, but with what the nation and the country needed. To a German who had before his eyes the spectacle of their own great nation degraded beyond belief and largely accepting that degradation, the voice of the people was hardly to be regarded as the voice of God: it had cried 'Sieg Heil!' far too often. On the other hand, as he well knew, the will of the people in our century is the only tolerable basis of government. It was a question of channelling that will to sensible and constructive ends by intelligent and peaceful means. An essential element of this process was that the political parties should, so far as possible, cease to consider the securing of advantages for any one class as their first duty. The atomization of society and its re-assembly in political groupings which are emotionally almost meaningless, should be halted. This must be done, not only by social rearrangement, but by the example and initiative of men possessing integrity, energy and good will.

Leber was clearly such a man. His widow has told the author that she once asked her husband what chances he really believed existed for the success of the attempt to overthrow Hitler. Leber replied:

'I don't know, and it doesn't make any difference. I have only one head to lose. I know of no better cause than this for which to risk it.'

He now earned his livelihood running a small coal business in

Berlin, and Stauffenberg and the others met frequently at his small house in the city's outskirts. One evening the men discussed the possibilities of going into hiding, of finding a place of refuge, should their plans miscarry. Fritz von der Schulenburg then made a remark which, in Frau Leber's opinion, sums up the attitude of these men. He spoke slowly and somewhat flatly.

'A hiding place?' he asked. 'I don't know if I'd try to find one. We'll still have to stand up for our beliefs, in one way or the other.'

Frau Leber has described the very real fear that these clandestine meetings, almost always held at night, could engender:

'One evening Stauffenberg and my husband had had a long conversation in our house. It was now the hour when the air-raids usually began. I was always anxious that such people should leave our house as soon as the alarm sounded. For should we be unlucky, a tragic accident might have revealed the plans of the long, secret preparations which finally resulted in July 20th.'

All that winter, crescendo, the bombs fell on blacked-out Berlin. In the darkness, which was also a protection, the conspirators made their way to one another's homes. The Stauffenberg brothers, who were living in Berthold's house out at Wannsee, nearly always had guests, and Claus once described his house as a home for bombed-out officers. (The brothers had sent their families to places of comparative safety in southern Germany.) These were nerve-racking months, but he himself never lost control of his nerves. His reluctance to go to an air raid shelter when the bombs were falling was a cause of anxiety to those about him. His friends were constantly urging him to be more careful of his own life, but if he did not snatch the few hours rest that remained to him each day, how could he carry on? Not for the avoidance of chance bombs had Brutus's page remarked: 'I have slept, my lord, already.'

Zeller quotes a description of an evening in the Stauffenberg household at Wannsee during this period, written by one who was there. Speaking of the Stauffenberg brothers, this unnamed witness says:

The power of conviction which they gave forth had a curious origin. One saw the effect which the condition of the world (of which conditions in Germany were only one manifestation) had upon oneself and other observant people: we were disgusted, depressed, fearful, anguished, upset, desperate, resigned, gloomily determined, highly incensed, clenched, ensnared, passionately aroused. . . . We argued, endured, thought, believed, complained, fell silent and so on. We all reacted, according to our strength, shouting or murmuring our answer to the inescapable which we both saw and foresaw. Sometimes, it is true, to judge by their remarks, the Stauffenberg brothers seemed to share the opinions and feelings of the rest of us; and yet one was surprised to discover that in their inner beings they were really quite unaffected by it all. They lived, thought, acted not as men answering a challenge or driven by an external force but as men following a curious inner certitude which indeed corresponded to the task imposed upon us all by the day and the hour—but which yet for them remained voluntary. They were not at all the victims of compulsion: without this compulsion they would still have fulfilled their destiny. From this strange and completely innate freedom there emanated a strength which in its results was and remains quite independent of success or failure.

And so did the winter pass, while all their plans were frustrated, while the net of the Gestapo drew tighter—Moltke was arrested in January—while some of them grew frightened and others, thinking that it was now too late to act, came close to despair. One more attempt was made on Hitler's life in March. A young orderly officer, accompanying Field-Marshal Busch to see Hitler, was persuaded by Tresckow to carry a Browning revolver in his trouser pocket. He was stopped at the door by S.S. men: no orderly officers today. With the spring, with the huge Allied invasion impending in the West and an enormous Russian offensive being mounted in the East, many of the conspirators would have given up, have resigned themselves to the inevitable and awaited the defeat of Germany which might at least have saved them their lives.

Not so Stauffenberg, who said:

'We have tested ourselves before God and our conscience, and it must be done, for that man is evil incarnate.'

Such was the basis of his curious inner certitude. For the last few months of his life he fills the stage on which he walked, al-most exclusively. But before going on to that tragic climax, it would be as well to examine the world which might have been created had he succeeded, the government that might have been given to Germany, and the ideas and ideals of that group of men known as the Kreisau Circle

CHAPTER V

'WE are to be hanged,' Count Helmuth von Moltke wrote to his wife, shortly before his execution, 'for thinking together.'

And so it happened; of that group of friends known as the Kreisau Kreis only three prominent members, Dr. Eugen Gerstenmaier, Dr. Harald Poelchau and Dr. Theodor Steltzer, survived the war. Though many of them did rather more than simply 'think together', and several were deeply involved with Stauffenberg, their thought was their offence against the Nazi tyranny and their service to humanity.

The Kreisau Kreis was never in any way a political party or even a conspiracy, save in so far that thought and discussion were illegal in National-Socialist Germany and that they therefore had to adopt conspiratorial methods in order to exchange their ideas. They were very diverse ideas that were exchanged, the members of the Kreisau Circle numbering amongst themselves socialists, land-owners, Jesuits, left-wing intellectuals, Protestant clergymen, right-wing politicians, economists, diplomats—in fact a cross-section of what should have been the German ruling class. Needless to say, they were all opposed to the morally nihilistic and criminal régime, but they had something more in common than this negative reaction: they set out to devise among themselves the fundamental principles on which a moral and cultural renaissance might, once the nightmare was over, be founded. Thus their thought was ethical, philosophical, theological. They went further, and in broad outline traced the form that the future German society and economy should follow. In this respect their thought was political. On the other hand they were not by intention the builders of ideological systems or abstract con-

94

stitutions. Steltzer speaks of 'those dreadful reformers and pure rationalists who by means of an ingenious patent solution or technical trick or logical system think to master the problems of reality.' 'Our thought,' he remarks elsewhere, 'was of a more practical cast.'

Kreisau was the estate in Silesia which belonged to Helmuth von Moltke. It had been bestowed as a national gift upon his great-uncle, the victor of the Franco-Prussian war, who was incidentally also the translator of Gibbon's *Decline and Fall*. The Moltke fortune was wiped out by the inflation, and the estate was for a time administered by an inspector put in by the creditors, but in the early 1930's Helmuth von Moltke restored it to solvency and regained full control of a property which he deeply loved.

Helmuth James von Moltke was born in 1907, his mother Dorothy being an Englishwoman, the daughter of Sir James Rose Innes, the judge whom Lord Milner appointed first Chief Justice of the Transvaal. England was a second home to Moltke, and he had and has many friends there, but his loyalties were not divided. Though his outlook was international, he was understandably proud of his paternal heritage and if perhaps his liberal principles can be traced to his mother's influence, his cool determination and unostentatious brilliance recall those of the great field-marshal.

He was brought up a Christian Scientist, but almost as soon as he reached manhood he decided that that faith was not for him. He studied law, and practised in Berlin. Meanwhile he had become interested in sociological matters, and his interest immediately assumed a practical form. To the annoyance of many among the other great Silesian landowners, he turned over a large part of Kreisau to the peasants: the age of privilege, he realized, was over, and though the responsibility of great possessions remained, it was very difficult for one man to fulfil those responsibilities towards hundreds in the twentieth century; therefore the cultivators should have the land which in any case they would eventually take were it not given them. During the depression years he was a leading figure in the organization of Work Camps, where young men of all classes could mingle and learn to understand one another. He hoped that thus a group of people would be created who, though they might have nothing else in common, would be free of the narrow political and social strait-jacket which is the curse of the century, men who would respect one another's humanity and who therefore might provide the seed for a kinder and more intelligent society in which self-interest would assume its proper, subordinate place. Such a society, needless to say, is the direct antithesis of the regimented, mindless 'People's Community', based on envy and aspiring to conquest, which the Nazis were to create. And when the Nazis came to power, among their first actions was the destruction of the Work Camps, or rather their incorporation in the *Reichsarbeitsdienst,* the pseudo-military National Labour Service.

Moltke was of course an anti-Nazi. Here is an episode which casts a light on his character. When Mussolini was to visit Berlin, the streets through which the procession was to pass were to be decorated. Workmen visited Moltke's office to erect a flagpole. Moltke sent them away. He even persuaded the other tenants of his office block that they do the same. So this one building remained unbeflagged. It may seem a small, even a futile gesture, but any man who has ever lived in a totalitarian state will recognize the courage that such gestures require and the effect, as of a stone thrown into a pool, that courage of this sort exercises on other and less enterprising citizens.

In the middle thirties he decided to read for an English law degree, not only because he wished to practise as an international lawyer—for a man of his views normal advancement in the German legal profession was closed—but also because the eating of dinners would necessitate frequent visits to London and temporary escape from the stifling atmosphere of the Third Reich.

The editors of his last letters, *A German of the Resistance,* Mr. Lionel Curtis and Mr. Michael Balfour, who knew him at the time of his visits to England, have described him thus:

> Physically, as well as intellectually, he was eminent wherever he went, for he stood some 6 feet 7 inches, with a spare and wiry figure. He was a supreme realist, quick to assess the essentials of any situation and impatient of words or plans which left out of account the facts of the case, the ultimate good aimed at or the resources likely to be available. A clear-cut sense of values enabled

Colonel Albrecht Mertz von
Quirnheim

Colonel-General Ludwig
Beck

Above. The Fuhrer's Conference Room, after the July 20, 1944 bomb explosion

(Imperial War Museum)

Below. Keitel, Goering, Hitler and Bormann on the afternoon of July 20. Hitler's damaged ear is stuffed with cotton wool.

(Planet News)

him to separate the gold in life from the dross and without any struggle to choose the better way. As a result it often appeared as though the ordinary pleasures of life meant little to him: he never smoked, seldom drank, and generally seemed indifferent to what he was eating. But this was not in fact due to lack of appreciation so much as to the fact that he had appreciated these things in their true proportion and in the light of his ultimate purposes felt them to be of minor importance. Unsparing of himself, he looked critically on people reluctant to make a similar effort, though he did not generally waste breath in condemning them unless he thought his remarks were likely to effect a reform. But his slightly dour concentration on the subject in hand was moderated by a lively sense of humour, puckish rather than cynical: no matter how much Helmuth loathed the things for which his opponents stood, he was much more likely to laugh at them than lose his temper, though his laughter was far from indicating any weakening in the resolution of his antagonism. Underlying all his strength of character and intellect was a deep love for the simple things of life, flowers and the country-side, his home, his children, his friends.

As an international lawyer in Berlin, he was much occupied with the affairs of Jewish clients who were anxious to leave Germany. On one occasion, shortly before the war, two people whom he was representing disappeared and Moltke's inquiries led him to the Gestapo headquarters in Vienna. The average German did not willingly visit the Gestapo, for it was doubtful if he would ever emerge again. But Moltke was not the average German. He went to see the secret police and discovered what he wished to know. It was the only way he could carry out his responsibilities to his clients.

When the war started Moltke was attached to the Supreme Armed Forces Command, O.K.W., as adviser on international law, being also somewhat involved in the legal side of economic matters. In this post he was able on more than one occasion to serve the causes in which he believed. He intervened, or led other more powerful figures to intervene, against the maltreatment of prisoners and of the civilian populations in the conquered Eastern territories. Hearing of an intended action against the Danish Jews, he was able to warn the Danish authorities in time for them to take counter-measures and for many Jews to escape. He, together with Steltzer, saved the life of the

97

Norwegian Bishop Berggrav. In 1942, when the British and American armies landed in North Africa, he learned that Hitler was planning to treat all Frenchmen captured fighting with the Allies as traitors, that is, to shoot them. He arranged that this intelligence reach the Allies and simultaneously that the German authorities learn that the Allies knew of the proposed atrocity. Next he submitted a memorandum pointing out the probability of Anglo-American retaliation and so ensured that this wicked order was dropped once and for all.

Meanwhile, in the summer of 1940, he had come to know Peter Count Yorck von Wartenburg, a relation by marriage, and the nucleus of the Kreisau Kreis was in existence. Like the Moltkes, the Yorcks were great landowners in Silesia and, like Stauffenberg, Yorck was descended from a famous general of the Napoleonic period, in his case that General Yorck who had signed the Convention of Tauroggen in 1812. The original text of the Convention was preserved in the magnificent library which Peter Yorck's grandfather had collected at Klein Oels, the family residence. There, too, was a first edition of Martin Luther's works, from which Peter Yorck's father read to his children. It was indeed a scholarly family, in the great tradition of early nineteenth century Germany, into which Peter Yorck was born in 1904. Like Moltke, he studied law and also economics, but did not practise at the bar, for he became a civil servant, being at one time assistant to the Reich Commissioner for Prices. He served in an armoured division during the Polish campaign, and was later attached to the Eastern Section of the Armed Forces Economic Staff in Berlin. He has been described as reserved, softly spoken, at first glance almost ineffectual in manner, an impression that was quickly removed when he began to talk in his forceful and pointed fashion. Unlike Moltke, there was nothing international about Yorck's point of view. He was proud of being a German and it was to him intolerable that Germany should be ruled by foreigners, whether they came from across the physical frontiers of the Reich or, like the Nazis, from across those moral and spiritual borders which mark the limits of our civilization.

Moltke and Yorck became close personal friends, as did their wives, and it was the conversation of those four persons which gave birth to the Kreisau Circle. One who soon joined in these conversations and plans, if plans they can be called, was Adam von Trott zu Solz who in the spring of 1940 had returned to Germany from the United States.

Trott was born in 1909, his father being the Prussian *Kultus-minister*, or Minister for Public Worship and Education. He studied law at Munich, Göttingen and Berlin universities and won a Rhodes Scholarship to Oxford, where he read Modern Greats, that is to say philosophy, politics and economics, from 1931 to 1933. While at Oxford he published a thesis on Hegel's philosophy of the state and international law. In 1935 he edited a selection of Heinrich von Kleist's philosophical and journalistic writings which, for those who could read between the lines, was an attack on the Nazi tyranny. For a couple of years he practised law and then in 1936 he went to China for two years where he was engaged on a research project in Peking. He also spent several months in the United States. In 1939 he was in the German Foreign Office in Berlin and was already involved with the group of anti-Nazis about Beck and Goerdeler. In July of that year he called on Neville Chamberlain and Lord Halifax in London, informed them of the forthcoming Nazi-Soviet pact and attempted and failed to enlist active British support for the democratic opposition within Germany. From then on he was, as it were, the foreign affairs specialist among the younger anti-Nazis. When war had broken out he visited Washington to attend a conference of the Institute of Pacific Relations. He devoted all his energies to an attempt to create an understanding of the great change in opinion which he believed imminent in Germany. He was anxious that the United States should support the opposition within Germany, as publicly as possible, and was convinced that if this were done German opinion, at that time overwhelmingly against the war, would be crystallized and the Nazi government overthrown. He asked for an interview with President Roosevelt, which request was at first favourably received but later turned down—on the prompting, it is said, of the British Embassy.

It is curious that the British should have regarded Trott as a probable Nazi agent and casts a sad light on the intelligence methods of the Foreign Office at that time. The Hon. David

Astor, who was at Oxford with him, has written, in a letter published by Eberhard Zeller: 'To me he was a teacher and elder brother as well as a well-loved friend. He was the greatest member of my generation in any country that I have met. . . . I believe that he was more deeply and thoroughly anti-Nazi than any Englishman or American.' But though an anti-Nazi, he was not anti-German, and during 1939 the spirit of hatred, with which the name of Lord Vansittart is perhaps unfairly associated, made great progress in Great Britain. The terrible simplificaions of warfare were at work—for many quite intelligent people Nazism and Prussian militarism had become synonymous, almost one word—and any German patriot, indeed any German who had not emigrated, was regarded as suspect. Furthermore, not all the men who had known Trott at Oxford had shared Mr. Astor's opinion of him. Trott was a forceful conversationalist and had little time for the woolly liberal emotions which were not infrequently produced as an alternative to thought in the late '30's. He had, in fact, made enemies. Many of those enemies were now in or close to Whitehall. And woolly sentimentalizing about the Spanish Communists was now replaced by an equally flabby hatred of 'Germany' as such and, soon, by a curious infatuation with Stalin's Russia.

Trott, then, was a link between Moltke and Yorck on the one hand and the 1938 conspirators on the other. He was also, of course, on terms of close acquaintance or friendship with the anti-Nazis inside the Foreign Ministry, Hans-Bernd von Haeften, the brothers Kordt, ex-ambassador Ulrich von Hassell, and the others who lived beneath the benevolent protection of State Secretary von Weizsäcker.

In Berlin Moltke had renewed an old friendship with Adolf Reichwein, the author, philosopher and celebrated *Wandervogel*, whose wanderings had led him all over Europe as well as through China and Mexico. In Germany he had been interested in the youth movement—hence his friendship with Moltke—and in education generally. In 1930 he became professor of history at the Halle Pedagogic High School. Basically non-political, though a Russophile, he had joined the Socialists shortly before the advent of the Nazis to power. He was now working at the Folklore Museum, in the Unter den Linden, and his little office there was a convenient meeting place for the enemies of the régime. It was he who introduced the leading socialists, Mierendorff, Haubach and later Leber, into the Kreisau Circle.

He was also a friend of Dr. Eugen Gerstenmaier, the Protestant clergyman who before the war had laboured chiefly among industrial workers, and who was now the representative of the Bishop of Württemberg, Bishop Wurm, in Berlin. Dr. Gerstenmaier was devoting himself to the spiritual welfare of the foreign workers in Germany. He was to be one of the leading figures of the German opposition and played an important rôle in the events of July 20th.

Two priests of the Society of Jesus who belonged to the Kreisau Circle were Father Delp of Munich and Father Roesch, the Father Provincial of the Bavarian Jesuits. They joined the Kreisau group—though 'joining' is too strong a word for membership of so loose an organization—in 1942. Through them contact was established with the Bavarian anti-Nazi movement, of which Colonel Sperr was the leading figure and which, by analogy with the Kreisau Circle, came to be known as the Augsburg Circle. They too were a link with Bishop Count Preysing, the Catholic Bishop of Berlin.

Other prominent members of the circle included Harald Poelchau, Lutheran chaplain of Tegel Prison in Berlin who was to have the sad and yet grateful duty of giving spiritual consolation to many of his closest friends during their last hours: Hans Peters, Professor of State Law at Berlin university: Paulus von Husen, another international lawyer; Horst von Einsiedel, an economist who, with Moltke, had worked in the Loewenberg youth movement in happier days: Hans Lukaschek, a former Oberpräsident of Silesia and a member of the Centre Party: and Theodor Steltzer who was much interested in the movement for the union of all the Protestant Churches. These, then, were some of the men of Kreisau, not all of whom knew one another, for such knowledge is extremely dangerous in a state where the police interrogate by torture, though all of them knew Helmuth von Moltke. There were others, on the fringes as it were of the movement. Though their views varied, as was only to be expected, they had one quality in common, or rather one attitude, a belief in justice and a sense of responsibility for the future.

Also they were, in the majority, profoundly religious men. Indeed it would not be an exaggeration to say that the Kreisau Circle was as much a religious movement—comparable, say, to the group of men about Erasmus and Sir Thomas More—as a political one.

The questions which preoccupied these men were three, or rather it was one question with three aspects. How had so disgusting a blight as National Socialism come to be accepted by a country as civilized as Germany? What should their attitude towards their infamous government and its suicidal war now be? And what preparations could be made for the future when the present infamy should have passed away?

In answer to the first question, they could not accept the Allied propagandist view that National Socialism was a purely German phenomenon, with its implication that the Germans were somehow endowed with more than their fair share of original sin. On the other hand they did not pretend that Germany was merely the victim of circumstances and thus attempt to shelve the responsibility of the German people for the crimes that were being committed in their name. On German soil, as they saw it, a poisonous plant with roots which stretched across all Europe had produced its monstrous blossom. The seed from which this plant had grown was the alienation of man from the society in which he lived through the destruction of his fundamental beliefs.

Steltzer speaks of the 'development of the mass-man' (*der Massenmensch*) into a being incapable of forming his own judgment, and describes the true crisis of our age as 'the loss of those fundamentals upon which a stable order can be constructed'. Without those fundamentals, mob propaganda, that insult to the human soul, has a clear field in which to build its bonfires. A man incapable of judgment can and will believe anything, no matter how foolish or wicked.

Father Delp put it thus:

Contemporary man is to a high degree not only godless, he has slipped into a way of life in which he is incapable of accepting God. . . . Wherein lies this incapacity for God? It lies in a withering away of certain human organs which no longer perform their normal functions. And also in the structure and form of human life which demands too much of the individual and prevents him from being himself. . . . What is to be done? There are three possibilities: To proclaim the Divine Order and to await everything from its renewed recognition: To mend the individual and from his restored health to await the general recovery: To put the framework of life in order and thence anticipate human triumph—all three courses must be followed . . . The twentieth century revolution acquires, at long last, its theme and the possibility of creating a new and durable compass for human beings.

Haubach, looking at the world about him, wrote on July 6th, 1944:

The more I attempt to penetrate the dark wisdom of the two testaments, the more I am forced to think that in the last centuries true understanding of God's message has become obscured; this message is that man is not only a fallen creature, sinful, petty and pitiful, but also that he can participate in the divine to an extent which is in no wise comprehended in our decadent age. . . .

Shortly before his death in 1943—and he was killed in an airraid, so this is not a death-bed remark—Mierendorff said to Father Roesch:

'I have long lived without religion. But I have reached the conviction that Christianity alone is capable of imparting meaning and strength to life. And now I follow this path towards God. I think, Father, that you will be happy to hear this from me.'

In a letter of Helmuth von Moltke's to Mr. Lionel Curtis, written in 1942, he said:

'Perhaps you will remember that, in discussions before the war, I maintained that a belief in God was not essential for coming to the results you arrive at. Today I know I was wrong, completely wrong.'

These quotations could be multiplied, but perhaps the point is made. The attitude of the men of Kreisau might be summarized as follows. Once Christianity is discarded, any *Weltanschauung* can take its place. Without God there can be no true law. The Goddess of Reason presides over the guillotine, the chimneys of Auschwitz, the starvation camps of the Russian north. It is all quite obvious: it is also quite frequently forgotten. The abandonment of the principles of Christianity has shown, perfectly simply, that sin is death. If our society is to live, then it must be so constituted that there is a place in it for God, and the only place for God is in the soul of man. These are platitudes. What is not a platitude is that Moltke and his friends, practical, active men, were prepared to live, think and die for these truths. In a letter to his wife, shortly before his execution, Moltke describes a dialogue with the judge, Dr. Freisler, who had condemned him to death:

'And so finally I am selected as a Protestant, am attacked and condemned primarily because of my friendship with Catholics, which means that I stood before Freisler not as a Protestant, not as a great landowner, not as a noble, not as a Prussian, not as a German even—all that was definitely eliminated earlier in the trial. . . . No, I stood there as a Christian, and as nothing else. "The cat is indeed out of the bag," as Herr Freisler says.'

This belief in the ethics of Christianity was, then, the common denominator of the very varied ideas of the Kreisau Circle. In Appendix I to this book are given the surviving Kreisau documents in which their views concerning the future were summarized. It will be seen that a section, perhaps the most important section, of the first paper and the greater part of the third are devoted to the question of how a future German society could be imbued with Christian principles. But also this acceptance of Christianity on the part of the men of Kreisau affected profoundly their individual behaviour towards the government in power. Here there was not unanimity nor consistency, nor was Christian doctrine an infallible guide.

On the one side there were those who inclined towards the Quietist view, that it is nobler to suffer the slings and arrows of outrageous fortune, that 'self-conscious will' is a poison. Though no Quietist—and Quietism is a metaphysic both deeply rooted and widely spread in Germany since the eighteenth century—could ever belong to such a group of men as those of Kreisau, there were some whose attitude was not far removed from it.

Theodor Steltzer, for instance, has written:

The underlying points of view which I let guide me throughout the war were as follows:

1. The moral criteria on which Western-Christian tradition is based apply as absolutely to individuals as to societies, whether the individual is dealing with friend or foe, in private life as in public. The statement that an ideal end excuses any means is false.

2. The political struggle against a criminal national government does not entitle the individual to escape from his responsibility as a member of that nation or even to place himself in opposition to the national community.

3. Personal political decisions must not be allowed to impose a burden upon outsiders and innocent men.

From these three basic principles a series of decisions follow automatically: Refusal of every form of revolutionary violence and of assassination as a political weapon: Refusal of sabotage, desertion and the passing of military intelligence to the enemy: Refusal of all measures which could damage the Armed Forces in which our sons, in truly tragic circumstances, are doing their duty.

Moltke, at least in the early years of the war, shared this point of view. And in one of the letters which he wrote to his wife from prison, he expresses his satisfaction that his arrest, in January of 1944, had prevented his becoming involved with Stauffenberg, as Peter Yorck von Wartenburg became involved. He says: 'I was and still am innocent of all connection with the use of violence.' Certainly to begin with, and perhaps to the end, he regarded it as the duty of himself and his friends simply to plan for the day when the Nazis would no longer be there. On the other hand, the plans that survive indicate that they envisaged a previous, successful *coup d'état* and it has been suggested that Moltke's advocacy of non-violence in his last letters was intended as much for the eyes of a possible Gestapo reader as for those of his wife. Be that as it may, in 1940 and 1941 his position was certainly close to Steltzer's.

On the other hand a man like Leber, while respecting such an attitude, explicitly refused to accept it for himself. He informed his Kreisau friends that he intended to fight against the Nazis with every means at his disposal, including the weapon of assassination. But then Leber always regarded Moltke somewhat from the point of view of the practical politician observing the theoretician. Gerstenmaier, in an article published in *Christ und*

Welt on July 20th, 1950, has shown how far removed he too stood from Steltzer's position.

The *coup d'état* of July 20th, 1944, in all its stages, in every phase of its preparation and in the will and consciousness of every participant, had at all times only one theme. This theme was: Germany's salvation. Undoubtedly there were and are people for whom this theme had and has no particular appeal, and this may be one reason why the *coup d'état* has been only slowly and grudgingly acknowledged by foreigners. So far as Germany's former wartime enemies are concerned, we can understand this attitude. For July 20th was neither planned nor executed for the sake of Allied war aims. No more was it carried out for the sake of this or that doctrine of national politics. It was planned and executed simply and solely for the salvation of Germany, for the salvation of German blood and German soil, for the salvation of German freedom and for the salvation of Germany's last claim to honour and dignity before the bar of world history. The attempt might fail—the odds were always two to one against success—but it must be made. For this attempt was the ultimate chance of using Germany's heart's blood to liberate Germany from a ruthless tyranny; it was also an attempt to save millions of degraded and humiliated men and women of many European nations from the fearful might of the murderers and ravishers of Buchenwald and Auschwitz, from those same murderers who had laden shame upon the name of Germany. No matter what the odds, this attempt must be made. At the same time there was the question of saving the Reich from that total collapse which would cost millions life and home alike.

Between Steltzer's and Gerstenmaier's points of view there is a great gulf. The explanation is that the Kreisau Circle, as such, was not involved in any of the attempts to kill Hitler, though many of its members were, and almost all died on the gallows, were beheaded or shot. But as a group, its responsibility, the terms of reference it set itself, were to study post-Nazi Germany and to prepare a group of men ready to take over when the Nazis were gone. To quote Gerstenmaier once again:

. . . the men of Kreisau occupied themselves almost exclusively with political, cultural, economic and legal problems, the problems which would confront a new, post-Hitler German government. Military matters were not their concern. They were neither army leaders, nor did they have at their disposal any organized power. Their field was that of thought. Their task, the drafting of a new order for a state based on law. Their intention, the overthrow of the ideology of the total state. Their aim, the rebuilding of Germany in the spirit of Christianity and of social justice, and its incorporation in a united Europe. . . .

It was in the winter of 1941–42 that the study of these subjects was systematically embarked upon. The system according to which they worked was that two or three men would study one particular subject, which would then be discussed at a larger meeting. On the results of this, a programme could then be outlined. If such a method seems remote and intellectual, it must be remembered that their aim was a consciously practical one, and, furthermore, that there was really no other method open to them. Political thought, with them, had to replace political action, though it might truly be said that in their case thought was action. And it was, of course, dangerous action. Moltke, writing in English to Mr. Lionel Curtis in 1942, said:

'The constant danger in which we live is formidable. . . . Can you imagine what it means to work as a group when you cannot use the telephone, when you are unable to post letters, when you cannot tell the names of your closest friends to your other friends for fear that one might be caught and might divulge the names under the pressure?'

So they worked in small groups, Steltzer and a few others studying the relationship between Church and State, Father Roesch Catholic matters, Professor Peters questions connected with the Concordat, Moltke the reform of higher education, Moltke and Steltzer again constitutional problems, Moltke, Gerstenmaier, Einsiedel and Trotha economic matters and so on. These groups met frequently in various parts of Germany. There were larger meetings, at which in theory at least the whole group was present. Three of these were held at Kreisau, the dates being Whitsun 1942, October 1942 and Whitsun 1943. At the first religious and cultural matters were discussed, at the second constitutional questions, at the third economic problems. A fourth meeting was held at Peter Yorck's house, Klein Oels, later in 1943. It was probably here that the *Instructions to the 'Land' Commissioners,* dated August 9th, 1943, were drawn up:

this document is the final, practical summary of the Kreisau Circle's work. With this achieved, their task as a group was over. As individuals, many of them were thenceforth involved in Stauffenberg's plans, and had he succeeded it seems at least possible that much of their thought would have been transformed into reality.

Moltke wrote, in English:

'For us, Europe after the war is less a problem of frontiers and soldiers, of top-heavy organizations or ground plans, but Europe after the war is a question of how the picture of man can be re-established in the breasts of our fellow citizens.'

There it is, in a nutshell. On the one hand we have the vast states of the modern world, growing year by year more centralized ever since the eighteenth century, with power more and more concentrated in the hands of a few administrators and bureaucrats in distant capitals: on the other an enormous pro-letariat, almost without responsibility, into which the middle classes are being steadily eroded, a shifting, unstable mass, in-capable of using the power which numbers, not talent, have thrust upon it and therefore at the mercy of demagogues and Caesars. In these enormous states the good of great numbers must be sacrificed to that of other millions. The peasants of Schleswig-Holstein, for instance, are left to starve in the '30's because the measures that would relieve their misery might possibly cause distress to other populations in other parts of the Reich. To Berlin, with bigger problems on its hands, or for that matter to the factory workers of the Ruhr or the miners of Silesia, the sufferings of the Schleswig peasantry are a very small matter. Similarly the collapse of an industry in Bavaria can mean little to those peasants in their salty meadows beside the North Sea.

A great political party needs five million, eight million, ten million votes. It is not and cannot be preoccupied, save on lowest common denominator terms, with the interests of those voters. And they, feeling themselves neglected, eventually decide that the democratic system is a swindle. They come to realize that, as individual men and women, they count for nothing. And then other voices, appealing directly to those emotions of loneliness and disillusion, are heard: *Ein Volk, ein Reich, ein*

Führer. King Stork has replaced King Log and the centralization is tighter than ever.

The problem, then, as they saw it from Kreisau, was how to re-create a democratic system in which power should exist in human, not numerical, form, or to put it in other terms, how the people could be enabled to administer their own affairs and therefore accept that element of responsibility without which no man can be a truly useful and satisfied member of his society.

Constitutionally, they saw it as very largely a question of size. In a country of three or four millions, in Denmark say, or Ireland, or Switzerland, it is possible for a man to know almost exactly what is happening and why, and in human terms. His public figures are also men of whom he has heard at least at second or third hand, whom he can judge almost as he judges his neighbours. That is certainly not the case in Germany or France or Britain. From a humanistic standpoint a country of half a dozen or less millions would seem to be of the optimum size. And indeed in those smaller countries there would appear to exist an emotional stability unknown in the great nations. The inhabitants of such countries may in fact be said to govern themselves.

But of course for economic, ethnic and many other reasons a country the size of Germany cannot be split up into twenty sovereign states. The solution, then, was federalization, that potent tradition in German political life. Germany, while remaining a unit, would be broken up into a number of Regions (*Länder*) corresponding not to the old kingdoms and principalities, but roughly to the military *Wehrkreise*. Prussia, for example, would be broken up. Fritz von der Schulenburg and others worked on the delineation of the Regional boundaries.

They did not propose to stop there. They looked back, beyond Hegel, Treitschke, Marx and the other nineteenth-century theorists of the centralized, omnipotent state, to Freiherr vom Stein who, it will be recalled, had rebuilt a Prussia wrecked by the Napoleonic hurricane. Stein, aware in his day of the intellectual and spiritual enfeeblement of the centralized administration, had devolved administrative power as far down as he could. Maximum responsibility for their own affairs was given to towns and even to villages. And, as is known, the response was immediate and great: a revivified Prussia took a leading part, only seven years after its total collapse, in the overthrow of the tyrant.

The constitution that the men of Kreisau desired is outlined in their own words in Appendix I to this book. The concept, which in this century is revolutionary, was that power should be far, far down, in Districts (*Kreise*) of a couple of hundred thousand and even in Parishes (*Gemeinden*) of many less. Each parish and district would have its own council or *Tag*, by which would be elected members to the *Landtag* and hence ultimately to the *Reichstag*. It was hoped that some supra-national federation of federations might provide, not a government in the ordinary sense, but an authority over all Europe which might ultimately be represented with the other continents and civilizations in a supreme legal body.

The central authority of the Reich, presided over by a Reich Commissioner (*Verweser*), would be responsible for foreign affairs, the armed services and those economic matters which were too extensive to be dealt with lower down. It would, with this last addition, have powers and responsibilities similar to, but rather less than, those originally envisaged for the federal government of the United States.

The future economic system is described in some detail in the second of the Kreisau documents. Briefly, a mixed economy was envisaged, the mines, steel production, the basic chemical industry and the power plants being nationalized, while in other industries competition was to be encouraged, any system of restrictive cartels or monopolies being liable to dissolution. It was considered essential that the workers be given a greater interest in their work and that industry become an act of co-operation between the owners and workers who were to receive their share of the profits. This was to be the responsibility of the trade unions, for whom a most important future was foreseen. It was hoped thus that the working man would regain that pride and interest in his work which the industrial revolution had often stolen from him. It was intended that the trade unions, like the state, be de-centralized as far as possible, at least down to the regional level, for the massive unions, too, had lost contact with their members in Weimar days. Each Region would have its Regional Economic Chamber, which would consist of members elected from the unions and from the representatives of industry, and which would arbitrate in cases of dispute. A similar chamber would exist for the Reich as a whole.

Such then, in broad outline, was the future condition envisaged by the men of Kreisau. It was proposed that this system of decentralization be begun at the earliest possible moment, as soon, that is, as Germany was freed of the Nazis. Since in these circumstances communications might well be disrupted for a longer or shorter time, Regional Commissioners were to be appointed at once, and the *Instructions to the 'Land' Commissioners* drawn up. Within the rather loose framework of these instructions, which are really a statement of principles, the Commissioners would, from the beginning, have great latitude of decision.

A minor question with which the men of Kreisau also dealt was the punishment of war criminals. Document D shows their views on this most thorny and dangerous problem. Briefly, they wished this matter put in the hands of the Hague Court, with a bench of judges, consisting of three representatives of the Allied powers, two neutrals and one German. They were anxious to avoid the farce of the war crimes trials that followed the First World War and also believed that the effect of the trials-to-be would be greatly increased if they could avoid the appearance of an act of legalized vengeance by the victors against the vanquished. There were several eminent lawyers among the Kreisau men and there can be no doubt that they knew what they were talking about. From a psychological point of view there is surely little question that they were right. To many people in Germany and to some, including Sir Winston Churchill, abroad, justice did not always *appear* to be done in all the endless trials which followed the armistice of 1945.

In December of 1943 Moltke learned that a certain man was wanted by the Gestapo. He warned him, but the man failed to escape and Moltke was incriminated and arrested in January. The charge against him was not a serious one, nor did the police uncover any of Moltke's more important activities. Indeed in the following July his gaolers were talking about his early release.

but then came the Stauffenberg *putsch,* papers were captured, including Goerdeler's, and all was blown open. Moltke was tried and executed in the following year.

With Moltke in prison, many of the men of Kreisau accepted Stauffenberg's thesis and his leadership, particularly Yorck, Trott and Gerstenmaier. He, in turn, was influenced by their ideas. He once remarked, *à propos* of the older leaders of the German resistance, that it was not his intention to make 'an old man's revolution'. Had he succeeded, on that hot and sultry morning in East Prussia, there can be no doubt that his prestige in the new Germany would have been enormous, and that he would have turned more and more to this group of young lawyers, socialists and theologians.

They were fully ready and willing to serve their country and their continent. Adam von Trott had made use of his position in the Foreign Ministry to establish contact with Mr. Allen Dulles, the American Secret Service agent in Switzerland, and had also visited Stockholm. By the spring of 1944 the Gestapo was taking an altogether unhealthy interest in his activities, as well he knew. In May he was in Verona. He could, quite easily, have gone to Rome, which was about to fall, and remained there until the Americans and British arrived. The idea crossed his mind, but he dismissed it. He knew that his sorely pressed friends needed him in Berlin, and he was determined to be at Stauffenberg's side when the attempt was made. He returned to Germany, was arrested on July 20th, tried on August 14th and executed on August 26th.

CHAPTER VI

D R. OTTO JOHN has described the political situation within the resistance movement at this time, 1943–44, in the following words:

After the elimination of Oster and Dohnanyi (in the spring of 1943) the executive branch of the conspiracy had to be reorganized. In October 1943 General Olbricht, in agreement with General Beck, handed over further staff planning for the *coup d'état* to Lieutenant-Colonel Count Stauffenberg, then Chief of Staff of the General Army Office. Stauffenberg inherited from Tresckow the military plans and preparations which the latter had drawn up, but not the central political leadership. This leadership crumbled away as a result of regrouping within the conspiracy since it was no longer possible—as in former days due to the combined activity of Oster and Dohnanyi—to keep the various resistance groups united under Beck's methodical and centralized control. Beck himself had to undergo a major operation and it was doubtful whether he would survive or, if he did, whether he would still possess the strength necessary for further leadership of the conspiracy. Furthermore Popitz and Goerdeler had become politically estranged. It is true that under Stauffenberg the conspiracy acquired a new military executive, but united political control was never recreated.

Yet a shadow cabinet did exist in various forms in the spring of 1944. The government of General Beck, who was to be Head of State, would probably have been formed more or less as follows:

Chancellor of the Reich: Dr. Karl Goerdeler (Conservative).
Vice-Chancellor: Wilhelm Leuschner (Social-Democrat).
Secretary of State in the Chancellery: Peter Count Yorck von Wartenburg.

113

Minister of the Interior: Dr. Julius Leber (Social-Democrat).
Secretary of State for the Interior: Fritz Count von der Schulenburg.
Minister of the Economy: Dr. Paul Lejeune-Jung (People's Conservative).
Minister of Justice: Dr. Joseph Wirmer (Centre).
Minister for Educational and Religious Matters: Dr. Kurt von Schuschnigg (if Austria were to remain a part of Germany, or alternatively Dr. Johannes Popitz or Eugen Bolz).
Minister of Finance: Dr. Ewald Löser (General director of the Krupp works).
Foreign Minister: Ulrich von Hassell (former ambassador in Rome) or Werner Count von der Schulenburg (former ambassador in Moscow).
War Minister: General Friedrich Olbricht.
Secretary of State for War: Claus Count von Stauffenberg.
Minister of Labour: Bernhard Letterhaus (Centre).
Minister of Transport: Dr. Raabe (Centre) or Matthäus Herrmann (Social-Democrat).

As already stated, General Witzleben was to be Commander-in-Chief of the Armed Forces and General Hoepner was to stand by to take over the Army, should Fromm fail to co-operate.

It was, in fact, a strong but scarcely a homogeneous team. And the man who should have controlled it was ageing and far from well. After Beck's death, Roland Freisler cross-examined his housekeeper during the trial of General Hoepner in August of 1944. Hoepner had maintained that Beck was a man strong and competent enough to save Germany from the impending disaster. Freisler, of course, was determined to discredit Beck, but nevertheless his housekeeper's evidence has a certain, tragic interest.

Freisler: You are the People's Comrade Frau Else Bergenthal. . . . How old are you?
Bergenthal: Forty-two. . . .
Freisler: What was your job? Whose housekeeper were you?
Bergenthal: Colonel-General Beck's.
Freisler: Good, Colonel-General Beck's. Would you say that his was a strong, firm personality which would have signifi-

cance if it were to be displayed to the people, if it were to make demands upon the people?

Bergenthal: I don't know; I'm not in a position to express an opinion on that.

Freisler: You might well say: 'That is a hard decision, which is beyond me: how can I, a woman, decide on such things?' You're quite right to be careful what you say. What do you know of his manner and way of life? Was he a man of soldierly determination or a man encompassed with worries and indecision?

Bergenthal: I can't express an opinion on that either.

Freisler: Well, let's put it this way. In the morning it's possible to see if a man has been thrashing about in the night.

Bergenthal: Yes.

Freisler: Well?

Bergenthal: During the last fortnight, when I was on holiday, Frau Kuster told me that he had sweated fearfully during the night and that he was terribly worked up.

Freisler: So that when he got up in the morning his bed was wringing wet!

Bergenthal: Yes.

Freisler: That hardly sounds like a man of especial strength. Have you anything else to say that struck you about this man recently, anything that seemed to you notable?

Bergenthal: No, there was nothing else that struck me.

Freisler: So the man who for fourteen days thrashed about in his fears all night until his bed was wringing wet, this is the man who said, 'It is a question of a trial of strength.'

Are there any questions to be asked of People's Comrade Bergenthal? There are not. You need not swear an oath. We believe you in any case, with or without oath. You may go now.

In July of 1944 Colonel-General Beck was sixty-four years old, having been born in June of 1880. His father was a scientist and ironmaster, who had entered industry in order to support his widowed mother, and he made a comfortable but not large income. His interests remained scientific—he had studied under the great Dr. Bunsen—and he wrote a number of papers on metallurgy and kindred subjects for which he was honoured by several academic bodies and finally created a Doctor of Engineering by Aachen Technical High School. His wife, the General's mother, was the daughter of a family of Hessian lawyers. Thus Ludwig Beck was born into the west German *bourgeoisie*, though he had soldierly relations on both sides of his family. He had uncles, paternal and maternal, who had been generals in the Franco-Prussian war.

When writing about his childhood at Biebrich, he quoted Theodor Vischer's remark: 'Morality is always self-evident.' His parents, who were Protestants, were church-goers but religiously tolerant. Their home life was quiet and solid, with much music in which the whole family—there were two other sons besides Ludwig—took part. In such an atmosphere no pressure was brought to bear upon the children in their choice of career. Ludwig Beck attended the Humanistic School at Wiesbaden, but in 1898 decided to become a soldier. He joined the 15th Prussian Field Artillery Regiment at Strassburg, being gazetted lieutenant the following year. His contemporaries have described him as a stern but cheerful junior officer and were much impressed by his force of character.

From 1908 to 1911 he was at the War Academy in Berlin, training for the General Staff. General von Thaer, one of his instructors, later said: 'Beck was a quite extraordinarily gifted soldier, who reminded me most strongly of the great Moltke, whom I had also known personally. He was undoubtedly the most capable officer of his class.'

He spent the years of the First World War on the Western Front, being in staff appointments throughout. He was with the VI Reserve Corps at the Marne, with the 117th Reserve Division during the Battle of Loos, the 13th Reserve Division at Verdun, and from the winter of 1916 with the staff of Army Group German Crown Prince, of which the Chief of Staff was Count von der Schulenburg who became a close personal friend of Beck's and whose son, Fritz von der Schulenburg, has already figured prominently in this story. Beck was also on terms of personal friendship with the Crown Prince; in August, 1919, the latter wrote of his pleasure at being visited in his exile by 'the outstanding Major Beck'.

He was at Spa in November of 1918 and witnessed the German collapse from the military centre. This was for him a tragic event, and he adopted and adhered to the theory that the civilians had stabbed the soldiers in the back. He did not, however, believe the German Army could possibly have won the war—indeed as early as 1917 he was a keen advocate of a negotiated peace—but he did believe that the revolution was an additional and unnecessary catastrophe. Since his attitude at this time foreshadows very closely his position a quarter of a century later, it is worth quoting from a letter that he wrote on November 28th, 1918.

'At a time when a state can only struggle out of defeat towards a tolerable peace and a healthy peace-time economy by straining its every muscle and by preserving its complicated organism fully intact, it is insanity to make a revolution as well.' He did not believe that the revolution was simply the result of the lost war, but rather that it marked the release of certain forces created by long laid anti-social plans. Of the war, he wrote: 'My views concerning the possible outcome of the war had become firmer during these past two years, in which I have gained a closer appreciation of the larger issues and factors involved: with only minor fluctuations my opinion has been that we must reach an understanding (with the Allies). That was also the view of the Chief of Staff and of the Crown Prince . . . Only a handful of men, with fearful anxiety, examined the future and foresaw the impending disaster. With the full co-operation of the home front, one possibility still lay open to us: to withdraw to a shorter line—Antwerp-Metz or Lèige-Metz—there to conduct another determined defence, and thus once again present our opponents with the alternatives of deciding on peace at once or of prolonging the war into 1919.'

Before and during the Second World War peace by negotiation was again his ambition, though he knew, before many of the authorities in London and Paris realized it, that negotiation with the Nazis was futile. Once war had begun he saw that only a new German government could talk to the Western powers, and it was a tragic disappointment to him that such a government, when still in embryo, should be treated with the utmost suspicion and should be offered really no encouragement whatsoever by the leaders of the democracies.   This perhaps shows a certain *naïveté* on his part.   He was well aware that the concept of total war is only the other side of the pacifist penny, a counterfeit coin: he stated this himself, and he regarded pacifism as a denial of God, arguing that war is a feature of the Divine Order here on earth. Did he fail to realize that when the democracies—the peoples of France and Britain and the United States—were compelled to abandon their pacifist beliefs, they were likely to slide into the alternative heresy?   Like many Germans with only an imperfect knowledge of our democratic systems, he ascribed too much importance and power to our elected leaders, who after all are usually men of responsibility and good sense, and not enough to the frequently irresponsible publicists who mould the opinion which controls those leaders.   In 1918, at least, it would surely have surprised him if he could have foreseen that in the years to come many of these publicists were to regret loudly and openly that the war had not gone on until 1919 and that several hundred thousand more men were not killed for the hollow gratifications of a victory parade down the Unter den Linden.

During the nineteen-twenties Beck filled various staff and command appointments in Seeckt's Reichswehr and by 1930 was commanding the 5th Artillery Regiment with the rank of Major-General. It was now that he first became directly involved in politics, and in a curious fashion.

Two of his junior officers were proselytizing for the Nazi Party, a most serious offence in the non-political army.   Beck firmly reprimanded them, reported the offence and assumed the matter closed.   A few days later, while returning from an exercise, the two officers were arrested in the streets of Ulm in broad daylight: nor had their commanding officer been informed.   He was furious and immediately sent in his resignation, which he was with difficulty persuaded to withdraw.   At the court-martial he spoke on behalf of his two officers vigorously and thus, by a curious paradox, first achieved national celebrity as a defender of Nazis.   From this fact, certain persons have since maintained that Beck was not then opposed to the Nazi point of view: this is quite untrue, he was merely doing what any decent commanding officer in any army would do, namely attempting to protect the men for whom he was responsible and whom he had already punished.   But the War Minister was intensely annoyed and only the insistence of the commander-in-chief, General Hammerstein, prevented Beck being dismissed from the service.

In 1932 Beck commanded the 1st Cavalry Division and in 1933 was made Chief of the *Truppenamt*, which was the camouflaged title of the General Staff.   In 1934 he swore the oath of allegiance to Hitler as Führer and Chancellor.   Beck's brother has reported that in later years he frequently expressed his regret that he had not resigned his commission rather than accept the oath.   It was Fritsch who persuaded him that his duty required him to remain in the army.

In May of 1935, when ordered to prepare a theoretical operational plan for the invasion of Czecho-Slovakia, he did offer to resign.   Such an operation, he said, could not be planned as an isolated campaign: it must lead to general war, and it was his belief that a staff study which was not based on reality was senseless.   In 1937 he refused to work on the plans for 'Special Case Otto', the invasion of Austria.   In July of that year he visited Paris as a private citizen and had a long talk with General Gamelin, the French chief of staff.   Gamelin quotes him as saying that a European war, no matter who won it, was 'bound to result in the destruction of Europe and of the civilization we share.   Bolshevism alone would profit.'

By 1937 he was already on friendly terms with Goerdeler, to whom he turned for advice on economic matters.   It was in November of 1937 that Hitler, at a conference of senior officers, first openly proposed to solve Germany's problems by force. Beck informed Goerdeler and began to consider how the army could be used to overthrow the government.   When Fritsch was framed by the Gestapo early in the following year, Beck looked to him to act, but Fritsch refused, first because he would not give even the appearance of rebelling from motives of self-defence, but also because, in his own words to Ulrich von Hassell, he had become convinced that Hitler was his country's fate.   'This man is Germany's destiny in good as in evil.   Should he now descend into the abyss he will drag us all with him.   There is nothing to be done.'

Beck believed that there was a great deal to be done.   From the early months of 1938 he, together with Goerdeler, Hammerstein,

Hoepner, the Berlin police president, Count Helldorf, and others, was planning a *coup d'état* in the event of war. During July and August Witzleben and Karl Heinrich von Stülpnagel, one of the four most senior officers on Beck's staff, worked out the military details. All was ready, only to be frustrated by the Munich Pact. In July of that year Beck had remarked: 'Soldierly obedience must cease at the point where knowledge, conscience and responsibility forbid the execution of an order,' and also: 'Exceptional times require exceptional measures.' But before this most un-revolutionary of men accepted force, he attempted to coerce his government by his own resignation.

Indeed he hoped that he might persuade Brauchitsch and, through him, the other most senior commanders also to resign in a mass gesture of protest against the policy of the Nazis. This 'generals' strike' was a concept which, as we have seen, endured. It was feasible, but it was hardly realistic. At Nuremberg, after the war, Manstein, who had been repeatedly approached to take part in, or lead, such a strike, explained his reasons for refusing to do so. A dictator, he said, can never give in to outside pressure: the moment he does so his dictatorship is automatically broken. Therefore a 'generals' strike', were it to succeed—and there was no other point in undertaking one—must be an act of mutiny against the political leadership of the state. But for a hundred and fifty years and longer the relationship of the military to the political leaders in Prussia, and later in Germany, had been based on the supremacy of the latter over the former. When Clausewitz remarked that war is the continuation of policy by other means, he meant precisely what he said. Decisions concerning war and peace are a matter of policy, a matter for the politicians and not for the soldiers, who at such times of decision are simply technical advisers.

This is true, not only of Germany, but of every modern state which is not prepared to slide into chaotic and pointless adventures on the one hand or rigid defeatism on the other. The army leaders cannot, as Bismarck knew, assume the role of the statesman, any more than one of the carriage horses can drive the coach-and-six. This basic principle, common to all modern civilized countries, had in Germany been reinforced since 1918 by Seeckt's insistence that the army stay clear of politics at all costs. Individuals such as Schleicher have been execrated for their dabblings in a field where they did not belong, by none more strongly than the German military leaders. Brauchitsch, Manstein, Rundstedt and the others were not the men to betray what they regarded as their primary tradition and the deepest interests of their service and country by following in his tortuous footsteps: they were even less willing to commit the army as such. Indeed it is open to considerable doubt whether they could have done so without actually ordering a mutiny. To expect generals to organize a mutiny is to have little regard for realities.

Yet, 'exceptional times require exceptional measures'. Beck realized exactly how exceptional the times were: the others did not, or if they did they lacked the clarity of vision to draw the necessary conclusions. To accuse them of civil cowardice is easy, and there is undoubtedly a grain of truth in it, but foolish inflexibility is an accusation closer to the mark. After all, one cannot expect men to be heroic in a civil or any other capacity. In fact, as in so many aspects of this tragedy, the problem is a subjective rather than an objective one.

Beck, who had clarity of vision and certainly did not lack courage, resigned alone, shortly before the Czechoslovak crisis reached its climax. Halder succeeded him as Chief of the General Staff. He inherited Beck's plans for a military *putsch*, which he amplified and which he was then prepared to put into operation in the event of war. Beck hoped that this would be unnecessary. He believed that his solitary resignation might open the eyes of the German people to the nature of the impending catastrophe. However, the position of Chief of Staff no longer carried the weight that it had in Moltke's or Schlieffen's time, as Beck well knew. Beck's departure was scarcely noticed outside the army, and, as Manstein and Weizsäcker had warned him, it made almost no difference to the course of events. From the autumn of 1938, Beck was without any official post and his name was soon forgotten by the mass of the German people.

From then on he lived in Berlin-Lichterfelde. He had married in 1916, only to be left a widower eighteen months later, with an infant daughter. This personal tragedy contributed to his increasing reserve of manner. Now, in his retirement, he was looked after by his daughter for a few months until she married.

Then he lived a very quiet life, alone at No. 9 Goethe-Strasse, growing his own vegetables and, like many another soldier-scholar, writing military history.

He was a sick man, worn by moral and mental conflict, when he left the Bendlerstrasse in 1938, though he wrote on October 31st that his health was improving and that he was sleeping better. But from that time forward he suffered from almost constant toothache which no dentist could cure. In 1943 he was seriously ill with cancer of the stomach. Sauerbruch, the celebrated surgeon and a close personal friend, saved his life by a most skilful operation and after a lengthy convalescence on Frau Sauerbruch's estate in Saxony Beck was fully restored to health.

During these years of retirement he wrote a history of Army Group Crown Prince and also edited the war memoirs of his old friend, General Count von der Schulenburg, who had died in 1939. Unpublishable at the time, these manuscripts were later destroyed by the Gestapo. He wrote numerous treatises on aspects of the 1914–18 war and on military matters generally, the essay entitled *The Doctrine of Total War* (1942) being of particular interest. In the last year of his life he was much preoccupied with the career of Foch, for whom he expressed a growing admiration. He was also interested in Robert E. Lee, in whose character and acceptance of self-denial he thought to see resemblances to his own personality and principles.

Many of these studies became papers which he read to the *Mittwoch-Gesellschaft,* or Wednesday Society, which had been founded in the mid-nineteenth century with the purpose of bringing scientists and humanists together. It was traditionally limited to sixteen members, each eminent in his own field, who met occasionally to exchange ideas. Each member in turn entertained the others to a simple meal and read a paper on his own subject. Sauerbruch was of their number, as were Planck, Jessen, Hassell, Popitz and a dozen more distinguished, older men. Beck was the only soldier amongst them. Professor Heisenberg, the physicist, has said how much wider than most soldiers' were Beck's interests. He could and did discuss existentialism with the philosopher, Eduard Spranger. Professor Heisenberg has described a meeting held on July 12th, 1944, at which Beck was present. Heisenberg spoke of the physical structure of the stars, the nature of the atom, the freeing of atomic energy and cosmic rays. Beck, he says, asked a number of acute questions, nor were they limited to the military potentialities of atomic energy.

Such, then, was the man who would, for a time at least, have been Head of the German State if Stauffenberg's bomb had done what it was intended to do. His political views were conservative without being reactionary. Though he himself would have liked to see a restored monarchy, he had no intention of further confusing what must already be a highly confused condition of affairs by drastic constitutional reforms. It seems likely that if he had had his way he would have made peace, seen order restored and then retired once again to his quiet and scholarly pursuits at No. 9 Goethe-Strasse. Devoid of personal ambition, it was only his high sense of duty which brought him to conspire against the government and which cost him his life.

During the discouraging months that were the spring of 1944, Beck's vitality had been low. Though frequently meeting with the other conspirators—we have a description of him visiting Leuschner, the trade unionist, wearing a pair of dark glasses as disguise—he had grown increasingly sceptical concerning the possibilities of success. On the other hand he had come to know Claus von Stauffenberg well and though in general Beck preferred the company of men of his own age, he developed a high respect for the young colonel. When, therefore, Stauffenberg was at last in a position to carry out the assassination himself, Beck sloughed off his depression. In the days immediately before July 20th, he was his old self again. At Jessen's house, on the evening of July 17th, he is described as alert and 'a changed man' after weeks of gloom, 'as though a burden had been lifted from him'. On the 18th Sauerbruch was with him and has written: 'He was quite calm, in excellent spirits and told amusing anecdotes about his past. He gave not the slightest indication that he was about to take part in an extraordinary and dangerous undertaking.'

Goerdeler was a man of Beck's generation, having been born in 1884. He came of a middle-class Protestant Prussian family which had produced many civil servants. He studied law, banking and commerce, and served in the First World War.

Returning to civilian life he entered local politics, first as a monarchist and later as a right-wing conservative republican. From 1920 to 1930 he was deputy Mayor of Koenigsberg and from 1930 to 1937 *Oberbürgermeister* of Leipzig. For a brief period in 1932 he also served as Reich Commissioner for Prices under Brüning, an office which he again held for a time under Hitler in 1934–5, but his advocacy of deflation and of a return to rigid financial orthodoxy suited neither the temper of the age nor of the politicians, and he soon returned to Leipzig.

The position of *Oberbürgermeister* of a German town was far more important than that of mayor of a large English or American city. Stresemann once described these powerful officials as being, after the great industrialists, 'the monarchs of everyday life'. They were elected for periods of up to twelve years, often had more power than the ministers of the government and provided many of the leading figures of Weimar days. These posts were the plums of the civil service, and election had to be confirmed by the Minister of the Interior. The *Oberbürgermeister* was the ruler, rather than the servant, of his city and frequently behaved as such.

Goerdeler, then, was a more prominent figure than his position might suggest to an Anglo-Saxon reader. His political views were very rigidly right wing. He was, in the early thirties, on good personal terms with Hitler, and was prepared to work with the Nazis so long as they were able to convince him that they were the nation's bulwark against bolshevism. His attitude, in fact, was close to that of Schacht, whom he numbered among his friends. However, he disapproved most strongly of Schacht's ingenious financial jugglings and described the economic policy of the Third Reich as 'insane'. He grew increasingly averse to the morals of the new state and its anti-semitism, and the persecution of the Churches disgusted him. When in 1937 the Nazi Party authorities in Leipzig refused to replace the statue of Mendelssohn before the *Gewandhaus* which had been removed in Goerdeler's absence and against his explicit orders, Goerdeler gave this as his reason for resigning from office. Henceforth he was to devote all his energies to the overthrow of the régime, which he had at last recognized for what it was.

In his 'Testament', written in America in 1937, he says: 'If the

Nazis wish to remain in power, they will of necessity turn against the Christian faith itself. The fight against the Church is only preparation and cover for the reality. This will be the fight against Christianity.'

He was a large, heavily-built man. His personal morals were rigidly, almost ridiculously, puritanical. Quite a number of people disapprove of divorced persons: Goerdeler would not allow in his house any woman who had so much as broken off her engagement. He regarded the possession of a silver cigarette case as proof of sybaritic luxury. He had no time for 'young men' which in his last years included men in their forties. He had even less time for 'ideologues' of all persuasions. In his earlier years he had been a convinced, indeed one might say a violent, Nationalist, and until the end of his life he was much preoccupied with Germany's eastern frontier. As late as 1944 he believed that it would be possible to restore to Germany, with British and American help, the territories lost to Poland in 1918: only in that year, too, did he apparently at last renounce German claims to Alsace-Lorraine. More practically, he was interested throughout his life in the reform of the German administrative system. He regarded himself, quite rightly, as an administrator of supreme ability. He believed that what he had done for Leipzig he could and should do for his country as a whole. As the years went by this conviction in his mission assumed almost Messianic proportions, clouding his judgment to the extent that he lost what little sense he had ever had for the political realities of the age. It was his duty to save Germany: it was Germany's duty to save Europe and the world from Bolshevism: therefore it was the duty of the Western Allies to support Goerdeler's Germany. But first, of course, Nazism must be overthrown, not only because it was intrinsically wicked but also because in its corruption and overweening ambitions it was incompatible with the Spartan, hard-working, puritanical Germany of Goerdeler's dreams. In his Germany there would be no luxury for the rich, no molly-coddling of the poor. The concept of the Welfare State, which we glimpse in the ideas of Kreisau, was anathema to him. He was violently opposed to the mildest socialism and believed in an absolutely free economy. It is hardly surprising that he was not popular with the men of Kreisau.

From 1937 on he was employed by the Bosch Works, a heavy-industry combine, as a sort of superior commercial traveller. This was camouflage arranged by Robert Bosch to enable him to move freely about the world before the war, and later to travel within Germany. He visited England and America, in 1938 and 1939, and attempted to enlist support for the German resistance movement. In England he was regarded as personally acceptable—nobody ever doubted Goerdeler's sincerity—but his tendency to talk wildly, to exaggerate his own importance in Germany and to promise more than could be achieved, undoubtedly did more harm than good to the cause he served.

Goering facilitated these lengthy travels abroad—Goerdeler was journeying in Europe, America, the Middle East and Africa almost continually from 1937 until the outbreak of the war—and on his return to Germany Goerdeler submitted reports of what he had seen and of the deductions that he had drawn to the Reich Marshal. These he hoped would strengthen Goering's hand in his spasmodic attempts to prevent Hitler from going to war. It must not be assumed that Goerdeler was engaged in any sort of espionage; he was not. He simply believed that he could influence Goering. Until the end, he cherished the belief that he could influence Hitler too, if given the chance, and always refused to approve of any plan to assassinate the dictator, though willing to serve or head a government brought into being by assassination.

Throughout the war, surprising though it seems, he still believed that if he could arrange an interview with Hitler, he could show the dictator the folly of his ways. He had a tremendous, and it would seem largely unfounded, faith in his own powers of persuasion. When he implied to foreign statesmen before the war that he possessed a large and influential following within Germany, he doubtless believed that he was speaking the truth.

Once the war had started, he applied the same tactics to the German generals, travelling from one front to the other, badgering them to act, exaggerating the possibilities open to them, often, and often correctly, insinuating moral cowardice on their part, and generally engendering more heat than light. On one occasion, during the spring of 1940, he succeeded in reducing Halder, then Chief of the General Staff, to tears. Guderian's reaction to Goerdeler, who visited him in March of 1943, is perhaps more typical and worth quoting:

It was during this time, when I was so extremely busy with my work, that my old friend, General von Rabenau, brought Dr. Goerdeler to see me, as the latter was anxious to talk to me. Dr. Goerdeler explained to me that since Hitler was incapable of performing his duties as Chancellor of the Reich and Supreme Commander of the Armed Forces, it was desirable that his activities as such be curtailed. He described to me in detail his programme of government and of reform: this programme showed high idealism and the social adjustments envisaged would undoubtedly have been most desirable, although Dr. Goerdeler's doctrinaire manner might not have facilitated the solution of the problems he posed. Dr. Goerdeler could not guarantee foreign support in the event of his plans succeeding. It was apparent that during his long-drawn-out attempts to establish contacts abroad he had been given a somewhat cold shoulder. Our enemies had refused to abandon the 'unconditional surrender' slogan, even in the event of Dr. Goerdeler being successful.

I asked Dr. Goerdeler how he envisaged setting limitations to Hitler's powers. He replied that Hitler would be retained as nominal head of the state, but would actually be interned on the Obersalzberg or in some other safe place. When I asked how the leading National Socialists were to be removed—since without doing so the proposed change of system was doomed from the beginning—I was informed that this was a matter for the armed forces to decide. But Dr. Goerdeler had not succeeded in winning over to his way of thinking a single commander of troops on active service. He asked me, when visiting the front, to promote his ideas and to let him know whether, and which of, the commanding generals were inclined to join with him. To my question as to who was actually in control of this undertaking, he replied: Colonel-General Beck. I was very surprised that a man like Beck, the hesitancy of whose character was well known to me, should be involved in such a business. A man of his type was the very last person suited to take part in a *coup d'état,* since he was incapable of taking a decision, and also had no popularity with the troops, to whom he was indeed more or less unknown; he was a philosopher but no revolutionary.

The weaknesses and mistakes of the National-Socialist system and the personal errors that Hitler made were by then plain to see—even to me; attempts must therefore be made to remedy them. In view of Germany's dangerous situation as a result of the Stalingrad catastrophe and of the demands made for unconditional surrender to all its enemies (including the Soviet Union) a way would have to be found that did not lead to a disaster for the country and the people. Hence the vast responsibility and the enormous difficulties that confronted anyone who tried to think quietly how he might best hope still to save Germany. I came to the conclusion that Dr. Goerdeler's plan would be harmful to our general interest and was furthermore incapable of being put into practice; I therefore declined to take any part in it. Like the rest of the Army, I also felt myself bound by the oath of allegiance that I had taken. I therefore asked Dr. Goerdeler to give up his proposed plan.

Disregarding my doubts, Dr. Goerdeler asked me, nevertheless, to procure him the information he had requested. This I agreed to do, since I hoped thereby to show Dr. Goerdeler that my attitude was not unique but that other generals thought as I did; by this means I trusted that I might persuade this undoubtedly idealistic man to abandon a course of action which I regarded as unsound. As a result I met Dr. Goerdeler again in April and was able to assure him that I had not found a single general who was prepared to join in his plan. The individuals I had sounded had all refused to take any part in the proposed action, not only on account of their oath of allegiance but also because of the grave situation at the front. I once again urged Dr. Goerdeler to give up the whole project . . .

I did not speak to Dr. Goerdeler again after April 1943, and I heard no more about his projects.

But there could be no question as to his personal courage. When another general complained that by such visits Goerdeler was endangering the lives of others, while himself remaining in the background, Goerdeler immediately composed a paper in which he stated in detail his reasons for opposing the Nazi régime, which he then signed and which he handed to the general in question. Courage or folly? He kept lists of the conspirators and also a journal which of course eventually fell into the hands of the Gestapo and cost many men their lives. When arrested, Goerdeler talked to the Gestapo incessantly, revealing all he knew about the conspiracy quite willingly. The fact that he also paid for his rashness with his own life is scarcely adequate excuse. It is hardly surprising that Stauffenberg was reluctant to trust him; though perfectly prepared to work with him once the *putsch* had succeeded, he would have preferred that Leber be the first Chancellor of post-Nazi Germany. Goerdeler was a brave and idealistic man, but whether he was more an asset than a liability to the German resistance movement is open to doubt.

Furthermore, his political friends were not of the best quality. They included Schacht, and for a time the authoritarian and near-Nazi Professor Popitz—who was trying, fatuously enough, in 1943 to attract Himmler of all people into the conspiracy—as well as Werner Count von der Schulenburg, who was a Russophile and would have considered making a separate peace with Stalin, and Professor Jessen, who at one time at least had foreseen a great future for the S.S. and whose star pupil, Ohlendorf, was the lunatic idealist responsible for some of the worst Jewish massacres in Russia. Goerdeler, in fact, was sadly lacking in discrimination.

In his description of his interview with Goerdeler, as given in his post-war memoirs, Guderian's reference to 'unconditional surrender' is characteristic. There can be no doubt that the 'unconditional surrender' slogan, propounded at Casablanca by Roosevelt and Churchill in January of 1943 and eagerly subscribed to by Stalin, had a great influence on the German generals: or, to put it cynically, that it gave them a first-class excuse for their continued refusal to act against Hitler. What was the purpose of overthrowing the government and perhaps risking the opprobrium of their fellow countrymen and the contempt of history, if by so doing they could not ameliorate the fate that Germany's enemies had prepared for her, the nature of which those enemies refused to divulge?

Both too much and too little can and has been made of the 'unconditional surrender' question. Too much, because there is no certain evidence that this gift to Goebbels prolonged the war, as many Germans have since stated. Would Guderian, for instance, have listened with more favour to Goerdeler's proposals if the catch-phrase had never been pronounced? It seems doubtful. On the other hand, the idea of 'unconditional surrender' does seem to have had a constipating effect on the policy makers of the Western allies. Having openly pledged themselves to this sterile and almost meaningless formula, they felt wellnigh incapable of talking to the men of the German resistance for fear lest such conversation reach Russian ears, be interpreted as a breach of faith and lead to a separate German-Russian peace. In retrospect the terror of thus creating a Russo-German *rapprochement*, which apparently lurked in the Foreign Office and the State Department in 1943 and even in 1944, seems very far-fetched indeed. Its effects were real enough. London and Washington refused to make any agreement with the conspirators: they were prepared to talk to them only in the interests of the Allied Intelligence services, that is to say, having accepted the Ludendorffian concept of total war, these tenuous contacts were to be employed for the Allied war effort, quite regardless of the fact that the men with whom they were dealing were German patriots, not Allied agents. These links were to be a one-way channel of information and no statement of intention or even simple co-ordination of plans was forthcoming from London or Washington. The British and American governments would not so much as pledge themselves to discontinue the aerial bombardment of Germany once the Nazis were overthrown. Despite the efforts made by Mr. Allen Dulles in Switzerland, nothing was offered to the men in Germany who were fighting the common enemy. They therefore found themselves with nothing positive to offer those generals who were wavering. Repeated attempts to discover what peace terms the Western Allies were prepared to offer a new German government were received in silence or were rebuffed.

The Allied refusal to state their terms was, in fact, a gross denial of responsibility. After 1918 they had been accused by the Germans of breaking their word, as outlined in President Wilson's Fourteen Points. Now, therefore, if they did not announce any terms at all they were making sure that they could not later be taxed with ill faith. Churchill's words, in the House of Commons on May 24th, 1944, were: 'The principle of unconditional surrender . . . will be adhered to . . . and that principle itself wipes away the danger of anything like Mr. Wilson's fourteen points being brought up by the Germans after their defeat, claiming that they surrendered in consideration of them.' The more one examines this statement, the more curious it appears. For a government to avoid a future accusation of lying by the simple expedient of saying nothing at all, surely implies a remarkable lack of faith by that government in its own integrity. The celebrated clarion call of the Atlantic Charter had been scarcely more explicit. It did not apply to the enemy. It did not apply to the neutrals. Nor to the Poles, when the time came. What then was the purpose of those sonorous and forgotten clichés about freedom? One of the more unpleasant and self-defeating aspects of total war is that pronouncements of policy tend to become subordinate to the excretion of propaganda, and responsibility for the future is cast aside in favour of immediate advantage and even of contemporary display.

As Professor Rothfels has pointed out, 'unconditional surrender' was a boomerang. It deprived any possible German government of responsibility for the future. Therefore the totality of that responsibility, for a nation of eighty millions toppling into an abysmal chaos, devolved on the Allies. Thus by their attempt to avoid any responsibility they in fact accepted the lot. Furthermore, by assuming that all Germans were evil, the Allies embraced Hitler's principles, and by refusing to help the German resistance in its attempt to shorten the war they also adopted Hitler's policy of nihilism, of leaving Germany a heap of rubble. Again, though he has since made ample amends, immediately after July 20th Churchill in the House of Commons exactly echoed Goebbels' speech about the conspirators, describing them as a small clique of officers, and expressing a certain satisfaction that 'dog eat dog'. Meanwhile Brendan Bracken was delighted that the *putsch* had failed since this failure would enable the Allies to win a 'total' victory. During the First World War it was ignorant eccentrics who went about stoning dachshunds and accusing elderly German Fräuleins of espionage. During the Second a similar hysteria, remarkably absent among the people, was occasionally in sad evidence among their rulers.

Did the Western governments not know what was going on in Germany? Unfortunately no such charitable explanation is possible. Mr. Allen Welsh Dulles, European head of the O.S.S. (the American secret service organization) from November 1942 until the end of the war, has stated in his book, *Germany's Underground*: 'Both Washington and London were fully advised beforehand on all the conspirators were attempting to do, but it sometimes seemed that those who determined policy in England and America were making the military task as difficult as possible by uniting all Germans to resist to the bitter end.' Yet in August of 1948 Lord Vansittart, who during the early years of the war had been Diplomatic Adviser to the Cabinet, could state: 'The whole basis of my attitude towards Germany was that there never was and never would be a real and effective opposition there.'

In any event, the attempts of Trott, John, Hassell, Müller, Goerdeler, Bonhoeffer and the others to co-ordinate their plans with those of the Western Allies were unavailing, even when, in the summer of 1944, the conspirators had reluctantly accepted the condition that they must surrender unconditionally to all their enemies, including the Russians. Those attempts were received by Washington in sphinx-like silence, by London with pious and non-committal reiterations of principle. Even today the conspirators are accused of having attempted to 'do a deal' when they tried to make the necessary arrangements for surrender and the essential preparations for a durable peace. It is hard to understand this reaction. The men about Beck and Goerdeler expected soon to be in positions of responsibility. It is surely only natural that they should have wished to clarify the attitude of the Western Powers. Indeed, since that attitude was bound to have the greatest effect on Germany's future, they would have been guilty of the grossest frivolity had they failed to do so.

They received no answer. Mr. Allen Dulles, in Switzerland, had most skilfully prepared the necessary channels of communication between the Allied governments and the conspirators—at great personal danger to the latter—but the Allies never saw fit to use them. Somewhere in London and Washington the speaking-tube was blocked by prejudice, suspicion and rancour. The conspirators received no answer, save the parrot-cry of unconditional surrender, let alone any active and imaginative help. If such help had been forthcoming—if, for instance, Allied airborne troops had landed in Berlin on July 20th, or if Rommel had been invited through the lines to discuss surrender terms earlier in that month or even before the invasion—it seems likely that the war would have ended ten or twelve months before it did, with the Red Army still on Russian soil and the German cities still standing and the atomic bomb an untried horror. If . . . Such speculations are as fruitless as they are depressing.

The Russians had no qualms about talking to the conspirators and were prepared to promise almost anything. Here, however, it was the conspirators who were reticent, for as already stated, they had no interest in a simple exchange of dictators. Yet the refusal of the Western powers to answer even very moderate suggestions eventually made certain of the younger conspirators consider the possibility of looking eastwards. The situation, from their point of view, was summed up by Adam von Trott in a statement which was passed to Mr. Dulles in January of 1944:

> The answer is always given (to the anti-Nazis within Germany) that Germany must suffer military defeat. Hence they conclude it is useless to continue the conversations in view of the failure of the Western powers to understand that the Germans are themselves an oppressed people who live in an occupied country and that tremendous risks are taken by the opposition in continuing its activity. As a result, the opposition believes the Anglo-Saxon countries are filled with bourgeois prejudice and pharisaic theorizing. There is a strong temptation to turn East. The reason for the eastward orientation is the belief in the possibility of fraternization between the Russian and German peoples, although not between the present governments. Both have broken with bourgeois ideology, both have suffered deeply, both desire a radical solution of social problems which transcend national limits, both are in the process of returning to the spiritual (but not the ecclesiastical) traditions of Christianity. . . . The opposition believes that the decisive development in Europe will take place in the social, not the military, realm. . . .

Early in April Mr. Dulles reported to Washington on the present state of the resistance movement. He said that the conspirators, headed by Beck and Goerdeler, were willing and ready to remove Hitler and overthrow the government, but demanded some assurance that once they had done so the Western powers would enter into direct negotiations with them concerning the next steps that must be taken. (Churchill had already given a completely unofficial undertaking, via the Swedish banker Wallenberg, that he would be prepared to talk to a new German government, but there was no reason to believe that Roosevelt would do anything without Stalin.) Mr. Dulles went on to say that though the conspirators were prepared to surrender to all the Allies, they did not wish to negotiate primarily with the Russians, as the Finns had done, but vice versa. Should it be necessary for them to deal directly with Stalin, then some other group of men must be found to do it. They were not prepared to co-operate with the German Communists, though they were prepared to work with any other left-wing group or party. Mr. Dulles said in this report:

> The principle motive for their action is the ardent desire to prevent Central Europe from coming ideologically and factually under the control of Russia. They are convinced that in such event Christian culture and democracy and all that goes with it would disappear in Europe and that the present dictatorship of the Nazis would be exchanged for a new dictatorship. The group points out most emphatically that the dangers of such development should by no means be underrated, especially in view of the completely pro-letarianized millions now inhabiting Central Europe.

And he added that the generals in the western occupied territories, particularly Falkenhausen and Rundstedt, were ready to facilitate the landing of Allied troops, while arrangements could also be made for the reception of British and American airborne forces at key points within Germany.

Later in April Trott managed once again to visit Switzerland, and in an interview with a close colleague of Mr. Dulles', Gero von Gaevernitz, he expressed his great disappointment at the continued silence of London and Washington. Gaevernitz, in a memorandum written at the time, quoted him as saying:

'Constructive ideas and plans for the rebuilding of post-war Germany constantly come from Russia. . . . The democratic countries offer nothing concerning the future of Central Europe. Socialist leaders in Germany emphasize the importance of filling this vacuum as quickly as possible if the ever-increasing Communist influence is to be counteracted.' Adam von Trott then made eight suggestions, all very moderate in tone, of which these three were the most important:

> 3. A fundamental statement (by the Western Allies) on the future self-government in Germany that includes some indication of how much independence the democracies intend to allow to a German administration. It is recommended that special emphasis be placed on the questions of regional and local self-government.

4. A pronouncement to the effect that the democracies do not intend to follow Hitler's methods and create a puppet government in Germany composed of German quislings to represent Allied interests and rule over the German people.

5. A message of encouragement from the American government to be passed on confidentially to the Socialist leaders in Germany.

He also suggested that leaflets be dropped, though not at the same time as bombs, and that bombings be concentrated 'as much as possible on military and industrial targets', for 'the bombings of large populated areas are rapidly completing the proletarianization of Central Europe.'

This information was passed on. Once again the only reply vouchsafed these mild suggestions was silence. And so, though the point of view of the conspirators had not changed, it became apparent that they must assume that a complete lack of interest in anything save 'total victory' in the field prevailed in the West, and that they must therefore envisage the necessity of surrender in the East. Hence the proposed substitution of Werner Count von der Schulenburg, a Russophile who had been on good personal terms with Stalin, as Foreign Minister in place of Ulrich von Hassell, a staunch 'Westerner'.

On July 12th Mr. Dulles informed Washington that an attempt to assassinate Hitler was imminent, and his chief informant, Dr. Gisevius, left Switzerland for Germany to take part in the events planned. Once again the American and British governments evinced no interest.

At about this time Adam von Trott was in Stockholm, where he apparently had a contact with, but probably did not himself meet, Madame Kollontay, who was Russian ambassador there. What results, if any, were achieved by this visit is not known, but they were certainly very slight. The Russians already had their Free Germany movement in Moscow, an odd collection of prisoners of war and Communist émigrés headed by General Seydlitz, and also the relics of a Communist underground in Germany, though most of this had been destroyed when the Gestapo broke up the *Rote Kapelle* Communist espionage group in 1942. Ideologically neither the Russians nor their Germans could accept the concept of an officers' *coup d'état*, a revolution from above. There had hitherto been no contact between Seydlitz's people and the group about Stauffenberg, while the relations of that group to the Communists were rather those of mutual antipathy. Trott was now attempting, in view of the apparent indifference of the West, to improve those relations, or at least to prepare a channel of communication for use once Hitler was out of the way. But the very nature of the Beck-Goerdeler group ruled out any but the most superficial co-operation with the Communists either before or after the *coup d'état*. Such co-operation was, as it happens, attempted within Germany during this same period, with disastrous results, as will be seen.

Thus by the late spring of 1944 the conspirators were, as they realized, quite alone. There was no help to be looked for from abroad, while at home they had made all the preparations that could be made. Every day's delay increased the danger of discovery, and still there was no opportunity to ignite the 'Flash'. And then, rather to their surprise, they acquired a new, spectacular and very powerful adherent. This was no less a man than Field-Marshal Rommel, commander of the largest army in the West, the most popular soldier in Germany and often described, in German and Allied newspapers alike, as 'the Nazi general'.

He was not a Nazi, but no more had he been until now an anti-Nazi. He was in fact a non-political soldier who had seen his army annihilated by the crushing might of the Anglo-American armies and air fleets in Africa. When he took over command of Army Group B in France, at the turn of the year, he had no illusions concerning the scale of the forthcoming invasion or the ability of the German armies to defeat it.

A friend of Goerdeler's, Dr. Karl Strölin, who was then *Oberbürgermeister* of Stuttgart, approached him in February. He discovered that Rommel was fully prepared to do what he could towards ending the war. However, he would not countenance assassination and it seems possible that he never knew fully of Stauffenberg's plans. Rommel's proposal was that Hitler be arrested and tried by a German court. It was, said Rommel, for the nation who had elected him to judge him. Rommel himself was prepared to become acting Head of the State or

Commander-in-Chief, positions for which his enormous prestige made him in some ways more suitable than Beck or Witzleben; he proposed to arrange surrender terms with the Western Allies before the invasion had begun.

In April, Dr. Speidel became Rommel's Chief of Staff and the drawing up of plans both for the overthrow of Hitler and for the armistice arrangements was accelerated. The military commanders of France and Belgium, Beck's old friend General Karl Heinrich von Stülpnagel and General von Falkenhausen, were fully involved already. Rundstedt, the Commander-in-Chief West, knew what was going on, but preferred not to be personally committed. It was Rommel's intention to carry out preliminary negotiations for an armistice with Generals Eisenhower and Montgomery without informing Hitler. The conditions he proposed to offer were: evacuation of the occupied territories, withdrawal of the German armed forces behind the 1939 German frontier and the orderly handing over of the administration of the evacuated territories to the Allies. In return he would demand an immediate cessation of the bombing of Germany. At home Hitler would be arrested and held for trial by a German court. This would be the duty of the O.K.H., though Rommel was ready, if necessary, to send panzer divisions to help. The whole Nazi apparatus would be dismantled and a coalition government headed by Beck, Goerdeler and Leuschner would take over. Rommel himself was prepared to serve this government in any capacity; he was not interested in a military dictatorship. In the East the fighting would continue, on a shortened front following the line of the Carpathians and of the Vistula. The ultimate end which Rommel had in view was a United States of Europe as outlined in a memorandum which had been submitted to him by Ernst Jünger and by which he was much impressed. It was agreed that preliminary negotiations with the West must be begun prior to the invasion. Failing this, a stable front was essential. But it was not believed that invasion was imminent. The German meteorological intelligence experts had told the Army Group that if the landings did not take place by May 18th they must be postponed until August. Therefore the tentative date for the action was fixed as June 15th.

This, then, was another conspiracy and Rommel's liaison with

Beck and Stauffenberg was, in the early days, far from perfect. While Rommel announced his willingness to serve under a Beck-Goerdeler-Leuschner triumvirate, he was patently too big a fish for a subordinate rôle. If his armies had ended the war, it would have been even more difficult to fit him into the new government in any but a supreme position. On the other hand his record and motives were such that he was not an attractive proposition to many among the convinced anti-Nazis of the Resistance. His adherence to the conspiracy, and particularly his refusal of assassination as a weapon, posed a number of problems which were never really solved. Stauffenberg proposed to visit the West and sort these out as best he could, but proved unable to do so. Instead he had to rely on various liaison officers and finally on his cousin, Cäsar von Hofacker, a son of Rommel's commanding general during the First World War and, as will be seen, an extremely determined man.

Meanwhile the invasion of June 6th had put an end to Rommel's original plan, which either never reached the ears of the Allies or, if it did, was ignored by them. His armies were committed and could not now be disengaged for an orderly withdrawal to the Rhine. If the Allies had accepted the full confidence of the men of the German Resistance, it is possible that there need never have been an invasion, that many thousands of men who died in Normandy would now be alive, and that France would not have been yet again a battlefield nor been rent by what was in some parts of the country neither more nor less than civil war and in others an anarchy recalling 1791. If, again. . . . However, the battle was joined.

On June 17th Hitler made his sole visit to France and called a conference of the army group commanders, Rommel and Rundstedt, at Margival. Rommel attempted to persuade Hitler that the war was lost and that it was his duty to capitulate. Hitler told him, in so many words, to mind his own business, which was the invasion front, and treated the Field-Marshals to a long and angry dissertation about the mythical powers of his wonder-weapons in which he apparently believed. Then Hitler returned to Berchtesgaden.

The rest of Rommel's story, as related by Dr. Speidel, is as follows.

In the days following the Margival conference Rommel and Dr. Speidel discussed the political situation with the army, corps and some divisional commanders and with the senior officers on their staffs. According to these men's known political views, Rommel was more or less open with them in disclosing his decision that independent action on the part of the armed forces in the West was now imperative. The two army commanders, Dollmann and Salmuth, and the general commanding the panzer troops, Geyr—that is to say Rommel's three immediate subordinates—expressed their full willingness to obey any orders he might issue, regardless of what might emanate from Hitler's headquarters.

On June 25th the new Quartermaster West, Colonel Finckh, arrived in Paris and had an interview with Rommel. Finckh had been sent by Wagner, the Quartermaster-General in whose plane Stauffenberg was to fly to East Prussia, with the mission of co-ordinating the *coup d'état* plans of the O.K.H. with those of Rommel. He told Rommel of the previous attempts on Hitler's life and of the plan to assassinate him at Berchtesgaden in the immediate future. Rommel expressed his displeasure at this, repeating his earlier conviction that Hitler should be arrested and tried by a German court. He also said that there were too many planners at work, and asked Finckh to arrange through Wagner that a central control be established. But without Oster and his *Abwehr* network, this was no easy matter. It must be remembered that the conspirators in the West could not use the telephone or the teleprinter to communicate any but the simplest code word to the conspirators in Berlin.

On this day there was heavy fighting in the Caen area. In the East the massive Russian offensive was now two days old and was already spectacularly successful. Time was running out. Rommel proposed to fly once more to Hitler in a last attempt to make him see sense. Meanwhile he demanded of Finckh that a strict time-table for the *coup d'état* be drawn up in the event of his mission failing, as he must assume it would. The commanders of the 2nd and 116th Panzer Divisions reported that they could rely on their divisions to follow them against the government if so ordered by Rommel.

Rommel and Rundstedt, who were in almost constant touch,

demanded an interview with Hitler. On July 28th they were ordered to Berchtesgaden immediately and arrived there in the morning of the 29th, but were not admitted into Hitler's presence until the late afternoon. There were many other officers in the room, nor would Hitler agree to the Field-Marshals' request that he see them in private. He ignored their demands that he end the war and treated them once again to a lengthy harangue concerning the miracle weapons, interlarded with references to the Seven Years' War. They were then dismissed the presence without being invited to dinner. (This interview is a mocking parody of the 'Field-Marshals' Strike' which the conspirators had been attempting for so many years to organize. Would it have proved more successful in 1942 than in 1944? Would Manstein, Kluge and Küchler have carried more weight with Hitler than Rundstedt and Rommel? It is possible.)

The Field-Marshals returned gloomily to France, where they found that one of the army commanders, General Dollmann, had died of a heart attack and had been replaced by an S.S. officer named Hausser. Two days later Rundstedt was himself dismissed—Hitler had lacked the courage to do this face to face. On July 4th Rundstedt said good-bye to Rommel and expressed his relief that he would not have to experience the coming catastrophe in a responsible position. On July 5th the general commanding the panzer troops in the West, General Geyr von Schweppenburg, was also dismissed. So of the five senior generals in command of troops who had agreed to make peace and overthrow the government a week ago, only Rommel and Salmuth now remained. But Rundstedt's successor was Kluge.

Kluge, it will be recalled, had been Henning von Tresckow's commanding officer and under the influence of that remarkable man and of his two aides-de-camp, Counts Hardenberg and Lehndorff, had been repeatedly led up to the very brink of rebellion. He, more than any other active field-marshal, was deeply compromised in the plans of the conspirators. During a conversation which he had held with Beck and Goerdeler during the previous autumn, Kluge had disagreed with Goerdeler's proposal that Hitler be taken prisoner and had insisted that he be assassinated. Once that had been done, he said, they could rely on him. It would have seemed that he would have been a far more valuable colleague for Rommel than the aged and cynical Rundstedt. But, alas, Tresckow, the keeper of the Field-Marshal's conscience, was far away in the East. Kluge, fearing his advice, had refused to take him to France as his Chief of Staff. Furthermore, Kluge had just spent a fortnight at Berchtesgaden and, temporarily at least, had fallen complete victim to Hitler's hypnotic powers. He arrived at La Roche Guyon, Rommel's headquarters, an ardent and optimistic Hitlerite.

He was an hysterical if not actually an unbalanced man (the year before he had challenged Guderian to a duel and had seriously suggested that Hitler be his second) and now he proceeded to give Rommel a tremendous dressing down in the best Berchtesgaden fashion, accusing him of defeatism here as in Africa, and of insubordination. He said: 'You, Field-Marshal Rommel, will henceforth obey your orders unconditionally! I'm warning you!' Rommel replied and the conversation between the two field-marshals grew so heated that their chiefs of staff were ordered from the room.

La Roche Guyon was the seat of the ducs de la Rochefoucauld. A portrait of the author of the *Maxims* surveyed this scene, which took place in the *salle des gardes*.

On the very next day Kluge visited the front and returned a changed man. *Il y a une inconstance qui vient de la légereté de l'esprit, ou de sa faiblesse qui lui fait recevoir toutes les opinions d'autrui; il y en a une autre, qui est plus excusable, qui vient du dégoût des choses,* la Rochefoucauld once wrote. Kluge apologized to Rommel. He realized now that the war was lost and that Germany's Western armies must see to it that the disaster was halted as soon as possible. He excused his rudeness of the previous evening on the grounds that he had been misinformed by Hitler and Keitel. Kluge's inconstancy was doubtless firmly based on both la Rochefoucauld's causes. Meanwhile in the East the Red Army was advancing fast.

On July 9th Cäsar von Hofacker arrived at La Roche Guyon. He was Beck's and Stauffenberg's emissary to Stülpnagel and he would be reporting to Berlin at once on conditions in the West. Rommel informed him that the front in Normandy could not be held for more than two or three weeks. After a talk with Kluge,

Hofacker set off for Berlin. He was to return on, or shortly after, the 15th with final instructions from Beck.

Meanwhile arrangements were pursued for making contact with the British and American commanders. The Allies had suggested, over the radio, a two-hour local armistice for the exchange of German nurses and female auxiliaries captured in Cherbourg against severely wounded Allied prisoners. Firing ceased for a time on a sector of the front held by the 2nd Panzer Division. It had been established that it was in fact just possible to talk across the fighting.

On July 12th Kluge was at La Roche Guyon again and Rommel spoke to him now quite openly about his plans. He expressed his willingness to canvas once again the opinion of the army and corps commanders. He said that Hofacker would be returning within the next day or two with first-hand information concerning the situation at Berlin and on the Eastern Front. Kluge vacillated once again, maintaining that his co-operation must depend on the answers which Rommel received from the other generals.

On July 13th, on Rommel's order, Speidel reported this conversation to Stülpnagel in Paris. Rommel wished it known that he was prepared to act no matter which way Kluge might finally incline. In Paris there was consternation owing to a wave of arrests which was now taking place in Berlin. It was debated whether or not the Western conspirators should await Hofacker's return. It was finally decided that they should.

On July 13th, 14th and 15th Rommel visited the generals under his command, including the S.S. generals Hausser and Dietrich who had the 7th Army and 1st S.S. Panzer Corps respectively. He spoke openly of his intention to act on his own initiative, 'should the front be torn open', and was convinced by their answers that the Waffen-S.S. would not cause him any undue trouble. At the same time Stülpnagel was quite satisfied that he could neutralise the Nazi police and functionaries in Paris and elsewhere. Rommel returned from those visits to the front convinced that the whole army expected him to act and that it was now his duty to do so.

However, he was determined to give Hitler one last chance, and on July 15th he drafted a long message which could only be regarded as an ultimatum. In it he described in detail the disastrous situation, contrasted the heavy casualties with the almost negligible replacements received alike in men and material, and the ever widening ratio between Allied and German strengths. He repeated to Hitler that the front must crumble within two or three weeks. He ended with the words: 'I must ask you to draw your conclusions from this state of affairs without delay. As Commander-in-Chief of the Army Group I feel myself in duty bound to state this clearly. . . . Rommel, Field-Marshal.' When this long signal had been sent, via Kluge, Rommel remarked: 'I've now given him one last chance. If he fails to draw the necessary conclusions, we shall act.' He did not know that several weeks were to elapse before Kluge sent on the signal.

Rommel, according to Speidel, cherished no illusions concerning the harshness of the peace terms which he might expect to bring back from the Allied commanders. But he believed he could anticipate a measure of statesmanlike vision, psychological skill and political foresight among the leaders of the Western Allies. Late in the evening of July 15th he spoke of these matters to Speidel and to the admiral who was his naval adviser, walking up and down in the gardens of La Roche Guyon.

On July 17th he visited the front again and told various commanders in the field of the demands he had made to Hitler and of what the results would be should these not be met. He was about to return to his headquarters at a comparatively early hour when he heard that a crisis had developed in the sector of 1st S.S. Panzer Corps. He therefore visited Dietrich and at 4 p.m. set off for La Roche Guyon. On the Livarot-Vimoutiers road his car was attacked by fighter-bombers, the driver killed and the field-marshal so severely wounded that he was unconscious for days and his life despaired of.

Kluge took over command of Army Group B in addition to his position of C.-in-C. West. On July 20th, therefore, Kluge was without a peer in the occupied territories. The decision, when the time came, was his alone. He had moved into La Roche Guyon and there, in solitude, his courage failed him. *La parfaite valeur est de faire sans témoins ce qu'on serait capable de faire devant tout le monde.*

CHAPTER VII

THE atmosphere in which the conspirators lived during the last few weeks before July 20th was hectic and the strain great. Stauffenberg knew that on July 1st he was to be appointed Chief of Staff to General Fromm and would therefore have, at least occasionally, access to Hitler. He decided that he himself would have to kill the dictator, though this was certainly not an ideal nor even a satisfactory plan. Stauffenberg was now the driving force of the whole movement. When the rebellion broke out his place would clearly be in Berlin, in control. Furthermore, in his capacity as Fromm's Chief of Staff, he and he alone could issue orders to the Home Army in Fromm's name without giving away the fact that a revolution was in progress. In the event of Fromm refusing to co-operate, this might prove vital during the first hours of the *putsch*. On the other hand, he also had to be at Rastenburg, since nobody else was likely to be able to plant the bomb in the near future with any certainty. And time was running short. Therefore Stauffenberg must, on one and the same day, attempt to play two major rôles in European history; within a few hours he must destroy one government and create another, and for a high proportion of those hours he must, for simple geographical reasons, be in an aeroplane, completely out of touch and unable to influence events.

Time was running short in two quite different respects. First, the German armies were losing two great battles. As the conspirators knew, it was only a matter of weeks before the American and British armies broke out of Normandy and rolled up Army Group B. Meanwhile, on the Eastern Front, Army Group Centre was in process of dissolution. Provided that the

Russians could deal with their tremendous logistical difficulties, there seemed no reason why they should not push straight on through Poland into Germany. In fact the end of the war was close. Had the Russians been able to solve their supply problems, or had the Western Supreme Commander exploited the victory in Normandy by a normal concentration of effort, the war in Europe would certainly have ended in the autumn of 1944. To the officers of the German General Staff it was apparent that they had very little time indeed. For if they were to act, it was essential from their point of view that they do so while the German army still existed. There would be no positive purpose served in overthrowing a government which could no longer govern, and only the negative one of attempting to avoid further unnecessary destruction. Were Stauffenberg and Beck to take over during the final spasms of total defeat, not only would they be incapable of making any sort of peace with Germany's enemies —even as Dönitz was to prove a year later—but, more important, their action would be void of moral significance. Their purpose was two-fold, to save Germany from further casualties and bombings and to prove to the world that there existed within Germany forces other than those which the nihilists had so long employed for their evil ends. To achieve these purposes, it was essential that Germans act before Germany was reduced to a mere geographical concept: in the circumstances this meant that the *coup d'état*, if it were to be more than the twitch of a moribund organism, must take place while the German army was still capable of exercising control within the home territories and of at least maintaining some sort of resistance along the frontiers. In July of 1944 these conditions still prevailed, but it was obvious that they would not do so for very much longer; perhaps for only a few more weeks.

Indeed, once the success of the Allied invasion of France was clearly established, a group within the German resistance began to express its doubts concerning the advisability of direct intervention at the centre. Goerdeler in particular seems to have given favourable consideration to the possibility of relying on the generals in the West—Rommel and later Kluge—to open the front to the Anglo-Americans, on the hypothesis that Churchill would do everything in his power to avoid a Russian domination of central Europe. Two strong arguments against action at this late date were, first, that if the conspirators succeeded in eliminating Hitler they would create a new stab-in-the-back legend: the German people might be led to believe that had Hitler remained his wonder-weapons might yet have won the war, and thus the ideals of the conspirators would be discredited in the eyes of their compatriots. On the other hand, should the conspirators fail, the massacre of all that was best in Germany would deprive the Germans of those very leaders whom they would need most desperately as soon as the dust of defeat had begun to settle.

These arguments, and particularly the final one, are formidable. Many honourable men believe, to this day, that action in the summer of 1944 was irresponsible, since the chances of success were too slight and the dangers as vast as they were apparent. In mid-June Stauffenberg sent his friend, Count Lehndorff, to visit Tresckow and ask him his opinion. Had the enterprise now lost its political purpose? Should they simply go to ground and await the inevitable end, or should they carry on as planned? It was clear to the men about Stauffenberg and Tresckow that this was not simply a question of risking their own lives: nor were they of the sort actively to desire the martyr's crown.

Count Lehndorff owned great properties in East Prussia and his castle, Steinort, had been requisitioned by Ribbentrop as his 'headquarters in the field' owing to its convenient proximity to Hitler's 'Wolf's Lair', near Rastenburg in the Mauerwald. Lehndorff, formerly a non-political man, had been aide-de-camp to Field-Marshal Bock in the early stages of the Russian campaign. At Borissow he had seen an S.S. man knock out the brains of a Jewish child and, as he then informed his wife, he decided that henceforth he would devote the rest of his life to extirpating such infamy. He became, in due course, one of the principal links between the Tresckow group and the Berlin group. In the winter of 1943–44 Stauffenberg arranged that he be classified as medically unfit—he was in fact a very healthy man of thirty-four—and attached to the O.K.H. His task henceforth was the extremely perilous one of sounding out dubious senior officers concerning their willingness to help in the overthrow of a régime which Lehndorff regarded as 'evil personified'. His tact, charm and high social position were his qualifications for these dangerous missions, of which he completed many.

Now, in mid-June, Stauffenberg sent him to see Tresckow who was the chief of staff of the Second Army on the Eastern Front and was again an active leader of the whole resistance movement. Tresckow had been summoned to attend a conference of army commanders and chiefs of staff in East Prussia, and Tresckow and Lehndorff met in Lehndorff's own house, where his family had retained their living quarters. Schlabrendorff, who had accompanied Tresckow, was present when Lehndorff expressed the doubts current in Berlin and he has recorded Tresckow's answer. It was, in Tresckow's own words:

'The assassination must be attempted, at any cost. Even should it fail, the attempt to seize power in the capital must be undertaken. We must prove to the world and to future generations that the men of the German resistance movement dared to take the decisive step and to hazard their lives upon it. Compared with this, nothing else matters.'

He also urged Stauffenberg, via Lehndorff, to visit Speidel in France and to bring all the pressure of which he was capable to bear on the generals in the West. Tresckow's own attempts to be summoned by Kluge were of no avail, but he did send Colonel von Boeselager, the cavalry officer who had once been prepared to lead an attack on Hitler's headquarters, to see that vacillating commander.

Lehndorff's message was enough for Stauffenberg. He replied that he would himself carry out the assassination attempt, at the first available opportunity, the only condition being that he be able to kill Hitler and Himmler with the same bomb. Meanwhile Tresckow was to remain with the Second Army on the Eastern Front. He would be summoned to Berlin by teleprinter as soon as Witzleben had assumed the duties of Commander-in-Chief of the Army.

In Berlin Stauffenberg, on his appointment as Chief of Staff to Fromm, spoke quite openly to that officer, expressing his opinion that the war could no longer be won and that Hitler must bear the full responsibility. Fromm accepted these 'treasonable' remarks and, indeed, seems to have agreed with the young colonel's point of view. This augured well for the forthcoming action: Stauffenberg, however, did not divulge his plans to Fromm.

There was, during these days of late June and early July, a last debate within the conspiracy concerning political methods. Dr. Otto John, who was director of a German-controlled air line in Madrid and was simultaneously the contact man between the conspirators and the United States military attaché in the Spanish capital, reported that there was no encouragement whatever forthcoming from General Eisenhower whose replies to all overtures remained the monotonous repetition of the words 'unconditional surrender'. Meanwhile from Stockholm Adam von Trott reported that the Russians had not been afflicted with such diplomatic *rigor mortis* by the Casablanca declaration and were, indeed, eager to open conversations with the anti-Hitler group.

On a previous occasion Stauffenberg, after talks with Trott and the former Ambassador von der Schulenburg, had expressed his opinion that it would be foolish for the conspirators to rely entirely on an 'American solution', in view of the apparent inability of the Americans to understand what was happening in Europe or even where their own interests lay. It would, he thought, be wiser at least to talk to the Russians, even though he was well aware of how carefully any such conversations must be carried out and with what reserve any statements that the Russians might make must be treated. But apart from that, the Russians were and would remain Germany's neighbours, while American policy, or rather the absence of any American policy in Europe (other than 'total victory') which was so sadly apparent in 1944, promised only a quicksand on which nothing lasting could be built. If it were possible to deal with the Russians and thus end the war, and if it were in fact impossible to get any sense out of the Western Allies, was it not the duty of the conspirators at least to attempt the first course, no matter how strong their aversion to Stalinism and its methods? Furthermore, could the conspirators even rely on the basic good will and humanity of the United States when a cabinet minister such as Morgenthau was advocating the 'pastoralization' of Germany, a word which was only a euphemism for mass starvation and depopulation?

There is a former Gestapo man, by the name of Hans Bernd Gisevius, who worked for the American Secret Service during these years and who wrote a book which appeared in 1946 with the title *To the Bitter End*. This book, much of which was first given as testimony during the Nuremberg trials, deals primarily with the struggle for power within and between the various police forces inside Nazi Germany. This struggle led certain police officials to work with the men of the resistance and Gisevius tells a fair amount concerning the events that led up to July 20th, as seen from his point of view. He is, however, a disingenuous writer and his book is rather unpleasantly slanted to make Dr. Gisevius appear as a central figure—he was, in fact, very much on the periphery, being usually in Switzerland where he acted as contact man with Allen Dulles—and to pay off certain old scores. Claus von Stauffenberg, particularly, disliked and distrusted this policeman, did his best to avoid him, and refused to discuss his plans with him. Gisevius paid him back by portraying Stauffenberg as an ambitious and frivolous soldier with totalitarian beliefs who aspired to play a great role in a German-Russian National-Bolshevist alliance. Since *To the Bitter End* was the first book dealing with the German resistance to reach any large audience, these fanciful fabrications were not immediately recognized as the tendentious rubbish that they are. Luckily, enough men who knew Stauffenberg's thought are left alive to discredit Gisevius.

In fact Stauffenberg, in these days of late June and early July, rejected the possibility of attempting to come to terms with the Russians. Not that he was a Russophobe, quite the contrary. It will be recalled that Stauffenberg, with Roenne, had been responsible for the creation of an anti-totalitarian force of Russian volunteers in 1942. He saw these men as his allies in the common struggle against the inhumanity of Stalinism and Hitlerism alike. He hoped that both Germans and Russians would realize the evilness of the Antichristian governments by which their countries were oppressed and that the mounting pressures of war and misery would enable the iron bands to be broken by men of determination in both hands. He was at all times deeply opposed to the attempts by the Nazis and by such Communist renegades as General Vlassov to create a militaristic, nationalist German-Russian block. Gisevius, in his malicious caricature of Stauffenberg, shows that he had learned at least one lesson from his former Nazi masters: when telling a lie, the greater it is, the better. His version of Stauffenberg's aims is almost exactly the opposite of the truth.

The decision that Stauffenberg actually made was as follows. As soon as Hitler was dead the German armies in the West must offer to surrender, while such divisions as were mobile and in a position to be moved were rushed to support the disintegrating front in the East. Within days there would be an armistice on the Western Front: the Allies could hardly continue to shoot at Germans who did not shoot back. What happened then would of course depend almost entirely on the British and American governments, but at least Germany should be occupied by them rather than by the Russians. Whether or not the Anglo-Americans would have approved of such a course remained, and in retrospect still remains, problematical. But within the extremely limited field of manœuvre that was now open to Beck and Stauffenberg, there was little if any alternative save the two unacceptable ones of continuing the war or of surrendering first to the Russians. In Berlin Colonel Hansen, who had succeeded Canaris as head of what remained of the *Abwehr*, was ready to fly to Madrid as plenipotentiary of the new government as soon as the *putsch* had succeeded.

Now, however, the relationship between the conspirators and the Communists assumed a new and disastrous importance. Adolf Reichwein, the socialist philosopher and head of the Folk-lore Museum in Berlin, had retained a link with what remained of the Communist underground within Germany. It was suggested, apparently by him, that it would be as well to establish contact with a group of Communists whom he believed trustworthy and thus to 'broaden the base' of the proposed action. Such contact was approved by Julius Leber, though on different grounds. According to Frau Leber, her husband had no intention of collaborating with the Communists: he knew them too well. But, she has told the author, he said that the conspirators must find out 'what those people are doing behind our backs', and what line they proposed to follow if the assassination were successfully accomplished; he was anxious that the Communists should not be able to exploit the action of himself and his friends for purposes which were utterly alien to his and their motives. Stauffenberg, who was very close to Leber, while agreeing that ignorance here might well be dangerous, was insistent that the Communists be told the minimum. Which, of course, was already Leber's intention, but it does seem strange that he should have been prepared to go even as far as he did. He must have known that the objectives pursued by himself and his friends were bound to be as unpopular in Moscow as they were with the Nazis. Nevertheless he knew that there were brave and anti-Nazi remnants of the Communist Party and perhaps he underestimated the control which, even in wartime, Moscow exercised over these individuals.

For years the rule among the conspirators had been that there would be no collaboration with the Communists, at least until after Hitler's fall. Emil Henk, the Socialist writer, in his book on the 20th of July, says that Leuschner knew nothing of these intentions of Leber's and Reichwein's, and adds: 'Had he known, he would have done everything in his power to prevent the meetings; afterwards he protested bitterly that he should have thus been kept in the dark.' The first meeting, however, took place, on June 22nd, in eastern Berlin, with Reichwein and Leber representing the Social Democrats, Saefkow, Jacob and a third man by the name of Rambow being the Communists present. Rambow was unknown to Reichwein and Leber.

The Communists seem to have been already far too well informed about the conspiracy. They demanded a further meeting, particularly with the military leaders, which was provisionally fixed for July 4th. When Stauffenberg heard of this he was incensed. Such unnecessary contacts were completely contrary to all the rules of conspiracy, as none knew better than the Communists themselves. However by then it was too late. Rambow was an informer. Reichwein attended the second meeting and was there arrested with Saefkow and Jacob. Leber was picked up by the Gestapo on the following morning. All four men were executed before the end of the war.

It has never been established whether the informer committed his act of Judas solely in the role of Nazi stool-pigeon or whether he was simultaneously acting as a Communist agent. Nor is it of much significance: whoever his masters were, he had carried out the wishes of both despotisms.

The conspiracy was now in the utmost peril. Leber could be relied upon not to talk. Reichwein, too, was a brave and trusted man. Yet how could anyone be utterly certain of even the strongest man's resistance to torture? In France, captured men of the maquis or of the British intelligence service were regarded as having done their duty if they kept silent for forty-eight hours. Furthermore, it was not known how much Reichwein had revealed on the occasion of this second meeting. Finally, the neatness of the trap implied considerable previous knowledge of the conspiracy on the part of the Gestapo. Time was indeed running short, for the noose was tightening. Stauffenberg realized that he must act at once, regardless of all other considerations.

Stauffenberg had another motive in acting with all speed. Within a few days of Leber's arrest he learned that Leber was being held in the Gestapo prison in the Prinz Albrecht Strasse. If he were to be saved from death, it must be soon. And not only was Leber a close personal friend of Stauffenberg's, but he was also regarded by Stauffenberg as an irreplaceable member of the government which must succeed the Nazis. When he learned where Leber was, his usual reserve broke down. In a conversation with Adam von Trott, he is said to have repeated over and over again, almost shouting the words: 'We need Leber. I'll fetch him out, yes, I'll fetch him out.' And to Frau Leber he sent a brief message by Schulenburg: 'We are aware of our duty.'

The sequence of events during the first nineteen days of July can best be summed up chronologically:

July 1st. Stauffenberg takes over as Chief of Staff, Home Army. On the morning of that day he is visited in his office by a junior officer from the East, a stranger, to whom Stauffenberg remarks: 'There is no point in beating about the bush: I am employing all the means at my disposal for the purpose of committing high treason.'

July 3rd. Field-Marshal von Kluge appointed Commander-in-Chief West, in succession to Rundstedt.

July 4th. On this evening a number of friends meet in the Stauffenbergs' house at Wannsee. Claus von Stauffenberg asks them whether or not it is now too late: whether it would not be better to preserve their strength for the period that must follow the inevitable defeat: whether the crime of tyrannicide will not make it impossible for them to create a renewal of values. His friends reply that success is not the point: that the act must be performed, if only for the sake of future and perhaps happier generations of Germans. These answers reinforce Stauffenberg in his convictions and he puts an end to the conversation with a phrase which was not one to which he was addicted: '*Noblesse oblige!*'

July 5th. Stauffenberg learns from Trott and Haubach that Reichwein and Leber have been arrested.

July 6th. Stauffenberg flies to Berchtesgaden, where Hitler's headquarters is installed. He has conversations with Stieff and others concerning the possibility of someone already stationed there killing Hitler. He is dissatisfied with Stieff's replies, and convinced that he must do it himself. He makes final arrangements with General Fellgiebel, the signals general, concerning that officer's role once the bomb has been exploded.

Returning to Berlin—perhaps not on this evening, however—Stauffenberg has a conversation with Professor Sauerbruch, the surgeon. The latter urges him to find someone else to perform the assassination. The dual role of assassin and of leader of the *putsch* would be too much for any man, let alone for one suffering from Stauffenberg's physical disabilities. Stauffenberg replies that earlier he might have agreed with these arguments: now it is too late, there can be no going back.

At La Roche Guyon, Kluge berates Rommel for defeatism.

July 8th. Army Group Centre is in dissolution. Beck and Tresckow believe that Russian tanks will be outside Berlin within ten days. Army Group North is about to be cut off.

There is deep depression in the Bendlerstrasse. A visitor notes that Stauffenberg seems for once as though borne down by a tremendous weight.

July 10th. Twenty-seven divisions of Army Group Centre have ceased to exist. An even more massive Russian offensive against the southern part of the front is expected daily.

Hofacker arrives in Berlin from Paris, to report on conversations with Stülpnagel and with Rommel, whom he talked to at length on the 9th. Rommel's opinion is that there will be an Allied break-through within a few weeks. Kluge has pronounced the 'Western solution' as advocated by Tresckow impracticable: if the war is to be ended, action in Berlin and at Hitler's headquarters is imperative. Rommel shares this point of view, though once the action has begun in Germany, he is prepared to give it his full support in France. However, he still disapproves of assassination as the means. A message comes from Otto John, in Madrid. Time is running out: immediate action is essential. Stauffenberg is ordered to attend a conference at Berchtesgaden on the following day and it is decided that he will commit the deed if Hitler and Himmler are both present.

July 11th. Stauffenberg flies to Berchtesgaden with Klausing acting as his adjutant—von Haeften is ill. Klausing remains at the wheel of the car, ready to drive Stauffenberg to Freilassing airfield, the moment the bomb has exploded. But Stauffenberg, finding that Himmler is not present, has already telephoned Olbricht in Berlin and asked whether he should go ahead or not. Olbricht replies that he should not.

On his return to Berlin Stauffenberg has a meeting with Beck and Olbricht at which it is agreed that the condition of Himmler's presence will henceforth be dropped. The sole aim from now on will be to kill Hitler.

July 12th. Kluge meets Rommel and they have a friendly conversation. Kluge now fully accepts the need for action against Hitler.

July 14th. Rommel drafts his 'ultimatum' to Hitler. Hitler moves his headquarters from Berchtesgaden to Rastenburg. Fromm and Stauffenberg are summoned to attend a Hitler conference at Rastenburg on the following day to discuss the urgent matter of new divisions for Army Group Centre.

The conspirators meet in the afternoon. Stauffenberg will act whether or not Himmler is present. It is decided to issue the initial *Valkyrie* order to Berlin at 11.00 hrs., that is to say two hours before the Hitler conference is due to begin. The troops will thus be available in central Berlin as soon as the bomb goes off.

July 15th. Stauffenberg flies to East Prussia with Fromm, who is in ignorance of his plans, Klausing and perhaps another officer also with a time bomb. (Or, more probably, there was a second bomb in Klausing's brief-case, concealed there in the hope that that officer might also be permitted to enter the conference room.)

At 11.00 hrs. Olbricht issues *Valkyrie* I for Berlin—the troop movements, but not the opening of sealed orders. He also summons General von Hase, the Commandant of Berlin, and tells him that it is probable that Hitler will be killed that day. Hase agrees to obey the orders of the Bendlerstrasse and Major von Hayessen, a full member of the conspiracy, is assigned to his staff. Troops begin to move into Berlin with orders to seal off the Wilhelmstrasse quarter.

At 13.00 hrs. the conference begins. Stauffenberg, having satisfied himself that Hitler is present, leaves the hall and telephones Berlin. All is in order at both ends. Then Stauffenberg re-enters the hall, to discover that Hitler has already left.

At 13.30 hrs. Stauffenberg telephones Olbricht again. The latter countermands *Valkyrie* and spends the afternoon visiting the units concerned, explaining that this was a training exercise.

In Brussels General von Falkenhausen is suddenly relieved of his command.

July 16th. In Berlin Stauffenberg has a meeting with Beck and Olbricht. Olbricht says that it will be impossible again to camouflage *Valkyrie* as training: Keitel is suspicious. The possibility of reverting to the 'Western solution' is discussed, but Beck declares that a central 'flash' is as imperative as ever. Stauffenberg states that next time he will act at the first possible moment, regardless of all considerations save the killing of Hitler.

That evening a meeting takes place at Stauffenberg's home at Wannsee. It is attended by himself, his brother, Trott, Fritz von der Schulenburg and Hofacker. Trott says that he has reason to believe that the Western Allies will deal with a new German government, but that they will insist on simultaneous surrender in the East. Nor is there any purpose in attempting to secure modifications to the 'unconditional surrender' slogan. This point of view is accepted, and it is decided that as soon as Hitler is dead, negotiations with the Russians will be undertaken by Werner von der Schulenburg and General Koestring, the former German military attaché in Moscow. Trott will be present when a meeting is arranged with representatives of the Western powers. In fact the decision is now finally taken to go ahead, regardless of what the future may bring. All that now matters is that Germans should deliver Germany from its shame.

July 17th. The Russian southern offensive opens.

The Allied offensive in the West opens: fall of Caen and of St. Lô imminent.

Rommel severely wounded and out of action.

July 18th. A naval officer named Kranzfelder, a friend of Berthold von Stauffenberg's, informs Claus of a rumour current in Berlin to the effect that Hitler's headquarters are to be blown up within the next week.

A report reaches the conspirators that during the midday conference at police headquarters in Berlin it was decided to issue a warrant at once for the arrest of Dr. Carl Goerdeler. Goerdeler is informed by Stauffenberg and goes into hiding.

That night Stauffenberg works on his report on the Volksgrenadier Divisions, which is to be submitted to Hitler within the next forty-eight hours: he has been summoned to attend a Hitler conference at Rastenburg on the 20th.

July 19th. During the course of the day the conspirators, so far as they can, send out warning orders. Witzleben and Hoepner are informed that their presence will be required at the Bendlerstrasse.

A visitor to the Bendlerstrasse, unaware of what was planned for the next day, has described Stauffenberg's calm and amiable manner.

At eight that evening Stauffenberg leaves his office and drives home to Wannsee. On the way he stops his car and enters a church, where he spends some time in prayer. It is believed that he had previously confessed, but of course could not be granted absolution.

Since so many of the men of July 20th were active Christians, before returning to the events of that day it is well to consider the attitude of the great Christian Churches towards tyrannicide. In 1952 Otto Remer, whose name will recur in the next chapter, was tried before the High Court of Brunswick on a charge of slandering the men of the German resistance. Three theologians, one Catholic and the other two Protestants, gave evidence concerning the judgment of their churches in this matter of tyrannicide.

Professor Dr. Rupert Angermaier, the Catholic, spoke as follows:

Up to the middle of the nineteenth century the Catholic Church consistently denied the right of any individual or individuals to remove by murder a man previously recognized as monarch. There was, in fact, no justification for tyrannicide.

Since the last pronouncement of the Church, in 1864, the powers of a modern tyrant have increased vastly, in his ability both to interfere in the life of the individual and to control the people's essential possessions. Many moral theologians have therefore considered that in moments of the most acute social crisis it may be a Christian's duty to take direct action against the tyrant in defence of his society. The analogy from private life is this: it is a man's duty to defend himself against a would-be murderer, even if in so doing he must kill his assailant. A closer analogy lies in the justice of defensive war: it is recognized by the Church that soldiers may kill the soldiers of a hostile power which attempts to conquer their nation. However, even though tyrannicide may possibly be regarded as an act of social self-defence, reasons for the committing of this deed vary in their validity.

One argument against the justification of tyrannicide is that a nation which has chosen for itself a criminal Head of State cannot in fact be truly 'saved' by being spared the final and most evil consequences of its choice. There is much scriptural authority for the belief that such a nation must, partly through those very consequences, overcome its own inner disposition before Divine Providence may lift the scourge from it. Another argument is the fact that 'tyrant' is a very loose word, which is often applied to heads of governments or states by men who would not think to kill those persons in power. If tyrannicide were justified, then every monarch, every government and therefore every society would be in permanent jeopardy.

It will be seen from these few examples that the arguments for and against tyrannicide are on different planes. Objectively no decision can be reached: objectively tyrannicide cannot be justified. The question can only be solved in individual cases, that is to say in terms of the subjective motives of the men who are prepared to kill the tyrant. An honourable and sensible man who acts in this, as in any other field, from the highest innermost convictions cannot, according to Christian moral theology, be guilty of sin.

But certain previous conditions must be fulfilled before tyrannicide can be countenanced. For example, every attempt must be made to remove the tyrant by constitutional means, or there must be absolutely no possibility of such attempts succeeding, before violence is resorted to. Further, the attempt on the life of the tyrant must bring about a diminution and not an increase in the misfortunes of the nation: that is to say the act of violence must be so prepared that those responsible can be reasonably confident of achieving their purpose. This does not mean that only actual success justifies tyrannicide, but that success must be foreseen by the men responsible. Finally the man who commits tyrannicide must be sure of the agreement and the silent support of the qualitatively superior majority of his compatriots. A man who commits tyrannicide can only invoke the plea of social self-defence if his action is intended to ward off an existing or clearly impending catastrophe from his people. Political differences or a desire for revenge cannot be construed as self-defence, since this would permit murder to become a normal political weapon.

In view not only of Hitler's past and present actions, but of his announced intention that the German nation should not survive his downfall, and in view of the fact that that downfall was imminent, the action of the men of July 20th was, according to the arguments of Dr. Angermaier, justified.

Stauffenberg said: 'We have tested ourselves before God and

our conscience: it must be done.' This was his innermost personal decision. He demanded no dispensation of the Church to kill Hitler, neither for himself nor for his friends. But he did tell the Bishop of Berlin, Cardinal Count Preysing, what he intended to do. The Cardinal has said that he honoured Stauffenberg's motives: nor did he regard himself as justified in attempting to restrain him on theological grounds.

The Lutheran point of view, as expressed at the Remer Trial by Dr. Iwand and, in other terms, by Professor Dr. Wolf, is rather different. Luther and his followers regard the Church as subordinate to the Prince in all secular matters. Render unto Cæsar . . . Tribute to whom tribute is due. . . . Nor had the Christian the right to resist his Prince if attacked by him for religious reasons, even though that Prince be a heathen. Should he be so attacked, pious submission and, if necessary, martyrdom for his faith provided the only course open to the Christian. Briefly, the duties of Church and State must not overlap, nor must the former attempt to assume the responsibilities or use the weapons of the latter. Whether the Prince be a tyrant or not, whether he be Christian or heathen, his tyranny was no excuse for the Christian as a Christian to defend himself with arms in his hands, for Christianity is concerned with the souls of men. Under the influence of the Pietists this doctrine of passivity came to be generally accepted by the Lutheran Church.

But there was another part of Luther's teaching which, in the gentle nineteenth century, had become largely forgotten. A man may defend himself against a highwayman by killing his assailant because in so doing he is acting as the representative of the State, though not as the representative of the Church. Had the power of the State been present, the State would have rendered the highwayman innocuous: such is the assumption. Furthermore, the man who thus acts on the State's behalf is shielding his fellow-citizens against the evil-doer. But what if the State itself be in league with evil? What, to put it bluntly, is to be done when the Anti-Christ appears, when 'that man of sin be revealed, that son of perdition who opposeth and exalteth himself above all that is called God or that is worshipped?' If the Prince himself creates that lawlessness, that ἀνομία to which Luther refers, then the State can no longer be regarded as a State but as a chaos.

And when such conditions exist, Luther himself has said: 'Were I able to foment a rebellion, I should do so.' Though Luther never went as far as Calvin, he did regard it as the citizen's duty physically as well as spiritually to fight against the Anti-Christ should he appear, even as it is the peasant's duty to kill a wolf, should one be loose in his village, without further ado or discussion. This is not a fight of Church against State, no matter how tyrannical that state may be, but of man against the devil.

Such a condition of affairs had arisen in Germany long before the war and should have been plain to all by that night of November 9th, 1938, when the synagogues were burning and the Jews were being publicly maltreated. By then, at the latest, it was the duty of those who could do so to resist, since the rulers of Germany had surrendered their title to rule: 'For rulers are not a terror to good works, but to the evil.' And now the evil was loose in the streets. To those who knew of the horrors being perpetrated in the concentration camps and, later, of the Jewish and Slav massacres, their duty should have been even plainer.

In fact, according to Professor Iwand, the only reproach that could be levelled against the men of July 20th by a Lutheran theologian, was that they had acted so late. The political consequences of their action were irrelevant, as was the failure of the attempt. 'Tribute to whom tribute is due. . . .'

...ler shows Mussolini the
...mb damage to the
...nference room
...ystone Press Agency Ltd.)

Helmuth Count von
Moltke

Carl Friedrich Goerdeler,
Lord Mayor of Leipzig

CHAPTER VIII

OWING to the fiasco of July 15th, no preliminary *Valkyrie* order was issued on July 20th. Nor had it been possible to inform all the conspirators that this was the day. The principals, however, knew that Stauffenberg was to make another attempt, Beck, Yorck, Trott, Schulenburg and the others in Berlin, Hofacker in Paris, Quartermaster-General Wagner at the Zossen headquarters some twenty miles south of Berlin, Witzleben at his home thirty miles or so beyond Zossen. Hoepner, too, was in Berlin with his wife. He was one of the first to arrive at the Bendlerstrasse, going to Olbricht's office shortly after half past twelve, that is to say at approximately the time that the bomb exploded beneath Hitler's conference table.

Colonel-General Hoepner was living in retirement in Mecklenburg, having been deprived by Hitler of his right to wear uniform though still drawing his pay. He was suspect, of course, to the Gestapo and it was not easy for him to make three trips to Berlin within ten days. On July 10th his mother had died and on that same day Olbricht had informed him by telephone that his presence was urgently needed on the 11th, and that he was to bring his uniform in a suit-case. He had done so. On the 15th he was again in Berlin, but by the time he arrived Olbricht knew that that attempt had failed. On the 19th he made the train journey once more, with the ostensible reason of accompanying his wife, who was to be fitted for a re-modelled fur coat, and of buying himself some cigars. He had spent that evening at his father-in-law's house in Wannsee, just outside the city.

In Olbricht's office he learned that Stauffenberg had left for East Prussia, 'fully laden', and then he and Olbricht went out to lunch together. They had a half bottle of wine with their rapid meal and drank a toast to the events of the day. They then returned to Olbricht's office where they studied the situation map. Hoepner was anxious to see where exactly his son's unit was fighting on the now fluid Eastern Front. While they were doing this, General Thiele entered the room. It was a little after one o'clock, and Thiele, who was chief signals officer with the O.K.H., had just spoken to Fellgiebel on the telephone. General Thiele, who was in the conspiracy, was extremely excited.

It will be recalled that Fellgiebel had been standing with Stauffenberg when the bomb exploded. Almost as soon as Stauffenberg had driven off, Fellgiebel learned that Hitler was alive. It took him a little time to get through to Thiele, for signals communication was particularly difficult on this day: the main signals centre was in the process of being moved from Rastenburg to Zossen, and even the Chief of Signals, Armed Forces, could not get through to the Chief of Signals, Army, immediately, for in view of the move all messages were being routed through Berlin and the lines were jammed. However, he got a line shortly after one o'clock. What exactly he said is not clear, nor was it apparently clear to Thiele. Doubtless Fellgiebel camouflaged his message, for he must assume that his conversation was being overheard. It may be thought that the time for camouflage was now past, but it must be remembered that it was essential for the conspirators in Berlin that they have a few hours' start over their enemies. Fellgiebel could not yet afford to reveal what was going on to a possible Gestapo telephone-tapper or even to the ordinary army telephonists.

Thiele told Olbricht and Hoepner that there had been an attack on Hitler's life, but that so far as he could understand, Hitler was alive. Thiele was of the opinion that if this was so, then the essential precondition to the uprising did not exist and therefore the *Valkyrie* and other orders should not be issued. At least they should wait for confirmation one way or the other. Olbricht and Hoepner agreed to this. And here is the first, fatal example of the rigid military mentality at work. There was a plan, a good plan, in existence. It had, apparently though not certainly, gone wrong at the start. These men were, they felt, not in a position to issue the orders which were drawn up in anticipation of another situation. This was exactly the reaction of General Stieff, at Rastenburg, who, knowing that Hitler had not been killed, simply went on with his job as head of the Organization Department of the O.K.H. as though nothing had happened. Had Beck been in the Bendlerstrasse, or Stauffenberg, there can be no doubt that a rapid decision would have been made, but neither was present. Olbricht and Hoepner decided that they must wait until Thiele got through to Fellgiebel again. This Thiele could not do.

For Fellgiebel, having seen the explosion and knowing that this must therefore be the last chance, assumed that the men in Berlin were acting. He therefore blocked the entire signals apparatus at Rastenburg. His words to his Chief of Staff were: 'Something frightful has happened. The Führer is alive. Block everything.' This was done, and for two and a half hours Hitler's headquarters was cut off from the rest of the world. Even the S.S. signals, it seems, were neutralized.

It has been said that Fellgiebel was supposed to blow up the signals centre, that he failed to do so, and that this failure was one of the causes, if not the main cause, of the disaster. That is not so. The 'signals centre' consisted in fact of four or five buildings, some of them blockhouses of the thickest reinforced concrete to give protection against air attack. To blow them up would have been a major feat of engineering and one which could not even be considered in the circumstances. All Fellgiebel could do was to use his personal authority to prevent any communications entering or leaving the 'Wolf's Lair'. He did this successfully and for the astonishingly long period of two and a half hours. It can only be assumed that Keitel, Himmler and the others ascribed this total breakdown of their signals centre to the signals move to Zossen. In any event Fellgiebel fulfilled his part of the conspiracy most adequately. The tragedy lies in the fact that during these two and a half hours Stauffenburg was in an aeroplane, and that for most of the time Olbricht and Hoepner were waiting for Thiele to get more definite news from East Prussia. Owing to Fellgiebel's thoroughness, this was precisely what Thiele could not do. Thus was vital time lost: and time was the one commodity which the conspirators could not afford to waste.

At Hitler's headquarters it was not at once fully realized what had happened. The bomb had killed four men, at the end of the table where the bomb exploded, those who died being Colonel Brandt, the man who had once been the innocent bearer of Schlabrendorff's 'brandy bottles', General Schmundt, the head of the Personnel Office and Hitler's Chief Adjutant, the chief of the air staff, General Korten, and the stenographer, Berger. All the others present, save Keitel, were more or less severely wounded; these included General Heusinger, himself a member of the conspiracy and, at the time of writing, about to become Chief of Staff of the new Federal German Army. The building was wrecked and a great hole blown in the floor. But the oaken support and the table-top had saved Hitler. He had been blown into Keitel's arms. His right arm had been so badly bruised as to be temporarily paralysed, he was deafened, in his right ear permanently, his right trouser leg had been torn off and both legs were burned as was his hair, while a falling beam had caught his back. He was, in fact, severely shaken, but as is often the case the reaction was delayed. Indeed, his calm for some three hours was astonishing. He was able to meet Mussolini's train at about four o'clock. He showed the other dictator over the wrecked building. And it was only during the tea party which followed that he had a nervous collapse, shouting and vowing vengeance with a frenzy unusual even for him. Even so he had recovered sufficiently by one o'clock that night to make a completely coherent broadcast.

The first assumption by the men about Hitler was that an aeroplane, perhaps a Mosquito, had made a sneak attack on the headquarters and dropped a single bomb. Jodl, badly cut about the head, soon produced another theory. This was that workers, probably foreign workers, of the Todt organization were to blame. It will be remembered that a considerable amount of building had been taking place at this headquarters while Hitler and his staff were in Berchtesgaden. Seeing the hole which Stauffenberg's bomb had blown in the floor, it was for a time considered likely that the builders had concealed a quantity of explosives and a slow burning fuse beneath the floorboards. Not for an hour or more was Stauffenberg's rapid departure remembered and connected with the attempt on Hitler's life. This, combined with Fellgiebel's efficiency, should have given the conspirators the time that they reckoned they needed.

Himmler, Goering and Ribbentrop soon arrived at the 'Wolf's Lair'. Bormann was already there and had been the first to congratulate Hitler on his escape. Shortly before half past one, that is to say just before Fellgiebel's closing of the wires became effective, Himmler spoke to Nebe at the headquarters of the Criminal Police in Berlin and ordered that detectives be sent to East Prussia at once to solve the mystery. There is no reason to believe that Himmler spoke to Berlin again before four o'clock. Shortly after this, at about half past one, an examination of the circumstances of the explosion revealed the facts concerning 'the one-eyed colonel's' rapid departure without his brief-case. Even then it was not immediately realized that this was part of a wider conspiracy, let alone of a military rebellion. It was assumed for some time that Stauffenberg had been acting in isolation. When Hitler walked to the tea-house with Mussolini, after showing him the bombed building, he stopped and spoke to a group of construction workers. He said he now knew that they had been falsely accused and told them that the police were on the track of the would-be assassin.

During the tea-party which followed a comprehensible atmosphere of hysteria prevailed: none of these Nazi potentates could be quite sure that one or more of the others was not involved or that accusations would not be levelled at himself. Ribbentrop and Goering had a noisy quarrel and the Reich Marshal is said to have threatened the Foreign Minister with his baton. When a reference was made to Roehm and the events of June 30th, 1934, Hitler became hysterical and vowed the most awful vengeance on all his enemies. The Italian visitors were quite bewildered and, indeed, embarrassed by the behaviour of their hosts.

By this time, it was now after four, the signals cut had been raised by a direct order of Hitler's and the Nazi counteraction in Berlin was about to begin, although remarkably slowly. In this counteraction a minor figure by the name of Dr. Hans Hagen was to play a conspicuous and quite fortuitous part.

Dr. Hagen was an employee of the Propaganda Ministry, and had been connected with the branch responsible for propaganda to the Russians. When two years ago, Stauffenberg had been involved in the creation of volunteer units of anti-Communist Russians, he had come to know Hagen officially. Owing to Hagen's not unfriendly attitude towards the Russians, the Gestapo, it appeared, were taking an unhealthy interest in his activities. In fact he feared that he would be deprived of his job, if not actually arrested. Whether this is so or not cannot now be known. A friend of the author's who worked in the Propaganda Ministry at the time has described Hagen as being an imaginative, excitable and self-important man. In any event, he asked his military acquaintances for their protection, which could be assured only by obtaining him a commission in the army, for the army was still, in theory at least, beyond the reach of the Secret Police. The trouble here was that Hagen had been wounded during the French campaign of 1940—a bullet was lodged immediately beneath his heart—and he was unfit for active service. However this was solved by obtaining for him the post of National Socialist Guidance Officer with the Berlin Guard Battalion of the *Grossdeutschland* Division. Hagen was not a fanatical Nazi: the *Grossdeutschland* Division, being the pick of the army, was officered by men who were also not Nazis. It suited them that such a man should be their 'Guidance Officer'. Hagen was thus secured from the Gestapo, could continue to work part-time in Dr. Goebbels' Ministry, and was of use to the staff officers responsible for the Russian volunteer units. It seemed a good solution all round.

In July of 1944 he was stationed in Bayreuth, whither he had been sent by the Propaganda Ministry to work on a book for Martin Bormann, a *History of National-Socialist Culture*. His presence in Berlin on this day was unusual—he was there to attend a memorial meeting in honour of a writer who had lost his life in Russia. He was also to address the officers of the Guard Battalion on the somewhat arid subject of 'National Socialist Guidance Questions'. During the 1939–45 war officers of all the armies engaged were compelled to attend this type of lecture from time to time.

On the morning of July 20th Hagen was at the Propaganda Ministry. His appointment at the Guard Battalion officers' mess, out at Döberitz, was for the mid-afternoon. This battalion was commanded by a young and non-political major, named Otto Remer, who had recently won a high decoration, the Knight's Cross, for gallantry on the Eastern Front.

Hagen, when he left the Propaganda Ministry for lunch, saw what he took to be a Field-Marshal in a car whom he immediately identified as Field-Marshal von Brauchitsch. Since Brauchitsch had been retired two and a half years ago, it struck Hagen as extremely odd that the former commander-in-chief should be riding about Berlin in full uniform. In fact there is no telling what, or rather whom, the imaginative lieutenant saw. It certainly was not Brauchitsch who was many miles away at home. Nor was there any other army Field-Marshal in uniform driving through Berlin at the time in question. But no doubt Hagen had heard the rumours of an impending military *putsch* and putting two and one together he immediately made four, or at least three and a half. Something fishy was going on, with Brauchitsch at the head of it. He went to his lunch and later to Doeberitz, where he made his speech to the officers who were presumably rather somnolent on this hot Thursday afternoon.

It is a pity that Hagen, when he saw the uniformed figure, did not immediately take his suspicions to the police, for Count Helldorf, the Berlin Police President, was a member of the conspiracy and was awaiting the order to act, in his office overlooking the Alexanderplatz. Gisevius had joined him there in the late morning and was present when, shortly after midday, a junior officer arrived from Olbricht with the maps showing the buildings that were to be occupied by the army and the order in which this was to be done. There was, apparently, a brief argument as to what the exact role of Helldorf's police officers should be: Olbricht wished them to accompany the military groups, while Helldorf desired that the buildings be occupied or at least cordoned off before his policemen arrived to arrest the more prominent inmates. The second course was the one adopted, or rather that would have been adopted had that stage of the planned operation been reached. For the rest, Helldorf kept his police force under close control during that day. He had arranged a conference with his senior subordinates for the early part of the afternoon, so that he would be in a position to issue immediate orders. He had also summoned the leaders of the Berlin Nazi Party to his office for a meeting at three o'clock. By then it was expected that the operation would be in full swing, and should these dignitaries turn up, their arrest would, of course, be made much easier.

Helldorf was in touch with Artur Nebe, the sinister and ambiguous head of the Criminal Police to whom Himmler had spoken at half past one. Nebe, a senior S.S. officer, had as foul a record as any man in Nazi Germany, having led one of the Jewish Extermination Commandos in Russia, where he is said even to have exceeded his monstrous instructions in order to ingratiate himself with his superiors. But for some time, perhaps as reinsurance, perhaps, who can say? from a higher motive, he had established contact with the conspirators. His close association with the heads of the secret police, Kaltenbrunner and Müller, had proved of some value. It was from him, for example, that the conspirators learned of the imminent issue of a warrant for Goerdeler's arrest. Whether or not he also reported on the progress of the conspiracy to Himmler is not and probably never will be known. He disappeared shortly after July 20th, according to Gisevius into a Gestapo prison, but this testimony, suspect by nature of its source and all the more so by the fact that Nebe was Gisevius' closest friend, has never been supported by documentary or other evidence. Nor do we have any record of Nebe's alleged execution. He simply vanished, and for all one knows may be still alive somewhere.

After the departure from the Alexanderplatz of Olbricht's staff officer, Helldorf and Gisevius waited together with Count Bismarck, the administrative president of Potsdam. Nothing happened. Finally, at two o'clock, Gisevius telephoned Nebe. Nebe had by then spoken to Himmler at Rastenburg. He now told Gisevius that something strange had happened in East Prussia and that he had to give instructions to two detectives who were to fly with Kaltenbrunner immediately to Hitler's headquarters in order to conduct the initial investigation. This at least showed the policemen that something had happened. But still no word came from the Bendlerstrasse, nor apparently did they attempt to telephone Olbricht. Helldorf presumably attended his conferences, the Nazi Party leaders went home, and it was not until another two hours had passed that Gisevius and Count Bismarck learned any more. 'At four o'clock Helldorf at last rushed excitedly into our room. "It's starting!" he exclaimed. Olbricht had just telephoned him to hold himself in readiness; there would be an important message within half an hour.'

In the Bendlerstrasse little more had occurred during the hours of the early afternoon. Peter Yorck von Wartenburg was there now, as was Ulrich-Wilhelm Count Schwerin von Schwanenfeld, who had once been Witzleben's aide-de-camp, who was a close friend of Ulrich von Hassell's, of Oster's and of the Socialists too: since 1938 he had been what might be described as the liaison man between the military and civilian wings of the resistance. Klausing, the young officer who had accompanied Stauffenberg on the 11th and 15th, was duty officer for the day and was to work with Colonel Mertz von Quirnheim, Olbricht's Chief of Staff. Fritz von der Schulenberg arrived at about this time and also Berthold von Stauffenberg in naval uniform.

At No. 11 Unter den Linden, the headquarters of the Berlin Command, Major von Hayessen had spoken to General von Hase at noon. He had informed him that the assassination was to take place on that day and that he would be reporting for duty, to act as Hase's chief of staff, at 16.30 hrs. The timing here seems curious, but such is the testimony that Hase gave when on trial. Perhaps what Hayessen actually said was that he would report for duty 'later'. It was, in fact, half past four when he did so.

Quartermaster-General Wagner, at Zossen, was informed that the bomb had exploded and at about half past two he passed on this information to Colonel Finckh, the chief Quartermaster in France, to whom he had already spoken at noon, warning him that today was the day.

Beck and Witzleben were told, but neither of them seems to have been in any particular hurry to reach the Bendlerstrasse, where they were to take over the duties respectively of Head of the State and Commander-in-Chief, Armed Forces. That afternoon Witzleben drove first to Zossen, where he had a conversation with Wagner, who told him that Hitler had been only slightly wounded, before coming on to Berlin. Beck did not arrive at the Bendlerstrasse until some time after four. Both these senior generals had strong views concerning the inadvisability of a commander's interfering in the work of his subordinates. Witzleben, indeed, appears to have had only the haziest idea concerning the mechanics of the uprising and during his trial he got Olbricht's rank and job wrong. But still, their slowness in arriving at what must be described as their command headquarters is surprising. The explanation seems to be that they did not wish to be seen in the Bendlerstrasse before the action had begun. They were, in fact, waiting to be summoned.

Hoepner's inactivity is more easily explained. He had no part to play in the rebellion unless and until Colonel-General Fromm refused to co-operate, when he was to take over Fromm's duties as Commander-in-Chief Home Army. Olbricht would then be Minister of War, and therefore Hoepner's superior. Thus Hoepner was never in a position to assume command in the Bendlerstrasse. Nor did he attempt to do so. These questions of rank and command powers may seem strangely unimportant at a time such as this, but it must be remembered that this was intended to be a legal revolution—or rather counter-revolution—for which a most detailed plan of operations had been drawn up by men accustomed to giving and receiving orders and who intended to go on doing so. They were not a group of political revolutionaries in which the man with the greatest drive and strongest personality will impose his will upon the others: the exception to this being Claus von Stauffenberg. Indeed, one criticism which might well be made of the plans drawn up for the *coup d'etat* is that, though basically simple, they were far too rigid.

In any event, there was this curious hiatus between half past one and a quarter to four, while Olbricht and the others waited for definite news from East Prussia. Perhaps the failure of these men to go into action becomes more comprehensible when one remembers that this was the third attempt. The other two had turned out to be false alarms and everyone had gone quietly home. Beck had already said that a horse which shies at a jump twice won't take it cleanly at the third approach. This gloomy forecast was now being fulfilled. They simply waited for definite news or for someone in authority—which could only be Beck, Witzleben or Stauffenberg, since Olbricht had not shown the necessary initiative—to tell them what to do. It is surely some-what eerie to picture those dozen or so men sitting about in Olbricht's and Mertz's offices on that hot afternoon for over two hours while what was possible success gradually changed into probable defeat. Not until Stauffenberg arrived in Berlin did the rebellion come to life.

His plane touched down at Rangsdorf at about a quarter to four, and Haeften immediately rang through to the Bendler-strasse. There the conspirators were still waiting for definite news. At a quarter past three Thiele had informed Olbricht that a communiqué was to be expected from the 'Wolf's Lair' in the near future, but there was no indication as to what it would contain. Shortly before Stauffenberg's call, Thiele seems to have got through to Rastenburg on a bad line. This must have been just about the time that Fellgiebel's block was being lifted. Thiele reported that so far as he could make out Hitler was either dead or seriously wounded. Now Stauffenberg crisply told Olbricht that Hitler was in fact dead. Nor could he understand why the men in the Bendlerstrasse had not issued the *Valkyrie* orders three hours before. They were to be sent out imme-diately. Then Stauffenberg and Haeften jumped into their car and drove with all speed to the old Defence Ministry. The streets of Berlin were normal and quiet on that sultry afternoon. The columns of tanks and lorried infantry which Stauffenberg had hoped and expected to see were far away in their depots.

The Bendlerstrasse now came alive. Olbricht's Chief of Staff, Colonel Mertz, took the file of orders from the safe where they had lain for so long. A telephone message was sent to Witzleben, who was still at Zossen with Wagner, summoning him to Berlin. Count Schwerin set off by car to fetch Beck. Olbricht went in to see Fromm, whose office was a few yards down the hall.

Fromm had a visitor whom he dismissed at Olbricht's request. Olbricht reported, in his usual dry fashion, that he had received a message from Fellgiebel in East Prussia: Hitler had been assassinated. He therefore suggested to his Commander-in-Chief that Fromm issue the orders designed for a state of internal unrest (*Valkyrie*) without delay. Fromm hesitated. He de-manded definite proof, before issuing the orders, for he recalled Keitel's anger at learning of the *Valkyrie* exercise five days before.

Olbricht, having spoken to Stauffenberg, had no hesitation in picking up the telephone on Fromm's desk and asking for a 'Lightning connection' with Keitel in East Prussia. To his considerable surprise, Keitel was on the line almost at once. He handed the telephone to Fromm.

Yes, said Keitel, there had been an attempt to assassinate Hitler, but it had failed. No, the Führer was not even seriously wounded. He was with Mussolini at the moment. There was no need for alarm or for any special measures to be taken. Keitel could not continue the conversation, since Marshal Graziani was in his office. By the way, he added, where was Fromm's Chief of Staff, Colonel von Stauffenberg? Fromm replied that that officer had not yet returned, and this ended the conversation. That, so far as Fromm was concerned, was that. Olbricht, puzzled and worried, returned to his office. This was at ten minutes past four.

Mertz had not been idle. The first order to go out was the one alerting the troops in the Berlin area. In order to send it through the proper channels, it should have gone by way of the District Command, *Wehrkreis III*, the headquarters of which were on the Hohenzollerndamm. But it will be recalled that the *Wehrkreis* Commander, General Kortzfleisch, was a known Nazi whose replacement by General von Thüngen was envisaged. Therefore in order to by-pass him, and also to save time, Major von Oertzen, who was to be the conspirators' staff officer in the *Wehrkreis* headquarters, ordered an Austrian officer to send the orders directly and by telephone to the units concerned. Mertz meanwhile spoke to Hase who immediately passed on the alert to the *Wachbataillon* out at Döberitz: the troops were to move into Berlin at once while the commander, Major Remer, was to report to the Unter den Linden with all speed to receive detailed instructions. The first *Valkyrie* order, to the other commands within Germany, was sent down to the signals centre for tele-printing. Klausing, who was acting as Mertz's orderly officer had to bring it back, for the signals officer had pointed out that Mertz had forgotten to ascribe a priority. This was now done, and the message went out. Count Helldorf was summoned by telephone as was General Kortzfleisch, the former to carry out his part in the conspiracy, the latter to be neutralized. By the time Olbricht left Fromm's office, Operation *Valkyrie* was under way. Even now, however, the rebellion could not truly be said to have begun. The issue of these orders might, at a pinch and with extreme difficulty, still have been explained away. But if this thought crossed Olbricht's mind, as perhaps it did, the decision was soon taken out of his hands. At about this time Beck arrived, wearing a lounge suit—which he doubtless regarded as the suitable dress for a man who was determined not to head a military junta government—and a few minutes later Stauffenberg came running up the stairs, breathing somewhat heavily, his face flushed and his hair matted over his forehead.

He first reported briefly to Beck, Olbricht and the others, describing what he had seen: the tremendous explosion, the tongues of flame, the crashing building and the screams of wounded and dying. The others told him of Thiele's ambiguous conversations and of Keitel's straightforward denial that Hitler was dead or even seriously wounded. What Thiele had said was indicative but nothing more. Keitel, on the other hand, must be lying, according to Stauffenberg. That Hitler had survived was credible, that he had been only slightly hurt was not: Stauffenberg knew where the bomb had gone off and had seen the force of the explosion. It was therefore plain that Keitel was simply playing for time, from which it followed logically that Hitler was not merely seriously wounded but dead. These arguments, for the moment at least, convinced Beck, Olbricht and the other officers.

Stauffenberg now put through a Lightning Call to Paris, where he spoke to his cousin, Cäsar von Hofacker, at Stülpnagel's headquarters in the Hotel Majestic. Here too there had been a hiatus of several hours. In Paris, as in Berlin, there were several headquarters involved and therefore much telephoning was necessary. First, the Supreme Commander West (Field-Marshal von Kluge) had his headquarters at St. Germain-en-Laye, outside the city. Since the previous day Kluge had no longer lived or worked here and the senior officer at St. Germain was his Chief of Staff, General Blumentritt, who knew well enough that there was a military *putsch* pending but did not know the details. Owing to Rommel's severe wounds, Kluge was now also acting as the

Commanding General, Army Group B, and he had moved to that Army Group's headquarters at La Roche Guyon, some forty miles downstream from Paris. Here his Chief of Staff was General Speidel, who was fully in the plot, at least to the extent that Rommel had been. For some reason, however, Hofacker had not, during the last forty-eight hours, informed Speidel of the definite plans for July 20th. Nor had Speidel found time or opportunity as yet to discuss the whole business with Kluge. Finally there was General von Stülpnagel's headquarters, as Military Commander France, in the Hotel Majestic near the Etoile: the officers' mess of this large administrative organization was across the street in the Hotel Raphael, where the senior officers and officials also had their living quarters. Stülpnagel was fully aware of what was to happen as was the Paris Commandant, General von Boineburg-Lengsfeld, who commanded the army troops in and about the French capital, and who had his headquarters in the Hotel Meurice on the Rue de Rivoli. Colonel Finckh, in his capacity of Quartermaster West, was attached to the St. Germain headquarters, but his offices were in Paris, in the Rue de Surène.

At a little after twelve Wagner had rung Finckh from Zossen and told him that today was X-day. Between two and two-thirty Finckh's telephone rang again. It was Zossen on the line, and a voice strange to Finckh pronounced the single word *Abgelaufen*, which might be translated as 'launched'. This was the code word which meant that the operation had begun. Finckh now could and did assume that the *Valkyrie* Orders were being issued to Stülpnagel from Berlin. He had his own job to do, which was to persuade Blumentritt and Kluge to make immediate contact with the Allies, while giving Stülpnagel a free hand to deal with the Nazis in France. In his role of Quartermaster there were also pressing decisions to be taken concerning the evacuation of the German forces from the occupied territories. Finckh drove at once to St. Germain.

He told Blumentritt the pre-arranged story. There had been a plot by the S.S. to seize power, Hitler had been killed and Witzleben, Beck and Goerdeler had formed a provisional government. Blumentritt showed considerable astonishment, but soon pulled himself together, remarking that it sounded like an excellent government which presumably would send out peace feelers at once. He then put through an urgent call to Kluge at La Roche Guyon. But Kluge was not there. He had gone forward and called a conference of his army and corps commanders in a small wood, out of sight of the Allied fighter-bombers. Speidel did not expect him back until the late afternoon, nor could he apparently be reached: he was probably on the road. What was up that it was so urgent to contact the C.-in-C.? Blumentritt, not wishing to discuss the event at length on the telephone, said that 'something had happened in Berlin' and spoke the word 'dead'. Speidel asked him to repeat what he had said. After a moment's silence Blumentritt replied that he would himself come to La Roche Guyon at once.

Then, for a few minutes, Blumentritt and Finckh discussed quartermaster matters, without referring to what was happening in Berlin. After which Finckh returned to Paris, and Blumentritt set off for Army Group B. He would ring Finckh as soon as he had seen Kluge. Finckh got back to Paris at about the same time that Stauffenberg telephoned Hofacker, that is to say at about half past four.

It is quite clear why Stauffenberg's first action was to telephone Paris. Not only was the Parisian group of conspirators the most organized and most powerful outside Berlin, but also the armies in the West held the key to the success of the uprising and to the future of Germany, if not of all Europe. Should Kluge and his subordinate commanders declare for the new government, then that government was almost certainly secure and the war surely over. On the other hand, should the Western armies remain loyal to the Nazi hierarchy, then the most that the conspirators could achieve was a brief civil war in Germany and certain defeat. To go back to the old metaphor of the 'flash', what Stauffenberg had done in East Prussia was to put the match to the fuse: the fuse itself should by now be burning in Berlin—it was, at last, thanks to Stauffenberg's arrival: the barrel of gun-powder which should blow the whole terrible régime with its murderous, pointless war to pieces was located in Paris and, even more, among the Norman *bocage*. Therefore Stauffenberg rang through to Hofacker immediately. Otto John and Colonel Hansen were standing by in the Bendlerstrasse, ready to fly at once to Madrid to establish preliminary contacts with the Western Allies.

As soon as he had spoken to Stauffenberg, Hofacker, who was intended to be the new government's ambassador to Pétain, hurried to see Stülpnagel. Stülpnagel had, during lunch, shown signs of strain. Now Hofacker told him that Hitler was dead, perhaps Himmler and Goering too, that the *coup d'état* in Berlin was in full swing and that troops were moving up to surround the Wilhelmstrasse quarter. Stülpnagel sent at once for his Chief of Staff, Colonel von Linstow, and for two or three other officers who were particularly close to him. He also summoned General Boineburg and his Chief of Staff, Colonel von Unger, who were waiting at the Meurice.

When they arrived they found Stülpnagel standing behind his desk. His orders were brisk and to the point:

'In Berlin the Gestapo has tried to carry out a *putsch*. An attempt on Hitler's life. All *Sicherheitsdienst* (which included the Gestapo and the Nazi espionage organization) personnel in Paris are to be arrested at once, as well as the senior S.S. leaders. In the event of resistance, open fire. Is that all quite clear?'

General von Boineburg and his chief of staff clicked their heels, saluted and left the Hotel Majestic at once. Shortly after they had gone, at about six o'clock, Stülpnagel's telephone rang. It was Beck, though the call had come through as from Fromm. Beck did not need to say who he was, since he and Stülpnagel had been close friends for many years.

Beck asked Stülpnagel if he knew of the latest events. Stülpnagel replied that he did. Beck said:

'Then I only have to ask you if you are prepared to accept my authority.'

'*Herr Generaloberst*,' Stülpnagel answered at once, 'I have been waiting for this opportunity.'

Beck's integrity would not allow him to deceive a friend, even by omission, and he now said:

'The blow has been struck. But we haven't received any precise intelligence yet. Are you with us, no matter what?'

'No matter what. I've already ordered the arrest of the entire S.D. It won't be long before we've got all the responsible S.S.

leaders inside. The troops here are reliable and so are their commanders.'

This reply satisfied Beck. He now said:

'Whatever happens, the die is cast: we can only go ahead.'

'I agree,' said Stülpnagel.

Then Beck asked:

'What will Kluge do?'

This was clearly a matter on which Stülpnagel could not express an opinion. He therefore advised Beck to speak to Kluge himself and had the call switched to La Roche Guyon. By now it was after six o'clock, and Kluge should be back at his headquarters. He was, and Beck spoke to him. But before describing further events in France, it is necessary to explain what had been happening in Berlin during the hour and a half that had followed Stauffenberg's return to the Bendlerstrasse.

Having spoken to Hofacker in Paris, Stauffenberg's next concern was to clarify Fromm's attitude and position. It seemed unlikely that he would collaborate, and therefore Hoepner went into Olbricht's lavatory and changed into his Colonel-General's uniform. Beck, for his part, did not wish to start with an argument or quarrel with Fromm. Thus it was Stauffenberg and Olbricht who entered the general's office. Mertz was nearby, probably in the adjoining map-room, together with Werner von Haeften and another junior officer, both of whom were armed with revolvers.

If it was unlikely that Fromm would play the part assigned him, it was yet worthwhile attempting once again to convince him. An experienced trimmer, he could be relied upon to join the side which he regarded as the stronger. And it would add great weight to the conspirators' orders if those orders were backed by Fromm's full authority: the *Wehrkreis* commanders would be far more willing to obey their recognized Commander-in-Chief than to accept instructions from Hoepner, whose ambiguous position was known to all. With Fromm in charge, the actions of the Home Army during the next few critical hours would be dictated by the routine of obedience: the subordinate generals, never anxious to accept moral responsibility, could console themselves with the thought that they were simply carrying

177

out the orders of their legally acknowledged superior. Should Hoepner have to take over it would be clearly apparent to all that they were engaged in revolutionary activities: reluctance, or at best indecision, was bound to be shown. Therefore, though their opinion of Fromm must have been low, Stauffenberg and Olbricht made one more effort to win him over. It was a failure, for though Fromm was a trimmer he was very far from being a weak character. And he had had some twenty minutes in which to consider what were the probabilities of the situation and what, according to his usual maxims of self-interest, his own attitude should be.

Olbricht, drily factual and correct as ever, made his report: Colonel Stauffenberg had confirmed Hitler's death. The beefy, red-faced Fromm replied:

'That's impossible. Keitel has assured me of the contrary.'

Stauffenberg now said:

'Field-Marshal Keitel is lying, as usual. I myself saw Hitler's body carried out.'

This must have caused Fromm to think rapidly, for he did not answer at once. Olbricht took advantage of Fromm's momentary indecision to present his Commander-in-Chief with the *fait accompli*. He said:

'In view of this situation, we've issued the code word for internal unrest to the various home commands.'

Fromm sprang to his feet, crashed his fist down upon his desk, and shouted:

'This is open disobedience. What do you mean, "we"? Who issued the order?'

Olbricht replied:

'My Chief of Staff, Colonel Mertz von Quirnheim.'

'Fetch him at once,' said Fromm.

Mertz appeared and confirmed what Olbricht had said: the *Valkyrie* Order was going out. The order to the Military Governor of Bohemia-Moravia was dispatched, we now know, at 16.45 hours, that is to say at a quarter to five. (The text of this order will be found in Appendix II, Document 1, page 252.) It and the identical messages to the other headquarters were therefore being sent out from the signals centre at this very moment. Fromm's immediate reaction was to arrest Mertz.

'You are under arrest. We'll see what's to be done with you later.' Then, according to one report, he ordered Mertz to go down to the signals centre at once and stop the orders.

Mertz replied woodenly:

'You have just put me under arrest, *Herr Generaloberst*, which makes it impossible for me to leave this room.' Upon which Colonel Mertz sat down.

Stauffenberg now made one last attempt, a hopeless one as he must have realized, to win Fromm over. He said icily:

'*Herr Generaloberst*, I myself set off the bomb during Hitler's conference. The explosion was like that of a 150-millimetre shell. Nobody who was in that room can have survived.'

Guilt by association was an accepted principle of National-Socialist justice. Stauffenberg was Fromm's Chief of Staff. Even if Fromm disbelieved Stauffenberg's first statement concerning Hitler's corpse, this remark was calculated to make him realize that for him, too, the bridges had been burned. But its only effect seems to have been to make Fromm even angrier than before. He said:

'Count Stauffenberg, the assassination has failed. You must shoot yourself at once.'

Stauffenberg replied coldly:

'Certainly not.'

Now Olbricht spoke again. He had preserved his customary calm and said:

'*Herr Generaloberst*, the time for action has come. If we don't go ahead now, our country will be ruined forever.'

Fromm said:

'Then you too, Olbricht, are involved in the *coup d'état*?'

Olbricht said:

'Yes, I am, though I'm only a minor figure in the group which is going to take over the government of Germany.'

Fromm said:

'I herewith pronounce all three of you under arrest.'

Olbricht answered this in level tones:

'You can't have us arrested. You don't realize what the actual situation is. We are in power, and we are arresting you.'

A scuffle ensued. According to one report Fromm simply shouted at Olbricht, according to another he struck the crippled

Stauffenberg, according to a third he reached for his revolver. Mertz and Olbricht quickly overpowered him, and Haeften and the other officer put an end to the squalid scene, entering the room with their revolvers in their hands. Fromm was led into the adjoining office, that of his adjutant, where Major von Leonrod was ordered to see that he remain. The telephone wires in this office were cut and Olbricht told Leonrod, in Fromm's presence, to shoot his prisoner should he attempt to escape. (Leonrod had some weeks before asked a chaplain friend, Father Wehrle, whether the Church tolerated tyrannicide. Father Wehrle had replied that it did not and had urged that Leonrod abstain from any such action. Nevertheless the priest was later executed for the crime of not having reported the young major's conversation. Leonrod, too, was hanged.)

Hoepner now took over Fromm's desk, but first he had the courtesy to express his regret to Fromm for the situation in which they both were placed. Fromm, who was an old friend of Hoepner's, replied:

'Yes, Hoepner, I'm sorry too, but I have no choice. In my opinion the Führer is not dead and you're making a mistake. I can't sign the *Valkyrie* Orders for you.'

The conspirators were now in control of the vital portion of the building; but it must be realized that in this huge, though partially bombed, edifice—it is built around a courtyard and is half a dozen or so stories high—the great majority of the officers still had no idea what was going on. Rumours were beginning to percolate, however. So Stauffenberg sent a young friend of Haeften's down to the gate to organize the guard, a section of infantrymen drawn from the Guard Regiment *Grossdeutschland*. Soldiers were posted at all entrances and also to cover the empty bombed shell which formed the rear side of the square. No man was to be allowed in or out without one of the orange-coloured passes previously prepared and signed by Stauffenberg or, failing that, direct authorization. It was a little after five o'clock when Stauffenberg thus assumed full control of the building, and Beck of the new government.

The scene with Fromm can be described in such detail, because Fromm himself recounted it fully to Fabian von Schlabrendorff when they were in prison together several months later. This account is partially confirmed by the evidence Hoepner gave when on trial for his life in August of 1944. Unfortunately, for the rest of that afternoon and evening in the Bendlerstrasse we have no such full report. Almost all the men who were present are dead. Dr. Eberhard Zeller has, however, reconstructed the series of events from the fragmentary and not always trustworthy evidence available, and has done so with his customary thoroughness and brilliance. In the pages that follow I have relied principally on the ninth chapter of his book, *Geist der Freiheit*, for the facts concerning those next seven hours in Berlin.

While Stauffenberg had been dealing with Fromm, Beck had a word with Count Helldorf. Olbricht had already given the Police President his instructions: the police was now subordinate to the army and Helldorf knew what his force would be expected to do. He was about to leave for the Alexanderplatz, when Beck stopped him. He did not wish Helldorf to be under any misapprehension. Whether Hitler was dead or not—and even at this early stage Beck seems to have inclined to the belief that he lived—the enemy would undoubtedly maintain that Stauffenberg's bomb had failed. Therefore Beck wished to make it perfectly clear to Helldorf and the others present what his point of view was and what he also wished theirs to be. No matter what the enemy might say, no matter even what the truth might be, so far as he, Beck, was concerned, Hitler was dead, and he intended to act accordingly. There could be no turning back. How differently events might have turned out if Beck had been in the Bendlerstrasse and had laid down this line four hours earlier. . . .

Helldorf left, and with him Count Bismarck, the administrative president of Potsdam. A few minutes after the police officer's departure another and very different sort of policeman arrived at the Bendlerstrasse. This was an S.S. officer with the curious name of Piffrader. He had come, he said, on behalf of the Reich Security Head Office and desired an interview with Colonel von Stauffenberg. He, together with his adjutant and two companions who were detectives—these people always went about in pairs—was shown up to Olbricht's office, where they waited: the rest of his posse also waited, in the car below. At Kaltenbrunner's Security Head Office the Gestapo authorities were as yet unaware of what was going on in the Bendlerstrasse. Piffrader's orders were simply to arrest Stauffenberg, as inconspicuously as possible.

When Stauffenberg, coming from Fromm's office, heard of his visitors he did not go to see them, as Gisevius has stated. He simply ordered them to be disarmed and locked up in an empty office, which was done by Colonel Jaeger and Lieutenant von Kleist. The other policemen at the gate were similarly incarcerated in the guardroom.

Another visitor to arrive shortly after five o'clock was General Kortzfleisch. He asked for Fromm and was shown in to Hoepner, to whom he refused to talk. Olbricht was sent for and then Beck. Kortzfleisch made a scene, loudly proclaiming his loyalty to Hitler, whom he did not believe dead, and refusing at the top of his voice to break the sanctity of the oath that he had sworn to Hitler as his supreme commander. Beck replied with a forcefulness unusual in that softly-spoken man. This matter of the oath was one to which he, like all the conspirators, had devoted much thought, and Beck had reached his conclusion long ago. Hitler had himself betrayed the oaths that he had taken to preserve the constitution and to the German people, betrayed them not once but a hundred times. By so doing he had rendered invalid any oath sworn to him. An oath is implicitly a contract. Hitler had torn up that contract many years before.

Kortzfleisch rudely refused to accept this argument and was locked up, General von Thüngen, who was standing by, being immediately sent to the Hohenzollerndamm to take over his command. A few minutes later Kortzfleisch attempted to escape, but was recaptured in the corridor: it surely speaks for the moderation of his captors that they did not shoot him.

Out at Döberitz Major Remer, having attended Dr. Hagen's lecture on National Socialist Guidance Problems, had been summoned to General von Hase's office at a little after four o'clock. He alerted his battalion, drove to the Unter den Linden, and received his detailed orders. He then returned to Döberitz, gave the necessary orders to his company commanders, and drove back to Berlin to supervise the operation entrusted to him. He had been told the story about the S.S. *putsch* and Hitler's death, and had not questioned it. It was all no concern of his: he was simply a junior officer with a job to do. By five-thirty the governmental quarter around the Wilhelmstrasse was sealed, as planned. However, Remer did not have enough troops to ensure especially effective roadblocks in the vicinity of the Anhalter Station where the Reich Security Head Office was situated: the necessity for this had been particularly stressed by Hase, and so Remer went once again to the Unter den Linden to ask for reinforcements. There Hase and Hayessen had alerted all the army units in and about Berlin.

But Hagen, so suitably named for the role that he was to play in this Wagnerian tragedy, had taken matters into his own hands. He had been present when Remer was summoned and also when he returned and issued his orders. Remembering the phantom of General Brauchitsch glimpsed in the passing car his reaction was immediate: 'Military *coup d'état*!' Borrowing a motor-cycle and sidecar from Remer, and acting entirely on his own initiative, he rode straight to the Propaganda Ministry and asked to see Goebbels.

At a little before half past five Hitler had telephoned Goebbels, had told him that there had been an attempt upon his life, and had asked him to make an announcement as soon as possible over the radio that this had failed. The conversation was brief, since Mussolini was still with Hitler. This was the sum total of Goebbels' information at that time, save that he had heard that the officers in the Bendlerstrasse had been misinformed and believed Hitler to be dead.

When Hagen now arrived at the Propaganda Ministry and asked to see Goebbels, he was told, with undoubted truth, that the Minister was busy. Hagen's self-important hysteria was well known in the outer offices, and no employee was going to risk his skin by allowing Hagen to inflict some cock-and-bull story about a Brauchitsch *putsch* on the Doctor. Hagen, it seems, more or less fought his way through to Goebbels' office, who was, as his subordinates expected, furious at being thus interrupted while drafting and arranging for an important and urgent broadcast. He was about to have Hagen thrown out, when, according to one story, that resourceful publicist persuaded Goebbels to walk across the room and look out of the window.

183

And there sure enough, at the end of the street or perhaps facing the building, were the pickets of Remer's battalion. Goebbels was immediately convinced and told Hagen to fetch Remer to the Propaganda Ministry at once. Were Remer not there within a specified time, twenty minutes or half an hour, Goebbels would assume that he was being either disloyal or held by force and would order S.S. troops to attack and capture the headquarters of the Berlin Commandant at No. 11 Unter den Linden.

Hagen, doubtless glowing with pride, set off at once for the Brandenburg Gate, which was Remer's command post. There he was told that the Major was with General Hase. He hurried along the Unter den Linden and again succeeded in forcing his way past the protesting orderlies and clerks, but did not manage to reach the general's office, where Remer was, and indeed suffered here a tactical repulse, being forced to retreat to the stairs.

On the stairs, however, were two lieutenants of the Guard Battalion who were waiting for their commanding officer. Hagen knew them both, and before he was finally ejected from the building he managed to give them Goebbels' message: Remer was to report to him immediately. This completes Hagen's dwarfish role in the tragedy.

Remer, emerging from Hase's office, overheard one strange officer remark to another: 'Goebbels is to be arrested by the Army Patrol Service, not by the Guard Battalion.' This, he subsequently maintained, was the first indication he had received of what was really afoot. When, a few seconds later, one of his lieutenants whispered Hagen's message, Remer realized how serious, not to say dangerous, his own position was. He therefore decided to go to see Goebbels, but suitably armed and escorted. His assumption at this point seems to have been that Goebbels' invitation was a trap. He therefore instructed the twenty men whom he had placed outside and in the hall of the Propaganda Ministry that they were to fetch him out by force if he had not reappeared within a specified time. Then, with revolvers drawn and cocked, he and his adjutant entered Goebbels' office. He had come, he said, to arrest the Minister: it was two minutes before the expiry of the time limit that Goebbels had given Hagen, and a little after six o'clock.

Between the hours of five and six the officers in the Bendlerstrasse had been fully occupied in sending out the orders already drafted and speaking on the telephone. The first of these orders was that signed *Witzleben* of which the copy to the Military Commander of Bohemia-Moravia was dispatched at a quarter to five, presumably in code, for its time of receipt at the Prague headquarters is given on the order as 18.30 hours, half past six. This order, which was probably dispatched to the Commander-in-Chief West at approximately the same hour, had to be re-routed from St. Germain and did not reach Kluge until half past seven. But within Germany it may safely be assumed that between half past five and six o'clock some if not most of the *Wehrkreis* commanders had received their first intimation of a change of government. The substance of this order, the text of which is given in Appendix II, was as follows:

A group of treacherous Nazi leaders had attempted to seize power. The army was therefore assuming control of Germany. All Nazi Party organizations, together with the police and the transportation system, were henceforth subordinate to the military district commanders within Germany and to the supreme commanders or army group commanders in the occupied territories and in the field. The entire Waffen-S.S. was to be incorporated into the army forthwith. The military commanders were to secure all signals installations and were to dissolve the *Sicherheitsdienst*. Signed: Stauffenberg, for Witzleben.

This set the wires humming, both to the Bendlerstrasse and to Rastenburg, as the commanding generals rang through for confirmation or further explanation of this startling order. By six o'clock, when Hitler said good-bye to Mussolini at the small railway station in the woods—they were never to meet again—Keitel was aware that a military *putsch* was in progress and had begun to battle by telephone and teleprinter against the men in Berlin. Hitler, freed at last of his guests, now also joined in. He telephoned the Foreign Ministry, where he spoke to Steengracht, the State Secretary. This official told him that the Wilhelmstrasse was blocked by troops, but erroneously believed them to be S.S. troops. 'Our people, then,' Hitler remarked with evident relief. Next he rang Goebbels once more, who was still waiting for Remer, and loosed a heap of invective on that Minister's head for his failure as yet to have broadcast the announcement that Hitler lived. At this point he seems to have suspected even Goebbels' loyalty, a reaction that can only be ascribed to a state of mind approaching panic. Then the Reich Chancellery telephoned: troops of the Guard Battalion had appeared outside that building and were demanding its surrender. The officials there were told to play for time: Goebbels was expecting to see the battalion commander in the immediate future.

At this point Himmler presented Hitler with a document for signature: it was the appointment of Himmler as Commander-in-Chief of the Home Army. Hitler was in the tea-house at the time and he signed it without even sitting down. While doing so he ordered Himmler to fly to Berlin at once and there crush the uprising in the Bendlerstrasse. The violence of his tone is said to have shocked even the leathery sensibilities of his entourage, recalling, as it did, his manner on June 30th, 1934. He said: 'If anyone offers any resistance, shoot him, regardless of who it is . . . The nation's destiny is at stake . . . Be pitiless . . .' There was a brief silence. Then Himmler, now the most powerful man in Germany, replied: 'My Führer, you can rely on me.' He raised his arm in the Nazi salute, a smile playing about his lips and his spectacles twinkling; he turned and was gone. The S.S. troops outside Berlin were already alerted.

In the Bendlerstrasse the second and more drastic order, also given in Appendix II, was going out. The copy to Bohemia-Moravia is timed 18.00 hrs., six o'clock. This ordered the occupation of all broadcasting and signals installations, both military and civilian: the arrest without exception of all senior Nazi officials: the arrest of all concentration camp guards: the arrest of all Waffen-S.S. officers who appeared unco-operative and the disarming of all units which displayed a tendency to resist: the occupation of Gestapo and S.D. offices: the appointment of a political representative, to be named by Berlin, to each *Wehrkreis* commander: the avoidance of all acts of revenge. This order was signed by Stauffenberg, for Fromm. It, too, had clearly been lying in Olbricht's safe.

Gisevius describes Stauffenberg, during this time, as follows:

Fromm's office was separated only by a sliding door from that of his Chief of Staff. There was a constant bustling back and forth between these two rooms.   One moment the telephone on Fromm's desk would ring, then one of the two telephones on Stauffenberg's. Each time Stauffenberg hurried the twenty or so steps from one desk to the other.   Everyone was asking for him—understandably. For the generals in the provinces scarcely knew Hoepner, and the switchboard operators had been instructed to say that Fromm was out.

Everyone listened to every conversation.   Sooner or later there were bound to be important messages from the provinces, and we really could do with a little good news.   At our end of the wire Stauffenberg incessantly repeated the same refrain: 'Keitel is lying ...   Don't believe Keitel ... Hitler is dead ...   Yes, he is definitely dead ...   Yes, here the action is in full swing....'

The questions he was being asked could easily be imagined. What was interesting was the variety of tones in which Stauffenberg responded.   One moment his voice was firm and commanding, the next friendly and persuasive, the next imploring.   'You must hold firm ...   See to it that your chief doesn't weaken ...   I'm depending on you ...   Please don't disappoint me ...   We must hold firm ...   We must hold firm....

While Stauffenberg, Olbricht, Mertz and one or two others were thus controlling, or attempting to control, this most complicated operation, there were several conspirators standing about, civilians like Gisevius, John, and, later, Gerstenmaier, or semi-civilians such as Yorck, Schulenburg and Schwerin, who had for the moment nothing to do save worry.   Their presence cannot have been helpful.   Beck, too, was largely unoccupied.   Several times during these hours he was heard to remark: 'A good general must know how to wait.'   Hoepner, whose passion for the observation of proper military procedure had no doubt been pathetically reinforced by his dishonourable dismissal from the army, began the tenure of his new office in the traditional manner: he summoned all his departmental heads at a little after six o'clock and delivered, as was customary, a short address.   He asked for their loyalty, a curious request.   This little speech seems to have been accepted by his audience as neither more nor less than routine.   Witzleben was still not there.   Calls to Wagner at Zossen revealed that he was on his way: they also revealed that Wagner did not believe in the success of the uprising, since he was now convinced that Hitler was alive, and after a little while Wagner ceased answering his telephone.

In the S.D. headquarters on the Berkaerstrasse in Berlin there was at this hour of six o'clock a state of near panic. In particular the S.S. General Schellenberg, who now headed the German espionage service as successor to Canaris, was extremely frightened, as well he might have been. But he recalled that the legendary Skorzeny was in Berlin, the man who had rescued Mussolini, nearly captured Tito, and who was to kidnap Horthy, and terrorize SHAEF by the mere rumour that he was loose behind the Allied lines. This formidable and highly unorthodox soldier would be, Schellenberg decided, just the man to deal with so irregular a situation, or at least to protect the clerks and policemen in the Berkaerstrasse. However, at six o'clock that afternoon Skorzeny boarded a train in the Anhalter Station, bound for Vienna where he was to supervise the training of a group of frogmen—those same frogmen who two months later destroyed one of the great Rhine bridges at Nijmegen far behind the British lines and thus contributed largely to the British defeat at Arnhem.

On this afternoon Skorzeny, unaware of what was happening, installed himself in his sleeper. At the last halt on the outskirts of Berlin, Lichterfelde, he became aware of his name being shouted along the platform. He got out and was told that he was urgently required by Schellenberg. He drove to the Berkaerstrasse, where, he says, he found an atmosphere of hysteria. First he advised the S.D. men to put their revolvers and tommy-guns away. The way they were handling them was, he said, most alarming and if they did not shoot themselves they were more than likely to shoot one another. Next he summoned a company of his men, his commandos, from their depot outside Berlin to guard Schellenberg's office building. After which, being a most capable officer, he set out on a reconnaissance.

He went first to the headquarters of the Inspector of Panzer Troops, where a Colonel Bolbrinker was in charge: Guderian, the Inspector, was on leave at his home in West Prussia where, according to his own rather disingenuous account, he knew nothing about what was afoot since he had passed the critical hours of the day going for an interminable walk in the woods, thus being conveniently out of touch to Keitel and Stauffenberg alike. His Chief of Staff, General Thomale, was in East Prussia. That was why Bolbrinker was in charge of the offices on the

Fehrbellinerplatz. He now informed Skorzeny that the commandant of the tank school at Krampnitz, a Colonel Gläsemer, had received his *Valkyrie* orders from Oertzen, the staff officer sent by Olbricht to *Wehrkreis* headquarters. These orders were to assemble his troops near the Victory Column in the Tiergarten, which is in the centre of Berlin, with all speed, and to reconnoitre the S.S. barracks in the suburbs of Lichterfelde and Lankwitz in anticipation of an ultimate attack on those installations. The commandant had queried these instructions with Bolbrinker before going, as he had been told to do, to the Bendlerstrasse for more detailed orders. Bolbrinker had instructed Gläsemer to go ahead, but to avoid any sort of an armed clash with the S.S. Gläsemer had therefore alerted his unit—the strongest in the Berlin district—and had sent a few armoured cars to drive about in the vicinity of the S.S. barracks, with instructions to act as though this were a simple training exercise. He himself reported with his adjutant to Olbricht. Now Bolbrinker was somewhat dubious as to whether he had done wrong even to give so tepid an approval, since he felt that he should take his instructions only from Guderian. Skorzeny, informing him that he had just come from Intelligence headquarters, persuaded him to do nothing more without further authorization. This suited Bolbrinker well enough, since in any case it would be some time before the whole unit was assembled; the tanks were only now reaching the outskirts of Berlin. Skorzeny, himself desiring more information, set off for the home of General Student, the commander of all the German airborne troops. His house was out at Lichterfelde, conveniently near the S.S. barracks should the shooting start.

At a little after six o'clock Remer had entered Goebbels' office. Much has been made of the highly dramatic scene, which now took place, by Nazi propagandists and by the former major himself, so that it is hard to disentangle truth from falsehood. The essence of the story seems to be as follows. Remer told Goebbels that he had come to arrest him. Goebbels, who though vicious and evil was certainly throughout his life extremely brave, asked calmly: why? on whose orders? Remer replied that since Hitler was dead, he was taking his orders from his military superiors. Goebbels told him that he was misinformed and that

Hitler was very much alive. Remer accused him roughly of lying: was not Goebbels the most notorious liar of the age? But this interchange had taken enough time for Goebbels' stronger personality to master Remer's, and the impetus of Remer's entry was spent.

Goebbels, noticing the Knight's Cross which Remer was wearing, asked him if he had received this high decoration from Hitler's own hands. This was so: it had been bestowed on him only a few weeks before. Would Remer, Goebbels now asked, recognize Hitler's voice? Remer replied that he would, and the quiet assurance of the Minister's manner must have almost convinced him that he had backed the wrong horse. However, with a last attempt at bluster, he threatened Goebbels that he would have no hesitation in shooting him were this a trap. For answer Goebbels picked up the telephone and asked for a Lightning Connection with Hitler. He got through at once. Hitler was presumably expecting this call, and he asked Remer if he recognized his voice. Remer, drawing himself up to attention, replied that he did. Hitler then told him that he, Remer, was to crush the rebellion in Berlin: he was to take orders only from Goebbels, Himmler or General Reinecke—a Nazi general who happened to be in the city: and he promoted him to the rank of colonel, there and then. Such was the end of the conversation and this, too, marked the beginning of the end of the Berlin rebellion, though this was not to be realized by either side for several hours.

Remer went down to his troops and ordered the immediate lifting of the blockade about the governmental quarter. He dispatched officers to halt and reverse the movement of troops into the city. He occupied the Commandant's offices on the Unter den Linden, but did not catch General von Hase who had gone at six o'clock to General von Thüngen's *Wehrkreis* headquarters on the Hohenzollerndamm. Finally he sent out patrols to discover where the headquarters of the rebellion was situated. He later maintained that it was not until three or four hours had passed that he realized the Bendlerstrasse to be the centre of it all.

Nazi propaganda, faithfully echoed by the politicians and press of Great Britain and America, made a great deal of the Remer-

Goebbels interview and of the young major's conversation with Hitler. The reasoning of the Nazi propagandists is obvious. They presented the events of July 20th as a very minor incident, carried out by 'a very small clique of ambitious, immoral and at the same time criminally stupid officers': it therefore suited their version of the events to pretend that this Lilliputian rebellion had been crushed by a single junior officer with a handful of troops who were conscious of their duty. In fact, by half past six, the forces of National Socialism, under the leadership of Himmler, Keitel and of Hitler himself, were rapidly mobilizing. The initial aim of the Beck group, to seize power without bloodshed, always an improbable hope, was by this time an impossibility. However, had Goebbels been arrested or shot, it is at least possible that a greater or lesser condition of civil war would have ensued which, with its inevitable repercussions in France and on the Eastern Front, might have brought the war to an end that summer. But this is purely speculative.

Another question that this interview poses is this. Why did Remer go alone to see Goebbels? Though some of the staff officers at the Bendlerstrasse were exceedingly busy, there were plenty of other supporters of Beck's who had for all intents and purposes nothing to do. If, for example, Fritz von der Schulenburg had been with Remer, one may safely assume that Goebbels would not have been allowed to pick up that telephone. The answer here would seem to be connected with the remark that Remer had overheard outside Hase's office: he was not supposed to go to the Propaganda Ministry at all. His job was simply that of providing the cordon around the governmental quarter. If this is so, why then *did* he go? Ambition, fear, curiosity, misunderstood orders? He is unlikely ever to say. But if he was not supposed to arrest Goebbels, if an altogether different officer —Colonel Jaeger—had been assigned this task, why had it not been carried out by six o'clock? The answer is that at seven o'clock or perhaps even earlier Colonel Jaeger did inform Hase that he had been ordered to arrest Goebbels but that he had not as yet enough troops. And indeed the other troops were slower mobilizing than was the Guard Battalion. But even so, since Goebbels was undoubtedly the most dangerous man in Berlin and was recognized as such, it would only have been sensible to send a platoon, composed of officers if need be, to seize him between four and five o'clock.

It is indeed a curious omission on the part of the conspirators that Remer should have been left to carry out his orders alone. They did not know him, he was only twenty-seven years old, and though they might trust him to obey their instructions—which he did until given contrary ones by the Supreme Commander himself—they should surely have realized that a man who had no inkling of what was going on could easily be swayed by some other authoritative senior officer. For at least an hour and probably longer his would be the only useful military force at the disposal of the rebels. Is it not extraordinary that they did not send an officer, as senior as possible, who was fully in their confidence, to supervise with his authority the actions of this young man on whom all might yet depend?

This was a mistake which was not being repeated in Paris. There the immediate military force at the disposal of General von Boineburg was the First Security Regiment, commanded by Colonel von Kraewel and stationed in the École Militaire, near the Invalides. This regiment, despite its ominous name, was an army unit and an honourable one. Only those men were eligible to serve in it who were the last male representatives of their families, whose fathers and brothers, that is, had been killed in action. They were assigned to this more or less non-combatant unit, usually if not always after service at the front, in order that their families might not be totally wiped out. It follows that a high proportion of the men in this regiment came of the military caste and that therefore the Nazi influence was small. Kraewel himself, though not privy to the aims of his superior officers, was known to be an anti-Nazi. Even so, Boineburg did not leave him to carry out his orders alone, but accompanied the troops himself. In Berlin Colonel Jaeger took command of troops and Colonel Müller, rather later, went from Döberitz to the Bendlerstrasse and back in an attempt to get the Infantry School on the march: otherwise the officers of the rebellion seem without exception to have remained in their own or each other's offices. When Goebbels later sneered at the uprising as a 'putsch by telephone' he was not far from the mark, as he saw it. But such are the pitfalls of a legal revolution, intended to take place on a

ius Leber

Colonel-General Erich Hoepner
(Paul Popper Ltd.)

neral Friedrich
oricht
ul Popper Ltd.)

Colonel-General
Fritz Fromm
(Keystone Press Agency Ltd.)

Above. Field Marshal von Witzleben on trial before the People's Court

Left. Major-General Helmuth Stieff on trial before the People's Court

(Paul Popper Ltd.)

nation-wide scale. If one of your principal aims is to avoid bloodshed, then a telephone is a more suitable weapon than a machine-gun. Nevertheless . . .

To return to events in France. At six o'clock Boineburg had been ordered by Stülpnagel to arrest all S.D. and senior S.S. men. Boineburg telephoned to the École Militaire, alerted the First Security Regiment, and ordered Colonel von Kraewel to report to the Hotel Meurice at once. And here another curious hiatus occurs. Kraewel had not been given any sort of warning order and, since his day's work was done, he had gone out. No one knew where to find him. It might be anywhere, playing tennis, swimming, having a drink in any of the countless Parisian bars or cafés. It was several hours before he was discovered. When at last he was found it was decided to postpone the round-up of the Nazis until after dark—darkness comes very late in July— because thus the Parisians would not be privileged to enjoy the spectacle of Germans arresting one another. Perhaps this was General von Boineburg's intention all along, which would explain why he did not appoint another officer to replace Kraewel. As it happened it made no difference whatever to the course of events in the West, but still the hours of total inactivity strike the observer as strange.

At a quarter past six Beck, after his encouraging conversation with Stülpnagel, was put through to Kluge at La Roche Guyon. Here he met a very different reception. Kluge had come back hot and dusty from his conference with the generals in the field, three-quarters of an hour or so before. After a quick wash and change he had, as was his custom, immediately settled down to work with Speidel, studying the situation map and examining the reports that had come in during his absence from his head-quarters. When that was attended to, he asked Speidel whether anything else had happened during his absence.

'Yes,' said Speidel. General Blumentritt had telephoned at half past three and had reported that he had been told of an attempt, apparently successful, to assassinate Hitler. Speidel, assuming that Blumentritt knew more than these bald facts, had asked him to come to La Roche Guyon. He should be arriving at any minute.

Kluge's reaction was curious, if not incredible.

'No other news?' he asked.

Speidel said there was none.

'Thank you,' said Kluge. Neither by his face nor manner had he betrayed the faintest emotion.

He was not allowed to remain so aloof for long. Within a few minutes of this conversation his telephone rang: Fromm calling him from Berlin. But it was not Fromm, it was Beck. Kluge listened while Beck told him of the measures that were being taken in Berlin and the provinces, and said that good news was coming from the Military Districts.

The time was now exactly half past six and Goebbels' brief announcement was being made over the Greater German Broadcasting Station: an attempt had been made on Hitler's life, but he lived; although some persons had been grievously wounded, Hitler had been only slightly hurt. An orderly was, on Speidel's orders, listening to the wireless for just such an announcement as this. The text was rapidly written down and the sheet of paper placed before Kluge while he was still talking to Beck. Beck said:

'Kluge, announce publicly that you're party to what is being done here in Berlin and give the word for a general revolt.'

Kluge, however, was not ready to commit himself, even less so when he had read the text of the broadcast statement which the orderly now laid on his desk. He asked Beck:

'What is the actual state of affairs at headquarters?' He was referring to Hitler's headquarters and he mentioned the radio statement of which Beck was presumably still unaware.

Beck replied:

'In the long run does it make any difference provided we're determined to go ahead?'

'Yes, but . . .'

'Kluge, I'm asking you for a straight answer: do you approve of what we are doing here and will you place yourself under my command?'

A straight answer was the last thing Kluge was prepared to give. He spoke once again of the radio announcement. As Commander-in-Chief West he must know what the facts were

194

before committing himself and his soldiers. Beck became more insistent:

'Kluge, in order to avoid any misunderstanding . . . I would remind you of our last conversations and of what was agreed between us. Will you unreservedly accept my commands?'

Kluge recalled those conversations, but the primary condition had always been a successful assassination. Since this had apparently miscarried, a new and unexpected situation arose. Kluge said:

'First I must consult with my people here, on the basis of the actual state of affairs. I'll ring you back in half an hour.'

And this ended the conversation. Although Beck had not achieved all that he had hoped, there was no reason for him to be particularly discouraged by Kluge's reaction. 'His people there' were Stülpnagel, Speidel, Falkenhausen, Blumentritt and the army commanders, all of whom were committed in a greater or lesser degree to Rommel's proposed operation. And then there was the fact of Kluge's past flirtations, and more than flirtations, with the resistance movement. Beck knew that Kluge was a cautious man, far from impetuous but easily influenced. He must have had every reason to believe that the influences to which Kluge was now willingly subjecting himself would bring him down on the desired side. All the more so since the operations inside Germany seemed to be going according to plan.

Beck therefore now rang Falkenhausen, who, though since July 15th no longer Military Commander of Belgium and Northern France, was still living outside Brussels, awaiting this day. The line was very bad. Beck could only tell Falkenhausen that Hitler was dead, all other news false, and that Kluge had been informed. Then they were cut off. Falkenhausen immediately telephoned Kluge and placed himself unreservedly at Kluge's disposal for the operation which he assumed Kluge was now about to initiate. Kluge replied that he had not yet decided what to do, but that the moment the situation had clarified he would ring Falkenhausen again.

Kluge told Speidel to summon Stülpnagel and Field-Marshal Sperrle, the commander of the Luftwaffe in the West, for a conference at eight o'clock. Blumentritt had by now reached La Roche Guyon, but had nothing to add to the picture of events. Kluge, like Beck, was a good general and knew how to wait. This most experienced soldier was not prepared to make a decision on an incomplete appreciation of the facts.

In the Bendlerstrasse, during the next hour, from about seven o'clock until about eight, a spirit of comparative optimism prevailed. The reports that were coming in from the provinces were, indeed, encouraging. In Munich and Vienna the S.D. were being rounded up and arrested. From Frankfurt, Hamburg, Stettin and Prague there came signals accepting the authority of the men about Beck, though it must be realized that these came from the officers who sympathized with Beck's and Stauffenberg's motives, and their signals were, as it turned out, in many cases merely the automatic acknowledgment of orders which were not being, or could not be, carried out. Beck and the others did not yet know of Remer's defection. Beck spoke on the telephone to those army group commanders whom he knew personally, and in one case at least gave a major strategic order. Army Group North was about to be cut off in Courland owing to the rapid Russian advance through Army Group Centre and also owing to a Hitler order forbidding all retreat. Beck now told the Army Group Chief of Staff that he was to withdraw with all speed in order to avoid being cut off. The general accepted Beck's authority, all the more willingly since this was the sensible order which he and his commander had been anxiously demanding and had not received from Keitel. He began issuing the necessary instructions for the withdrawal to the formations of the Army Group.

But there was one serious flaw in the calculations of the Bendlerstrasse. Beck and the others had now accepted the fact that Hitler probably lived. They assumed that the operation had reached a stage in Berlin and the provinces alike at which this inconvenient fact made little difference, that the rebellion was sufficiently far launched to be carried forward of its own momentum. They do not seem to have realized that in the provinces affairs were not nearly so far advanced as they perhaps assumed, and that the radio announcement of Hitler's escape was causing consternation and second thoughts. They did not, however, simply ignore the announcement. At a quarter to seven the following signal went out from the Supreme Commander of the Home Army. It was presumably drafted by Stauffenberg.

The communiqué given out over the wireless is incorrect. The Führer is dead. The measures already ordered are to be carried out with maximum speed.

Hoepner, in his subsequent statement to the police, gives us a picture of Beck's attitude at this hour, a little after seven o'clock:

> I said to him (Beck) that there was still no confirmation of Hitler's death, and it all depended on that; if that weren't so, then what we were doing was all rot. Beck pointed out that the others were so good at propaganda and were so used to bluffing that they were bound to maintain the fiction about Hitler being alive. I argued against this: How about if the Führer himself were to broadcast? Beck replied: 'Yes, that's why I must speak first,' and he said that on all accounts everything possible must be done not to let the Führer have a chance if he was in fact alive. So I said: 'Then it would come to a trial of strength?' He said: 'Certainly; that is the job we've got to do for the sake of the German people in the present circumstances.'

Presumably Beck would not have spoken of a trial of strength, had he not believed that there was a fair chance of emerging from it victorious. What in fact was happening in the provinces at this time? Our information is scanty, and of course it varied from city to city, but here are a few brief chronicles of events, principally as recorded by Walter Goerlitz in his history of the German General Staff, *Der Deutsche Generalstab*.

Munich. The orders of the Bendlerstrasse were carried through without a hitch, and the arrests made. This was the only District Command in which this happened.

Vienna. After Stauffenberg had spoken to the commanding general, Freiherr von Esebeck, that officer said dryly that if Stauffenberg regarded it as necessary, he was perfectly prepared to gaol the *Statthalter* of Austria together with the senior Party and S.S. functionaries. He did so, though by eight o'clock they were freed again.

Frankfurt am Main. The town commandant expressed his loyalty to the new government. This seems, however, to have been all he did do.

Hamburg. The District Commander of *Wehrkreis X* was not on duty. His Chief of Staff went to see the Gauleiter and told him that he had received orders to take him into custody. Kaufmann was not a keen Nazi, and indeed it had been his pleasure, more than once, to visit Rommel's headquarters in France for what he called 'a breath of fresh air'. He was probably aware that a *putsch* was impending and prepared to collaborate, but he did not wish to be too precipitate. He therefore suggested to the *Wehrkreis* Chief of Staff that they drink a bottle of wine together before telephoning Hitler's headquarters to find out what exactly the situation was. This they did. Then they rang the 'Wolf's Lair'. After which there was no question of Kaufmann's arrest.

Stettin. The town commandant, another General von Stülpnagel and a distant cousin of the Military Commander, France, attempted in vain to persuade the District Commander to act.

In the other cities it was much the same story.

Nuremberg. The District Commander showed the order he had received to a Major-General Meyerhoefer, under an oath of secrecy. Meyerhoefer immediately broke his promise and informed the Gauleiter of what was happening, so that the latter was able to mobilize his forces and anticipate any steps that the Commander might have been planning to take.

Koenigsberg. Count Lehndorff attempted to persuade the Commander of this most vital Military District to obey Beck's orders. Although the general did not arrest Lehndorff, who was later able to make his way to his home at Steinort, neither did he act. Had he done so, he might conceivably have been able to overpower the Supreme Headquarters at Rastenburg, which was within the district.

Prague. The Military Commander Bohemia-Moravia, General Schaal, has described in some detail what happened here. At half past six he was enjoying a glass of beer after a hot day inspecting an S.S. training school, when he heard of the radio announcement concerning the attempt on Hitler's life. He therefore went to his office. At seven o'clock he received the first order, signed by Witzleben, concerning the pretended S.S. mutiny. Expecting popular uprisings, he immediately ordered out the army to protect military installations. At thirteen minutes past seven he telephoned Fromm but spoke, of course, to Stauffenberg, who told him that Hitler was dead—he had himself seen the corpse—and that the radio was lying. The men of the *Sicherheitsdienst* were to be arrested at once. A new government was being formed.

Schaal's reaction was to telephone the Protector of Bohemia-Moravia, the notorious Frank, at the Czernin Palace. But Frank had left his office and was on his way home. However his deputy, Dr. Gies, came to see Schaal as requested. The commander of the Prague Home Defence Division was also with Schaal, awaiting orders. It was eight o'clock before Schaal spoke to Frank on the telephone: the Protector then said he would come to Schaal's office at once.

A few minutes later the second long message arrived from Berlin, ordering the arrest of all Nazi dignitaries. Schaal decided that it would be unwise to send troops or otherwise arrest Frank openly, since this would undoubtedly lead to rioting on the part of the Czech populace and it was his duty to keep the peace. In his perplexity he again attempted to ring Fromm—it will be recalled that the order in question purported to come from Fromm—and this time spoke to Hoepner, who informed him that he had succeeded Fromm as Commander-in-Chief, Home Army. When Schaal expressed his doubts about the wisdom of arresting Frank, Hoepner told him to do whatever he saw fit, provided he kept full control of all forces in Bohemia-Moravia. Hoepner also told Schaal that Beck was the new Head of State and that developments were proceeding.

Meanwhile Frank, instead of coming to Schaal's office, had gone to his own in the Czernin Palace. He now telephoned to Dr. Gies, and ordered his deputy to join him there. Schaal therefore arrested Gies. Schaal attempted to telephone Frank, but without success.

At five minutes past nine Schaal received the telegram from the Bendlerstrasse concerning the untruth of the six-thirty radio statement and ordering the carrying out of previously issued orders with all speed. Schaal says that he now realized that this meant war between the army and the S.S. But in a hostile, occupied country such a war could only be suicidal. Furthermore, the S.S. in Bohemia-Moravia enjoyed such tremendous numerical superiority over the army, that there could be no doubt which side would win. Therefore he again tried to ring Fromm and again got Hoepner, whose reply was non-committal and unsatisfactory. Now he telephoned Frank again, only to learn that he was at his 'battle headquarters' with his staff. In order to avoid civil war, Schaal therefore released Gies from custody. A little after ten o'clock Schaal at last spoke to Frank who demanded the immediate cancellation of the orders alerting the army, and Schaal's word of honour that he would henceforth accept Frank's direction in all political matters. If Schaal did not immediately agree to those terms Frank would send an S.S. unit to arrest him. Schaal says that in view of the fact that Hitler was still alive—'and within the larger political framework nothing had changed'—he felt that he had no option but to agree immediately.

Finally, here is a quotation from the S.S. Report on the events of this day, which was drawn up for Himmler:

'The effect of the teleprinted messages quoted above was in many places a comical one, for the commanders of the Military Districts reported at once to, and asked advice of, those very men whom they were supposed to arrest first of all, namely the Gauleiters. There were no intuitive revolutionaries [sic] within the German Armed Forces.'

Only in Paris, as will be seen, was the story a different one for an hour or two.

Such, then, was the state of affairs in the provinces on which Beck's belated optimism was based. But of course there was still the hope that Kluge would play the part assigned to him.

At about half past seven Field-Marshal von Witzleben at last arrived at the Bendlerstrasse. With his *baton* he saluted Colonel-General Beck as his supreme commander, a charming, even a touching gesture. There was little else that was charming about Witzleben this evening, for he was in a towering rage. He led Beck into Fromm's office, where they were joined a little later by Stauffenberg and Schwerin. Witzleben's angry voice could be heard in the next room. The whole business had been bungled, miserably bungled. There was, he said, no sense in continuing. Stauffenberg and Schwerin are reported to have stood 'like marble pillars' while the Field-Marshal abused them for their clumsiness and inefficiency. Nor would he listen to Beck's arguments. Such, at least, is the story that Gisevius tells, which is therefore suspect. Witzleben himself, when on trial, says that he realized the *putsch* had failed, because Beck and Stauffenberg were not in control of the capital and particularly of the broadcasting station. He was also perhaps annoyed that the order bearing his name had been sent out before his arrival. The time schedule had required the occupation of Berlin by H plus 2, to be followed only then by the seizure of power in the other cities. What exactly was said during this desperate interchange between Beck and Witzleben will never be known. It would seem likely that Witzleben, convinced of failure, saw no point in going on, whereas Beck saw even less point in surrender. They talked for half an hour, Hoepner being also called in. At a little after eight Witzleben left the Bendlerstrasse, having first signed Hoepner's appointment as Commander-in-Chief of the Home Army. This futile gesture, performed apparently at Hoepner's request, was Witzleben's sole contribution to the events of the day. Witzleben drove back to Zossen, where he saw Wagner again. He told Wagner what was happening in Berlin. Wagner said: 'Well, let's go home.' This they did, Wagner to commit suicide, Witzleben to await the arrival of the Gestapo.

The sequence of events in Berlin, outside the Bendlerstrasse, is not easy to establish for the next hour or so. By now Remer's defection was being felt. At a quarter past eight Major Hayessen reported that that officer was with Goebbels and that he was not carrying out his original orders. For the last hour and a half the scattered pickets of the Guard Battalion had been behaving oddly and it was now apparent that they were acting against the Bendlerstrasse. An attempt to supplant Remer by a new commander had failed.

The Krampnitz Tank School commander, Colonel Gläsemer, had reported for orders to the Bendlerstrasse at some time after seven. When he realized what was happening he refused to co-operate and was imprisoned by Colonel Mertz in an office on the fourth floor. Orders sent to his unit were for a time carried out, and the tanks began to assemble by the Victory Column. Soon, however, Colonel Bolbrinker at the Inspectorate received contrary orders—perhaps from Himmler—and by half past eight or a little later the tank school was under Nazi control again. Part of it returned to Krampnitz, while some of the tanks were moved to the Fehrbelliner Platz, where they spent the rest of the night under the immediate supervision of the Inspectorate.

The Armourers' School and the Artillerymen's (*Feuerwerker*) School had occupied the Schloss and the *Zeughaus*, or Arsenal. Neither building was an important acquisition. Nor were these troops either numerous or impressive in quality. Colonel Jaeger, at the Schloss, did not have enough assault troops to capture Goebbels, particularly in view of the now problematical reactions of the Guard Battalion.

The other sizeable unit available was the Infantry School out at Döberitz. The commandant of this school, General Hitzfeld, had been for some time fully informed of the plans for the uprising, which he was keen to assist. As energetic as he was reliable, he had no doubt that the men under his command would follow him, and he was therefore assigned what was perhaps the most vital task of all, the seizure of the Berlin radio stations and installations including the powerful *Deutschlandsender*. His troops were also to capture the two great concentration camps at Oranienburg. On July 15th, when the *Valkyrie* Order was first issued, the speed and efficiency with which he had called out the units under his command had won Olbricht's commendation.

Unfortunately it had not been considered necessary to warn Hitzfeld that July 20th would be the day. And he, because of a death in his family, had that morning gone to Baden. The only other officer at Döberitz who was in the know was Colonel Müller. He too was away, in his case on duty, when the school was alerted at a little before five o'clock, and the first he heard of what was happening was when he arrived at a Berlin railway station later that evening. He went straight to Döberitz, which he reached at about half past eight, to find the officers in a state of indecision. Some were in favour of obeying the orders from the Bendlerstrasse, others not. Müller, after considerable difficulty, managed to speak to Hitzfeld in Baden; Hitzfeld was astounded at the news and immediately ordered 'a ruthless attack on the S.S.' The majority of the troops, according to Müller, greeted this order with approval, many boisterously so. But the School Demonstration Battalion, its best unit and the one destined for the Oranienburg operation, had gone out on a night exercise. It was some time before it could be brought back. Since the S.S. troops were by now on the move into Berlin, Müller went to the Bendlerstrasse with all speed for fresh instructions. By the time he arrived back at Döberitz with written orders it was almost midnight and all was over.

Here was another tactical and psychological error, comparable to that made with Remer. The initial orders for the Döberitz School should have been taken there by an officer, preferably a senior officer, at five o'clock. Then Beck might at least have had a chance to deliver his broadcast at about eight o'clock. The effects that this broadcast would have had, particularly in the West, are incalculable.

For in the West, between half past seven and eight Kluge was, it seems, prepared to act.

Blumentritt was with Kluge now, having arrived at about a quarter to seven, that is to say shortly after Kluge's non-committal conversation with Beck. While Speidel took over, for the rest of the evening, effective command of the German armies in the West, Kluge and Blumentritt discussed the political situation. Blumentritt was an old and trusted colleague: he had been Kluge's Chief of Staff at Fourth Army during the terrible winter of 1941 in Russia. Men who have worked so closely, in such circumstances, learn to trust one another. If there was one man in the West in whom Kluge could confide, it was General Blumentritt. Blumentritt, however, neither was now nor ever had been an active member of the conspiracy. All the same, it seems that while observing the impartiality which, in his professional capacity at least, is becoming to a staff officer, he definitely influenced Kluge during the next three-quarters of an hour to side with the conspirators. When, at a little after half past seven, the first long order signed by Witzleben came in, Kluge's mind was almost made up.

He discussed with Blumentritt what action he should take, and it was decided that the first step must be the discontinuing of the

V-1 (pilotless plane) attacks on London. This direct gesture to the Western powers, and particularly to Great Britain, should help to create the atmosphere in which to discuss terms for an honourable surrender. Furthermore, it would be a comparatively simple measure for Kluge to order. He and Blumentritt agreed to do this at once. Nor was this all. Accepting Witzleben's statement that Hitler was dead, Kluge was within an ace of declaring himself and his armies for Beck. It is at this point of time that one cannot help wondering what would have happened if the Western Allies had, in the past, given the conspirators the slightest encouragement. The balance, in Kluge's headquarters, was tipped now, though only slightly, in favour of revolt against Hitler and surrender to the West. Had there been any positive offer, or even any clear statement of Western aims, would not Kluge now have taken an irrevocable step? If there had been, for instance, some means arranged by which Kluge could get in touch with the Allied command in Normandy, might he not now have used it, if only to inform Field-Marshal Montgomery that he proposed stopping the discharge of V-1s? And had he done this, is it not logical to assume that Winston Churchill, who was at this hour, and for the next three days, on board a cruiser in the artificial harbour of Arromanches, would have taken immediate control of the situation? General Eisenhower's enormous headquarters was still in England on July 20th. He would perhaps have been by-passed and the disastrous slowness and indecision which had marked that Allied commander's reaction to the Italian surrender a year before were hardly likely to be repeated with Churchill on the spot. But no arrangements for any sort of communication had been tolerated by the Western Allies. Churchill knew nothing of what was happening only a few miles away. At almost the exact time that Kluge was making up his mind, the British Prime Minister was teaching the words of *Rule, Britannia* to the officers in the wardroom of H.M.S. *Enterprise*.

While Kluge and Blumentritt were discussing the immediate future, the telephone rang again.

'What the devil is it this time?' Kluge asked, as Blumentritt picked up the receiver.

It was Colonel Zimmermann, the first operations officer at St.

Germain. Another message had come in, this one signed by Keitel. It was a teletype signal to all supreme commands and larger formations, and simply said that Hitler was still alive. Kluge's new-found resolution weakened at once.

Or rather he was determined to discover what in fact the truth was, before making the decision to which he now inclined. He therefore told Blumentritt to establish the actual state of affairs once and for all. And so now Blumentritt began putting through Lightning Calls. It should be easy enough to get at the facts.

But it was not. The first call he put through was to Keitel. The adjutant at the 'Wolf's Lair' told him that Keitel was not available, which was odd. Very well then, he would speak to Jodl. Jodl, too, was unavailable. In that case he would speak to Jodl's deputy, General Warlimont. The adjutant would see if he could find him. For nearly a quarter of an hour Blumentritt and Kluge waited. At last the officer came back to the telephone. He was very sorry, General Warlimont was in conference with Field-Marshal Keitel and was not able to take the call. Blumentritt hung up.

To him and Kluge it seemed not only curious, but highly suspicious, that none of the three authoritative generals at Hitler's headquarters would speak to the Commander-in-Chief West's Chief of Staff. They could not know that Jodl was wounded and that Keitel and Warlimont were attending a meeting with the Italian generals. Their first assumption was that chaos must prevail at the 'Wolf's Lair', or possibly that the three generals were dead or under arrest. This would imply that the Keitel message was bogus, the Bendlerstrasse telling the truth and Hitler dead. But Kluge was not the man to be satisfied with negative information and suppositions. He told Blumentritt to telephone General Oberg in Paris.

Oberg was senior S.S. officer and police commander in the West. If Hitler lived and the Nazis were reacting against Beck's men, it was logical to assume that Himmler or some other Nazi leader would have informed Oberg. But when Blumentritt spoke to him, Oberg knew nothing beyond what had been announced on the radio at half past six. This, again, was negative information tending to support Witzleben's signal.

But still Kluge was not satisfied. He wanted a plain statement of fact, and therefore another Lightning Call was put through to East Prussia, this time to the Army headquarters called 'Anna' which adjoined the 'Wolf's Lair', and now Blumentritt spoke to General Stieff.

When Stieff, who had flown to East Prussia with Stauffenberg that morning, had realized that the bomb had failed and Hitler lived, his reaction had been the opposite of Fellgiebel's. Fellgiebel had taken for granted that the men in Berlin would act. Stieff had assumed that they would not, and had therefore gone about his day's work as though nothing had occurred. When, several hours later, he learned that Beck and Stauffenberg were acting, he was convinced that they were wrong to do so, and for himself had no intention of taking part in the rebellion. He said as much to the Bendlerstrasse: nor, indeed, was there much that he could do, save in this single and unforeseen contingency. Had he now told Kluge a lie, had he given his support to Stauffenberg's story, it seems probable that Kluge would have declared for Beck. But Stieff, who had once worked on Kluge's staff, had on July 20th attempted to step back out of the conspiracy. And so now he told the truth.

Hitler lived. Kluge took the telephone himself and asked Stieff if he were quite certain of this. Yes, there were officers with Stieff at this moment who had been in the *Lagebaracke* when the bomb exploded. There had been casualties, but Hitler was not among them. Keitel's statements were true, those of the Bendlerstrasse false. There was no question of a shadow of doubt: the assassination attempt had miscarried.

And that, for Kluge, was decisive. It had failed, he had been misinformed, he would therefore do nothing. He did not even telephone Beck or Falkenhausen, as he had said he would. And now, while awaiting the arrival of Field-Marshal Sperrle and of General von Stülpnagel, Kluge remarked to his Chief of Staff:

'Blumentritt, you know or you must at least have suspected that at one time I was in contact with those people. There is no need for me to tell you what my reasons were. Those were days in which it was still possible to hope. But now I no longer hope, because there's no point to it.'

Had Kluge, that sad soldier, been given to quoting French

poetry, he might have remembered the words of another soldier, Alfred de Vigny, which so exactly describe his attitude from this hour until his suicide by poison, thirty days later. *Puis après, comme moi, souffre et meurs sans parler.*

When Sperrle arrived at La Roche Guyon, at about eight o'clock, there was little to be said. Sperrle had no news either to amplify or to deny what Kluge now told him. Like most of the Luftwaffe, he was a supporter of Hitler if not actually a Nazi. He and Kluge therefore simply exchanged a few words, confirming that all would continue as before; then Sperrle drove back to his headquarters in the Luxembourg palace. Kesselring, another Air-Marshal who was at this time Supreme Commander of all German forces in the Italian theatre, was similarly uninformed, though Witzleben's signal was presumably sent to his headquarters. He says in his memoirs that the first he heard of the attempted rebellion was when Goering telephoned him later that evening.

At a quarter past eight or so Stülpnagel arrived at the headquarters of Army Group B. With him were a Dr. Horst, who was Speidel's brother-in-law and a full member of the conspiracy, his aide-de-camp, Dr. Baumgart, and Lieutenant-Colonel Cäsar von Hofacker. Hofacker, who had his cousin's, Claus von Stauffenberg's, quality of extreme determination and also his powers of persuasion, was here to explain the motives and programme of the conspirators to Field-Marshal von Kluge and, it was hoped, to fire him with his enthusiasm. Stülpnagel's Chief of Staff, Colonel von Linstow, had remained in Paris to supervise the carrying out of the orders for the arrest of the S.S. and the S.D. This was about to start. Colonel von Kraewel had at last been found: the 2nd Battalion of the 1st Security Regiment was ready to march out of the École Militaire as soon as dusk fell: and at General von Boineburg's headquarters in the Hotel Meurice a high state of excitement prevailed. A Swedish countess had telephoned Boineburg and had told him that according to her embassy Berlin was in rebellion and the end of the war at hand.

Stülpnagel, Hofacker and Dr. Horst were taken in to Kluge's work-room, which was one of the several large drawing-rooms of the château. Blumentritt was present and, for a while, Speidel, though that officer was soon summoned to the operations room to deal with urgent messages from the front. The officers sat down: and for fifteen minutes Hofacker spoke.

He told of the plans for, and the carrying out of, the assassination. He explained the patriotic motives of the conspirators. He placed his life in Kluge's hands by stating that he had himself been Beck's and Stauffenberg's liaison with Stülpnagel since the autumn of the previous year. He referred to the private conversation which he had had with Rommel in this very room on July 9th. And with all the persuasive intensity which he could command, he urged Kluge to do what Rommel would have done were he here now. Events in East Prussia and Berlin were comparatively unimportant. The ultimate decision was Kluge's. For the sake of German honour, of Germany's future and of mankind itself, he asked that Kluge break with the Hitlerite government and lead the movement for peace and freedom in the west.

Kluge sat motionless while Hofacker spoke and the light that fell on to the carpet through the long open french windows grew weaker. No change of expression revealed what, if any, effect Hofacker's words were producing on the Commander-in-Chief. Even when Hofacker had finished, and the room was filled with silence, Kluge did not speak at once. For a few moments he sat, staring at his hands. Then he got to his feet and walked up and down. At last he spoke. All he said was:

'Yes, gentlemen, in fact an attempt that has failed.'

Stülpnagel flushed and then turned pale. He leaned forward and said:

'*Herr Feldmarschall*, I was under the impression that you knew all about it.'

'No,' replied Kluge, sharply now. 'I had no idea whatever.'

This denial, Stülpnagel knew, was untrue: he also knew what it meant. Kluge was abandoning them, he was abandoning Beck and the others in Berlin, Tresckow and his friends in Russia, his country and the future. Kluge's moral courage had failed him, and he had sought refuge in his soldier's oath. Stülpnagel stepped through the open window and for a few minutes walked up and down between the beds of roses outside.

Only one faint hope remained. Once Boineburg's action in

Paris was under way, Kluge might realize that at this stage there could ultimately be no retreat, that for better or for worse his head too was at stake. As with Fromm in Berlin, Kluge, despite his denial, knew too much for his own safety. Therefore it was just possible, though unlikely, that motives of self-interest would induce him once again to change his mind. It was a faint hope indeed. Stülpnagel, like Kluge, was a Prussian, and he knew that Prussian generals do not usually allow considerations of personal safety to influence their more important decisions.

Kluge now invited his guests to come in to dinner, and they took their places about the table in order of seniority. It was scarcely a cheerful meal, though Kluge ate and drank heartily. Stülpnagel and Hofacker scarcely touched their food or looked up from their plates. The conversation was a monologue by Kluge who spoke solely of the events in Normandy, of the impending Allied offensive and of the measures he intended to take in order to delay the inevitable Anglo-American break-through. He also told anecdotes concerning his experiences at the front, but these too called forth only monosyllabic answers from his guests. Speidel was repeatedly summoned from the table to the telephone. There were heavy Allied attacks in the St. Lô and Caen areas. The generals were begging for reinforcements and supplies. Also they wished for information concerning the events at the 'Wolf's Lair'. Speidel told them what he knew, and added that it should not effect the fighting troops: the front must be held.

When Speidel came back, the candles had been lit. He has described the atmosphere around the table as resembling that of a morgue. At last Stülpnagel, glancing at the now dark windows, realized that the time for the last attempt had come.

'*Herr Feldmarschall*,' he said, 'may I have a word with you in private?'

Kluge frowned and hesitated. Then he got up and led Stülpnagel into an adjoining room. Now the silence of the men seated about the flickering candles was total.

After a few minutes the door opened again and Kluge called for Blumentritt. When Blumentritt entered the room he found Kluge in a state of high excitement and anger. Stülpnagel had ordered the arrest of General Oberg and the entire S.D. They might even be in jail already. It was a presumptuous and unpardonable act of insubordination to issue such an order without first obtaining the approval of the Commander-in-Chief. Stülpnagel stood in silence during this outburst, his hands on his hips. His last attempt had failed. Kluge would not play the part assigned him. For Kluge, scarlet in the face, said to Blumentritt:

'Get on the telephone at once. Countermand the order immediately. Otherwise I can't answer for anything, I can't answer for what will happen.'

Blumentritt got through to Colonel von Linstow, who said:

'The operation is already under way. It's too late to put the brakes on, the troops are out.'

This caused another outburst on Kluge's part. Why, he wanted to know, had Stülpnagel acted in this high-handed and independent fashion? Because, Stülpnagel replied, neither Kluge nor Blumentritt had been accessible by telephone. This was, of course, only partly the reason, but the answer seems to have satisfied Kluge. At least his temper subsided and he invited Stülpnagel to come back into the dining-room and finish his meal. This they did, or rather Kluge ate and drank what was placed before him. Not even he now spoke. And at last, at nearly eleven o'clock, the dinner was over.

At half past ten the round-up in Paris had begun. The deputy commandant of the city, Major-General Brehmer, took personal command of the troops which occupied Gestapo headquarters on the Boulevard Lannes. The guards and orderlies here were mostly Russians or *Volksdeutsche*; only a single shot was fired, and that by accident. Brehmer himself arrested Oberg in his nearby office while he was talking on the telephone to Otto Abetz, the German ambassador to Pétain's government. The headquarters of the *Sicherheitsdienst* were on the Avenue Foch and here Colonel von Kraewel took charge. General von Boineburg had had a word with the troops assembled in the darkness under the trees. They were, it is said, enthusiastic at the task assigned them, and it was as simple in the Avenue Foch as it had been in the Boulevard Lannes. The senior S.D. official, Dr. Knochen, was, however, not immediately caught. He was in a night club, from which he was summoned by telephone. On arrival at the Avenue Foch he too was arrested and taken to the Hotel Continental, in the Rue Castiglione, where he was held with Oberg and the other senior prisoners. The smaller fry were bundled into lorries and driven to Fresnes prison, which had been partially cleared for their reception, and to the old Fort de l'Est out beyond the walls of the city. Smaller bodies of troops rounded up other undesirables and only a very few managed to escape. One or two junior S.D. men who got away through the garden of the building in the Boulevard Foch succeeded in telephoning the commander of the S.S. *Hitlerjugend* Division and an S.S. teleprinter installation was also apparently overlooked, so that the Reich Security Head Office in Berlin was informed, but there was no reaction either from Sepp Dietrich's Waffen-S.S. in France or from S.S. headquarters in Berlin for several hours. By midnight 1,200 of the most unpleasant people in France were safely under lock and key. It was intended that the more notorious criminals among them be tried at once by drumhead court-martial. Sandbagged execution stands were being set up in the courtyard of the École Militaire.

The whole operation had been carried through without bloodshed or confusion. Shortly after midnight most of the Security Regiment marched back to its billets and the men were dismissed. They are reported to have been in high spirits. By then Stülpnagel's car was approaching Paris.

As soon as dinner was over Kluge had ordered him to return to his headquarters and release his captives. The entire responsibility, Kluge said, was Stülpnagel's. Furthermore, he proposed to relieve him of his command at once. Stülpnagel had made one last appeal, in which he was supported by Hofacker. According to Hofacker, Kluge listened quite sympathetically, but his sole comment was:

'Yes, if only the swine were dead.'

Blumentritt now said to Kluge that they must do what they could for Stülpnagel. Kluge therefore suggested to the Military Commander, France, that he change into civilian clothes and disappear. This was certainly not Stülpnagel's style, and he appears to have accepted Kluge's well-meant offer in silence. Kluge now was anxious, so far as he could, to make amends for his decision.

He accompanied Stülpnagel down the steps outside the château and as far as the door of his car. There he held out his hand. Stülpnagel did not shake it. He saluted, got in and drove off.

In Berlin, with the departure of Field-Marshal von Witzleben from the Bendlerstrasse, the last act had opened. Skorzeny and General Student had telephoned Goering. Then Skorzeny had returned to S.S. headquarters in the Berkaerstrasse where Schellenberg had asked him for an officer and ten men to arrest his former rival, Admiral Canaris, who was living in retirement at his home, guarded only by his dachshunds. Skorzeny, who had just one company of his commandos, told Schellenberg that he must make do with a single officer, and prepared to take command of the S.S. troops now marching into the city.

Olbricht and Stauffenberg were telephoning in all directions, attempting to find troops.

At a little after nine o'clock Radio *Deutschlandsender* broadcast for the first time that the Führer would speak to the German people later that evening. This announcement, repeated over and over again, was the monotonous death knell of the rebellion. The reason the broadcast was delayed for so long was that a broadcasting van had to be brought from Königsberg to the 'Wolf's Lair'. Hitler's rage at the inevitable delay is said to have been atrocious.

By now it was clear that the rebellion in the provinces was collapsing, and that only in Paris were the orders of the Bendlerstrasse being carried out. An eye-witness describes Stauffenberg on the telephone at this time, speaking loudly and clearly:

'Stauffenberg speaking . . . yes, all orders from the C.-in-C. Home Army . . . yes, of course . . . that's right . . . all orders to be carried out regardless. You must occupy all the broadcasting stations and signals installations. . . . All resistance must be smashed. . . . It's likely that counter-orders will come from Supreme H.Q. . . . They're not to be believed . . . no . . . the army has assumed complete authority, nobody apart from the C.-in-C. Home Army is entitled to issue orders . . . do you understand? . . . yes, the nation is in danger and as always in the hour of danger the soldiers have taken over . . . Yes, Witzleben has been appointed Commander-in-Chief . . . It's only a formality, you're to occupy all the signals installations . . . have you got that? *Heil!'*

But it was no good. Within the Bendlerstrasse itself, the announcement that Hitler would speak was having its effect, and outside the company of Remer's *Wachbataillon* which had been guarding the building was moving off. Only the small regular guard at the front gate remained. By half past nine there were no longer any tanks to be seen in the Wilhelmstrasse area.

At about this time General Herfurth, the deputy commander of the *Wehrkreis*, who had so far co-operated with the conspirators, changed sides. General Reinecke was now in command of the forces supporting the National-Socialists. General von Hase, the Commandant of Berlin, left *Wehrkreis* headquarters and returned to his own on the Unter den Linden. There Reinecek telephoned him at about nine-thirty and told him that all his troops were now to be put under his, Reinecke's, command for an assault on the Bendlerstrasse block. Hase, as a last hope, drove to the Propaganda Ministry to find Remer. He found Goebbels instead, who smoothly placed him under arrest.

Fromm, under guard in his adjutant's office since a quarter past four, asked at about eight that he be allowed to retire to his private quarters, which were down one flight of stairs. He gave his word of honour to Hoepner that he would attempt nothing against the conspirators, nor would he try to establish contact with the outer world. He was therefore allowed to go to his flat. He complained of hunger: sandwiches and a bottle of wine were brought him.

Towards half past eight three of Fromm's departmental chiefs, the Major-Generals Specht, Kunze and Strecker, came to his office, where they found Hoepner. This may be the occasion of the 'address' which has been described above as taking place three hours earlier or it may be another meeting altogether. In any event, Hoepner tried to win these men over, but they quite refused to have anything to do with the conspiracy. They demanded that they be taken to Fromm, and this was done, though it was arranged by Hoepner that they be kept in custody in his flat. Fromm told them of an unknown rear exit, and the three generals escaped. Despite his promise to Hoepner, Fromm had ordered them to find troops loyal to Hitler and to capture the building by assault.

But that was to prove unnecessary.

During the course of the afternoon all the junior officers in the Bendlerstrasse had, naturally, become aware of what was going on, nor had any of them objected to what Olbricht and Stauffenberg were doing. Some are said to have torn the national emblem, which bore the swastika, from the left breast of their tunics. However, with the announcement at half past six that Hitler lived, second thoughts began to prevail. In particular Olbricht's second general staff officer, a Lieutenant-Colonel Herber, decided that re-insurance was highly advisable. He arranged that sub-machine guns and ammunition be brought from the Arsenal to the Bendlerstrasse. They were stored on the second floor and made ready for use. In what might be described as the conspiracy against the conspiracy, Herber, a former police officer, had with him two other lieutenant-colonels of Olbricht's staff, named Priduhn and von der Heyde, and a Major Fliessbach. Von der Heyde—who must not be confused with the celebrated parachutist Colonel von der Heydte, who was at this time commanding the 6th Parachute Regiment in Normandy—was a devout Nazi who had broken down and cried when told that Hitler was dead. The others were opportunists who would undoubtedly have continued to obey Olbricht had they not been convinced that the *putsch* had failed. Indeed Herber later explained the motive for his action in the words: 'We would all have been hanged.'

At about half past ten, that is to say when the round-up of the S.S. was beginning in Paris and the possibility of a successful 'Western solution' therefore still existed, but when the Bendlerstrasse was practically without guards, Olbricht assembled his officers. He told them that since the men of the Guard Battalion had marched off, it was necessary for the officers themselves to ensure the safety of the building. He assigned them their tasks, nor was there any word of protest. Those officers not of the General Staff were dismissed. The staff officers remained.

Colonel Bernardis, when on trial in the following August, has described what happened next:

Lieutenant-Colonel Herber goes up to General Olbricht and tells him he'd like to know what exactly his game is, who is the building being guarded against, and above all why? General Olbricht spoke briefly, along these lines: 'Gentlemen, for a long time we have been observing the developing situation with great anxiety; it was undoubtedly headed for catastrophe; measures had to be taken to anticipate this; those measures are now in process of being carried out; I ask you to support me.'
I remember those words exactly. They were dismissed. They went into (Priduhn's) office. There Lieutenant-Colonel Herber and Lieutenant-Colonel von der Heyde . . . made their plans. Something shady was going on. Against who and why should the O.K.H. be defended? Something was wrong. The gentlemen armed themselves . . .

While this was happening, Colonel Müller arrived from Döberitz. He asked for a written order giving him full command of the Infantry School. With this authority he proposed to capture the broadcasting station, which would infuse new life into the entire rebellion. He also suggested that the Infantry Demonstration Battalion be sent at once from Döberitz to guard the Bendlerstrasse. The necessary order, dictated by Mertz, was signed by Olbricht at a quarter to eleven. Müller departed, taking with him the last order to be issued by an anti-Nazi O.K.H.

Five minutes later Herber and his men, some six or eight officers and N.C.O.s, appeared in the corridors armed with pistols, sub-machine guns and grenades. They forced their way into Olbricht's office, and demanded an explanation for his actions. Schwerin, Yorck, Klausing, Gerstenmaier, Berthold von Stauffenberg and a Major Georgi were in this room. Stauffenberg looked in, saw what was happening, and was about to go out again when Herber's men seized him. However, in the confusion he escaped a few moments later through Mertz's adjoining office and reached the corridor. He was making for Fromm's office, where Beck and Hoepner and the others were assembled, when he was shot at and hit in the left upper arm, his only one. He stumbled but, bleeding heavily, reached Fromm's office. There had been a number of shots in and around Olbricht's office. The shooting lasted for some five minutes, but curiously there is no record of anyone save Stauffenberg being even wounded. Herber's men ran down the corridors asking all they met: 'For or against the Führer?' Klausing and Georgi managed to escape from the building; Gerstenmaier was turned back. By eleven o'clock it was over. Mertz, Olbricht and Olbricht's A.D.C. were disarmed and brought to Fromm's office where Herber's men mounted guard over them, together with Beck, Hoepner, Stauffenberg and Haeften. The remainder of Beck's supporters were shut up, also under guard, in Mertz's office.

Herber demanded to know where Fromm was, and Hoepner told him. A few moments later Fromm appeared, flanked by armed men. He told his prisoners that he intended to treat them as they had treated him that afternoon. Haeften drew his revolver and would have shot Fromm, had Stauffenberg not stopped him. It was all over: there was no point in further bloodshed. Fromm informed the men assembled that they were all under arrest, and demanded that they surrender their revolvers. Beck said:

'You won't make that demand of me, your old commanding officer. I shall find my own way out of this unhappy situation.'

Beck picked up his revolver from off the safe behind his chair: Fromm told him to point it only at himself. Beck began to say:

'At this moment it is the old days I recall . . .'

But Fromm interrupted him:

'We're not interested in that sort of thing now. I ask you to do what you are going to do.'

Beck squeezed the trigger but succeeded only in grazing his forehead. He collapsed in his chair. Fromm told an officer to take the pistol from him. Beck asked that he be allowed to keep it for another attempt. Fromm agreed. He also granted Olbricht's request that he be permitted to write to his wife, telling him, with strange sentimentality, to 'sit at the round table, where you always used to sit opposite me.' Hoepner also wrote. The others stood in silence. Fromm left the room for a few minutes.

Down below a platoon of the Artillerymen's School, now acting under the orders of General Reinecke, had arrived at the main gate and taken over from the guard at a few minutes past eleven. They were joined almost immediately by a well-armed company of Remer's Guard Battalion.

When Fromm re-entered his office he was accompanied by officers of the Guard Battalion. Hoepner and Olbricht were still writing, Beck still slumped in his chair, his pistol in his hand. Fromm said:

'Well, gentlemen, are you ready? I must ask you to hurry, so as not to make it too difficult for the others.'

Hoepner blotted his letter. Olbricht asked for an envelope and sealed his. Then Fromm announced that he had convened a court-martial which had pronounced the death sentence on four officers: 'Colonel of the General Staff Mertz, General of Infantry Olbricht, this colonel (Stauffenberg) whose name I will not speak, and this lieutenant (Haeften).' He ordered a young officer to assemble a firing squad which was to carry out the sentence, immediately, in the courtyard. The four were led away and shot in the headlights of the cars below. Stauffenberg is said to have died with the name of Germany on his lips.

Upstairs Fromm took Hoepner into another office. He offered him the choice of suicide or arrest. Hoepner chose arrest and was taken off to the Military Prison. While this conversation was taking place, Beck made yet another attempt to shoot himself, and again failed. Fromm told an officer 'to help the old gentleman', but this officer did not feel he could give the *coup de grâce* himself. Beck was taken next door and killed by an N.C.O.

A few minutes after midnight Skorzeny and his S.S. men reached the Bendlerstrasse. He found the road outside blocked with cars, and got out of his own. On his way to the entrance he met Fromm and Kaltenbrunner. He heard Fromm say:

'I'm going home now, you can always reach me by telephone there.'

Then he and Kaltenbrunner shook hands.

It did Fromm no good. He was arrested next day as an accomplice, eventually court-martialled for cowardice, and executed in January of 1945. His last words were: 'Heil Hitler!'

Skorzeny took over the Bendlerstrasse. The conspirators who were still alive were manacled to one another and taken to the

Gestapo prison in the Prinz Albrecht Strasse. Skorzeny ordered the other staff officers back to work. For the next thirty-six hours, until Himmler took up his new appointment, Skorzeny acted as Commander-in-Chief of the Home Army.

In Paris, at midnight, Boineburg and Linstow, unaware of what was happening in Berlin, drank a bottle of champagne together in a private room of the officers' mess at the Hotel Raphael. There they were joined by Stülpnagel and Hofacker. In the main hall many officers were drinking to the success of the evening's operations. Stülpnagel seems to have considered even now the possibility of going ahead on his own.

But at one o'clock Hitler spoke, and that harsh, unmistakable voice from the loud-speaker put an end to what were, in fact, no longer real hopes at all.

The naval and Luftwaffe troops in Paris were preparing to fight the army. Sepp Dietrich's S.S. divisions were also now ready to crush the dying rebellion. Stülpnagel ordered the release of the S.S. and S.D. men at half past one. He sent Boineburg to fetch Oberg and Knochen to the Raphael, where Abetz was also present.

And now a most curious scene took place. Stülpnagel, Boineburg, Abetz, Oberg, Knochen, Linstow, later joined by Blumentritt and Admiral Krancke, drank several bottles together, while in the main hall army, navy and S.S. officers fraternized until long after dawn, by which time the execution stands in the courtyard of the École Militaire had been quietly demolished. And this strange party undoubtedly saved the lives of many of the conspirators, for it was decided by army and S.S. alike to make the minimum of what had happened.

It did not save Stülpnagel, as he knew it could not. Later that day, on his way to Germany whither he had been summoned, he attempted to shoot himself outside Verdun. He succeeded only in blinding himself. He was led, blind, to the gallows. Hitler had promised that his revenge would be terrible. It was.

CHAPTER IX

'A VERY small clique of ambitious officers, devoid of
conscience and at the same time criminally stupid, had
forged a conspiracy to remove me. . . .'
Thus spoke Hitler at 1 a.m. on July 21st, and this remained
the official Nazi propaganda line.

To deal with this 'very small clique', a special police commission, consisting of eleven sections in which were four hundred
detectives and officials, was set up on Himmler's orders. The
commission remained active until the end of the war. It was
responsible for some seven thousand arrests, some five thousand
deaths. Many, indeed most, of those persons were of course not
directly connected with the events of July 20th. The net was
deliberately made as wide as possible to eliminate once and for all
the leaders, actual or potential, of any anti-Nazi movement within
Germany. Similarly members of the active opposition who were
already in prison or in concentration camps, some since long ago,
were executed. Those who still remained alive in April of 1945
were, so far as possible, shot out of hand by the S.S. guards lest
they survive the war and play the part that would naturally have
been theirs in post-war Germany.

The ultimate intention of the Nazi leaders was even more
monstrous. It included the destruction of the aristocracy and of
the officer class. The elimination of socialist and clerical leaders
was already well under way. In August of 1944, Goebbels
addressed the Gauleiters at Posen. He said that it was not
Hitler's intention at that time to launch 'a general attack upon
the German army, or a general attack upon the officers of the
army or a general attack upon the German nobility. In so

far as it would prove necessary to attack these occupants of various positions, these members of a class or of a profession, such action would be postponed until the times were more suitable. . . .'

Himmler, addressing this same gathering, made a speech of a violence that echoes Marat or Desmoulins. The General Staff was a criminal conspiracy, and had been for generations : a collection of cowards and traitors, it was responsible for the loss of the First World War and for the defeats in the Second. Only half the officers in the army as a whole were reliable. Drastic 're-organization' was promised.

If this was the Nazi attitude towards the German opposition as a whole and to the huge German army, the treatment of the men actually involved in the conspiracy can be foreseen. Everybody in Germany who bore the name of Stauffenberg, men, women and children, many of them very distant cousins who in some cases had never even met Claus von Stauffenberg, were arrested. 'The family of Count Stauffenberg,' Himmler said at Posen, 'will be wiped out root and branch,' and indeed many members of it died in the camps. The children, even babies, were taken from their mothers and, under false names, given to strangers. People bearing the name of Goerdeler were similarly treated, as were the relations of other leading conspirators.

The conspirators were tortured, tried before the People's Court, condemned to death, but in many cases kept alive for further months of torture in the hope of extracting from them information which would incriminate others. Hitler personally ordered that the condemned be refused the last rites of the Christian Churches : if this foul order was in many cases ignored, it was owing to the courage of the prison chaplains.

The trials were conducted as circuses. The President of the Court, Roland Freisler, had observed Vishinsky in action in Moscow and modelled his court on that of the Russian. The prisoners, bruised, weak and in some cases—Hoepner for instance—apparently suffering from the effects of drugs, were treated with the most spiteful ignominy. Witzleben, for example, was deprived of braces and belt so that he had to stand clutching his trousers. His false teeth had also been taken from him. The purpose of these trials was to humiliate the accused before executing them in the cruellest fashion.

They were strangled by piano wire, suspended from meat-hooks while drunken warders screamed and jeered at them. The death agonies of Witzleben, Hoepner, Stieff, Yorck, Klausing, von Hagen, Bernardis and von Hase, tried and executed in August, were filmed and the films rushed to Hitler so that he, his adjutants and his women, might enjoy the spectacle that very evening.

Enough of such disgusting detail. Three Field-Marshals, Kluge, Rommel and Witzleben, paid with their lives, as did half a score of generals. A wave of terror raged through the General Staff. A price of one million marks was placed on Goerdeler's head. A wretched woman betrayed him and he died. So did Leber, Leuschner and countless other Socialists and Trade Unionists. So did almost the entire Kreisau Circle. Likewise many clerics. In fact only a minute proportion of the men involved escaped, owing always to a fortunate accident. It is scarcely an exaggeration to say that during the winter of 1944–45 what remained of the spiritual *élite* of Germany was behind bars; the cells of the Prinz Albrecht Strasse contained a nation's conscience. And Goerdeler wrote from prison:

'I beg the world to accept our martyr's fate as penance for the German people.'

The world has not, and indeed probably could not. The crimes committed in the name of the German people, and in many cases with that people's tacit approval, were too abominable, the hatred thus created far too intense, for this most Christian plea by a man facing certain death to be acceptable to Germany's conquerors. And Germany was punished, as no great European nation save Russia has been punished in modern times. But it is curious that the world has been so slow to honour, or indeed to recognize, the men of July the 20th.

The reasons for this reluctance are several. The first is that the world was not informed. It suited the Nazis to maintain their legend of a 'very small clique of officers', and for several years after 1945 many, perhaps most, Germans were anxious to to obliterate the immediate past. While the war went on, and in the years when the Germans were being punished, it was similarly in the interest of the Western Allies and its Press to ignore the fact that there had been so many brave and honourable men in Germany. Total war and the proclamation of collective guilt required a propaganda of the crudest black-and-white. Since those days much of the German history published in Britain and America has been written by men who were connected, directly or indirectly, with the formulation of the policy. summed up in those two phrases or with the enunciation of that coarse propaganda. The world has scarcely had a chance to be informed.

And then, of course, the rebellion failed. Hegel's views on history, popularized and ill-understood, have perhaps exerted an influence on the thinking of our century more widespread even than we realize. Marx, too, would have been surprised by the moral nihilism which is a bye-product of Marxism. An action which fails to influence the course of history becomes a mere anecdote, at best a drama, if the unrolling by which future becomes past is regarded as devoid of moral content or meaning.

Why did it fail? First, and most surely, because Hitler was not killed. Secondly, and less surely, because the conspirators in Berlin did not go into action as soon as they knew that the bomb had been exploded. Thirdly because the Berlin broadcasting stations were not captured: that is to say, the military plans were inadequate. Fourthly because Kluge did not act in the West, a fact for which the elimination of Rommel was certainly responsible; nor did the intransigent silence of the Western powers offer Kluge or any other of the conspirators the slightest encouragement or help.

Once it had failed, the utterances of London and Moscow were remarkably similar. The Royal Air Force dropped leaflets urging the 'workers' to rebel. One such leaflet, with extraordinary frivolity in view of the circumstances, said: 'A million German workers can achieve more in a hundred hours than all the Generals in Germany rolled into one.' Another said: 'The German workers can expect as little permanent good from a revolt led by German generals as can the workers of any other land.' The responsible British Press took up this same inspired line. On July 24th, 1944, the *Daily Telegraph* said: 'Even if the plot had succeeded, caution would still have had to be the dominant note, for the one certain thing about it is that a military junta planned it and that such an authority would be no less untouchable by the Allies than the political junta which was its target.' The tone of the press in the United States was similar. Two years later, on July 14th, 1946, the *Sunday Times* was still taking the same line: 'It was just as well that the attempt did fail. Had it succeeded, the army officers who planned it would have sought peace at once and might have saved the German army.' No mention here, it will be noted, of the men, women and children killed between July of 1944 and May of 1945 on battlefields, in concentration camps or in the bombed cities of France, Italy, Germany and Britain: no mention of the enslavement of Eastern Europe, nor of the presence of the Red Army in the centre of that continent: above all, no mention of how the precious 'workers', that extraordinary *deus ex machina*, were supposed to rise spontaneously in a Gestapo-controlled country nor why a government containing former soldiers should be 'untouchable' to the West. Seydlitz, speaking over Radio Moscow on August 10th, 1944, expressed the same ideas, far more comprehensibly, when he ascribed the rebellion's failure to the fact that it was not placed on 'the broadest possible basis both in Germany and in the armies' (i.e. that it was not dominated by Communist Workers and Soldiers' Councils), and that it 'lacked new political (i.e. Communist) assumptions'. But then Stalin did not share our declared war aim to create a decent, independent Germany.

The evidence both before and after July 20th clearly shows that the authorities in the West did not desire a successful rebellion within Germany and were glad that the attempt to bring one about had failed.

The obvious reason, so frequently alleged, was their fear of German militarism. It is an unsatisfactory one. The Western powers would have been as free to deal with Germany in 1944, under Beck and Goerdeler, as they were to deal with Germany in 1918, under Ebert, or with Germany under Dönitz in 1945. Is it unfair to suggest that the governments in Washington and at Westminster wished to regale their nations with the spectacle of total victory? That is to say, that they were debasing policy to gratify exactly those same furious and diabolical emotions in their own countries which had raised Hitler to power in his? Such a motive for the relief expressed by some responsible newspapers and politicians at the failure of July 20th was certainly never avowed, and in most cases was probably quite unconscious. The intention, previously announced by London and Washington, to 'wipe out German militarism'—whatever such a phrase may mean—and the contrary fear that a successful German military rebellion would have led to a new 'stab in the back legend', were the overt reasons for the Western refusal to encourage the rebellion and, later, to regret its failure. However, more squalid emotions were obviously at large in the background.

Nazi Germany was certainly the disgusting abscess of the age, but the poison that burst at Buchenwald, Dachau and the other camps had infected to a certain extent all the West in the first half of our century. It could be described, very briefly, as an abdication of personal responsibility in favour of the dense pressures created by mass organizations aware primarily of their own, largely primitive but none the less real, interests. If such was the climate of opinion of the age, then the motives of the men of July 20th became suspect if not actually incomprehensible to its representatives. For theirs was the action of individuals willingly aware of their responsibility to and for others less fortunate, less intelligent and less courageous than themselves.

And it is this which gives the action of Stauffenberg, Beck, Goerdeler, Leber, Tresckow and the hundreds of others involved, its lustre. They acted not at all from self-interest: they were men prepared to take charge of events because they knew it was their duty to do so, regardless equally of what would happen to them or of what would be said of them after their death. And this was a startling departure from the principles and practices of the century. These men, who had nothing to gain and everything to lose, acted primarily for ethical, moral or religious reasons, not for economic reasons nor for purposes of enjoying power. That is why they appear so paradoxical a group, unmilitaristic soldiers such as Beck or Stauffenberg, trade unionists and socialists who saw far beyond a class or a doctrine, such as Leuschner, Kaiser and Leber, great landowners who were prepared and willing to see their estates divided, such as Moltke and Yorck, men of God who after what must have been acute spiritual anguish were prepared to countenance murder, such as Father Delp and Pastor Gerstenmaier. But then truth is a paradox. And in this century it is paradoxical, indeed almost unknown, for a man to act politically with neither doctrine nor party but only his conscience behind him. They acted for their nation, for Europe as a whole, but they did this as men, not as the representatives of some great intellectual theory or inhuman machine. They acted because they knew that as decent, God-fearing men they had no choice. 'It must be done,' said Stauffenberg, *'coûte que coûte.'*

It was done. And it proved simply this: that in the most atrocious situations, subjected to the most appalling moral and emotional pressures, such as those which existed in wartime Germany in 1944, it is still possible for men to stand up and act as men are intended to act.

APPENDIXES

APPENDIX I

THE KREISAU DOCUMENTS

Document A

Draft of 9 August, 1943

FIRST INSTRUCTIONS TO THE 'LAND' COMMISSIONERS

The internal and external misery of the German people can only be lessened, and a vigorous rejuvenation of its fortunes only be undertaken, on the basis of a clear and coherent vision of Germany's future. Such a closely reasoned design is all the more necessary since military and political developments may produce a state of affairs in which certain regions are under military occupation and separated from the rest, or even in which there is no government of the German Reich or at least no means by which such a government can communicate its orders.

It is a matter of urgent necessity that in such circumstances responsible leading persons in the individual *Länder* and districts will act on uniform lines and on identical principles, even though they may be unable to consult one another or exchange their views: this must be ensured in order to maintain and strengthen the cultural homogeneity of the German *Länder* as parts of one national body.

The principles, outlined below, are limited to basic matters in view of the great diversity of possible future developments; they are intended to ensure that should the military situation take an unfavourable turn, the German people will be able to present a homogeneous attitude to the other nations.

The German working class, which believes in freedom, and the Christian Churches represent and lead those popular forces

229

with which the reconstruction can be undertaken. At this time only they, on account of their enduring spiritual traditions, offer a guarantee that the cultural substance of the German people be preserved and that its national coherence be saved from the perils which now threaten it. Supported by those forces, we assign to you the high responsibility to assume the office of a *Land* Commissioner in the region delimitated on the attached map, and to take possession of the necessary powers to perform your duties. The commanders of the Military Districts are being told to follow your instructions.

The *Land* Commissioner is responsible to the Reich for shaping the political, cultural and economic forces of the *Land*:

1. He will ensure Law and Order, liberty of the person, and a genuine co-responsibility on the part of the entire population of the *Land*. By so doing he will make prevail the natural course of political self-determination, and see to it that self-administration will develop according to the particular character of each district.

2. In close co-operation with the recognized representatives of the cultural activities, the Commissioner will take steps to re-create a Christian system of education and thus a genuine renewal of spiritual life. In this field it is essential that collaboration between *Land* and Church, based on mutual trust, be initiated forthwith.

For this purpose you are immediately to establish contact with the leaders of the Churches within your *Land*.

3. In particular, the *Land* Commissioner is to arrange for responsible co-operation by the workers in administrative and industrial matters. You will therefore establish immediate contact with the officials of the German Trade Union who are to be recognized as the only rightful representatives of the workers.

For further details see Annex I.

The following general lines will be pursued in carrying out these principles:

ANNEX I

1. In the matter of appointments, you have complete freedom to carry out all measures you may consider necessary to ensure an orderly administration and the preservation of law and order.

On principle all leading National-Socialists are to be dismissed from important positions.

After selecting your closest colleagues, you will first appoint absolutely reliable persons to fill key positions. Your right of appointing personnel also extends to officials of Reich departments and regional authorities operating within your *Land*.

Final appointments carrying civil service status can only be made after your confirmation in office as *Land* Commissioner.

2. In the case of the proclamation of a State of Siege (Martial Law) the military plenipotentiary will remain subject to your general political directives.

3. As regards necessary arrests, the amount of personal guilt, particularly with regard to the provisions of Annex II concerning law-defilers, will be the criterion; offences are so far as is possible to be tried and judged according to the normal processes of law. In addition, all persons are to be arrested who may be suspected of attempting to hinder the State in carrying out the measures deemed necessary. Persons unjustly deprived of their freedom are to be liberated at once.

It is your responsibility to take all the necessary steps without awaiting instructions from higher authorities.

4. The adjustment of frontiers, necessitated by the re-division of the *Länder*, is to be carried out at once in co-operation with the Commissioners of the adjoining *Länder*. Means for a constant exchange of views with the *Land* Commissioners of all neighbouring *Länder* are to be ensured as a matter of urgency. The spheres of the postal and railway administrations, as well as of the Armed Forces, will for the time being remain unaltered.

ANNEX II

1. All laws and decrees directed against individuals as members of a nation, race or creed will be suspended; all discriminatory measures based on such laws or decrees will be lifted immediately. Apart from those, the laws and administrative decrees at present in existence will, in principle, continue in force.

2a. All measures intended to serve the battle-worthiness of the German armed forces or, at a later date, their orderly demobilization, are matters of Reich responsibility and as such to be carried out with priority over all other tasks; the necessary actions will be taken regardless of any possible resistance.

2b. The orderly continuation of the existing economic system of production and distribution must in no circumstances be interfered with. Requisitioning of supplies in transit and a breakdown of the rationing scheme present the greatest danger.

3. In addition to maintaining the integrity of your *Land* and ensuring law and order with your *Land*, your primary task is to build up a system of self-administration in accordance with the principles laid down in Annex I above. In so doing the economic interests and the political forces existing within your *Land* are to be incorporated in the self-administrative edifice to the maximum extent, while the bureaucratic administration is to be reduced and your own personal authority is to be placed on a firm basis of support derived from below.

4. You will do what is needed to ensure that industry is capable of carrying out the necessary measures of re-organization, if possible without external help and while maintaining a proper level of employment. In order to stabilize conditions, the emigration of non-resident workers is to be encouraged. No regulations limiting the immigration or residence of Germans will be permitted.

5. To fulfil your necessary cash obligations you are entitled to claim the necessary disbursements on the basis of the Reich Appropriation Law.

Document B

Draft of 9 August, 1943

BASIC PRINCIPLES FOR THE NEW ORDER

The government of the German Reich regards Christianity as the basis for the moral and spiritual renewal of our people, for the overthrow of hatred and falsehood, and for the rebuilding of the European community of nations.

The point of departure is man's obligation to recognize the Divine Order which supports both his inner being and outward existence. Only when this Divine Order has been made the standard of relations between individuals and between states can the disorder of the age be overcome and a genuine condition of peace brought about. The internal reconstruction of the Reich is the basis on which a just and lasting peace is to be built.

With the collapse of forces that have become rootless and are founded exclusively on technical mastery, it is above all the Europeans who are confronted with this task. The way to its solution lies in a determined and energetic realization of the Christian way of life. The government of the Reich is therefore determined to fulfil the following indispensable demands, using all the means at its disposal:

1. The principle of legality, now trampled under foot, must be elevated once again to a position of supremacy over all conditions of human life. Beneath the protection of conscientious and independent judges, freed from the fear of men, this is the basis for every aspect of the peaceful state of affairs which is to come.

2. Freedom of belief and freedom of conscience will be guaranteed. All laws and decrees which contravene these principles will be repealed immediately.

3. Totalitarian moral compulsion will be broken: the inalienable dignity of the human individual will be recognized as the basis for that legal and peaceful order which is the objective. Each man will work, in full responsibility, in his own field of social, political and international activities. The right to work and the right to property are under public protection regardless of race, nationality or creed.

4. The family is the basic unit of the peaceful life of the community. The family is under public protection which, in addition to education, will ensure that the family is provided with the material necessities: food, clothing, lodging, garden and health.

5. Work must be so organized that it encourages rather than restricts the will to personal responsibility. In addition to promoting the material conditions of work and a programme of vocational training, this requires an effective co-responsibility on the part of every worker not only towards his own industrial unit but also towards industry as a whole, to which his work contributes. He shall thereby co-operate in developing a healthy and enduring way of life in which the individual, his family and the community shall be capable of organic growth within a well-

balanced economy. Industrial leadership must guarantee these fundamental requirements.

6. Everybody's personal political responsibility requires his right of co-determination in the administration, which is to be revived on the basis of small, easily comprehensible communities. Rooted and tested in such communities, his participation in the affairs of the state and of the community of nations will be ensured by his elected representatives: thus will he be given a living awareness of his personal co-responsibility for the general course of political events.

7. That especial responsibility and loyalty which each man owes to his national origin, his language and the spiritual and historic heritage of his people must be respected and protected. However, those emotions must not be perverted into the concentration of political power, nor must they be used to vilify, persecute or oppress foreign national groups. The free and peaceful expansion of a national civilization can no longer be combined with the maintenance of absolute sovereignty on the part of individual states. Peace requires the creation of an order embracing the individual states. As soon as the freely given approval of all the nations involved has been obtained, the representatives of this order must be given the right to demand of each individual obedience, respect, and, if necessary, the sacrifice of life and property, for the sake of the supreme political authority of the community of nations.

Organization of the Reich

The Reich remains the supreme authority of the German nation. Its political constitution shall be based upon genuine authority and the co-operation and co-responsibility of the nation. It is founded on the natural organization of the people: the family, the parish and the *Land*. The structure of the Reich follows the principles of self-administration. Within it, freedom and personal responsibility combine with the requirements of order and leadership.

This structure shall ensure the unity and coherent leadership of the Reich and its incorporation in the living community of European nations.

The people's political will shall be realized within a framework that remains comprehensible to the individual. Parish and district form the natural bases of the *Länder* which consist of geographical, economic and cultural units. In order to ensure an effective self-administration, the *Länder* shall contain from three to five million inhabitants each.

Functions will be distributed according to the principle that each public body will be responsible for the independent performance of all duties which it can reasonably be expected to execute on its own.

It is the immediate duty of all public authorities to ensure that all measures and pronouncements lead towards the final objective of a constitutional system embodying the rule of Law. Together with the elimination of the chaos and abuses caused by the National-Socialist war and the collapse, which now threaten the very existence of the German people, the constitutional organization of the Reich must be undertaken with all speed and with all the forces that shall become available for this purpose, according to the following principles:

1. *The Parish*

Parish councils will be chosen by the entire electorate by secret and direct ballot.

The right to vote belongs to everyone who has completed his twenty-first year or who has served in the armed forces in wartime; heads of families will have an extra vote for each child below the voting age; everyone is eligible who has completed his twenty-seventh year and whose candidature has been sponsored by a number of enfranchised citizens, the number to be determined according to the size of the parish; members of the armed forces are not eligible.

2. *The District*

District and borough councils will be elected according to the principles outlined for parish councils. This applies also to the ward councils within the boroughs. Constituencies which exceed the comprehensibility of the voter have to be sub-divided.

3. *The* Land

1. The *Land* Diet (*Landtag*) of the *Länder* and the Town Council of the boroughs will be elected by the district and

borough (or ward) councils. Every male citizen of the *Land* or town who shall have completed his twenty-seventh year is eligible. Political officials and members of the armed forces are ineligible. The electoral Law will ensure that at least half of the men elected do not belong to the elective bodies.

The following are the functions of the *Land* Diet: decisions concerning budget, taxation and laws of the *Land*; the right of interpellating the *Land* governor (*Landeshauptmann*) and to pass resolutions concerning all matters of general *Land* policy and administration. The election of the Representative of the *Land* on the proposal of the Land Council (*Landrat*).

3. The *Land* government consists of the *Land* Governor and of the required number of State Councillors. The *Land* Governor is elected by the *Land* Diet on the nomination of the *Land* Commissioner. The State Councillors are appointed by the *Land* Governor on the nomination of the *Land* Commissioner. Members of the *Land* government must permanently reside within the *Land*.

In addition to governing its *Land*, the *Land* government performs the functions of the Reich government within the *Land*.

4. The *Land* Council proposes to the *Land* Diet the names of candidates for election to the post of *Land* Commissioner, makes recommendations to the *Land* Diet and exercises disciplinary jurisdiction over the members of the *Land* government.

5. The *Land* Commissioner will be elected by the *Land* Diet on the nomination of the *Land* Council for a twelve years' term of office. He will be confirmed in office by the Reich Commissioner.

The *Land* Commissioner is responsible for the supervision of the entire *Land* administration and for the appointment of the civil servants. He is responsible for the realization of Reich policy within the *Land*. He presides at meetings of the *Land* Council.

4. *The Reich*

1. The Reichstag will be elected by the *Land* Diets. Every male citizen of the Reich who has completed his twenty-seventh year is eligible. Political officials and members of the armed forces are ineligible. The electoral law will provisionally ensure

that at least half the deputies elected do not belong to an elective body.

The following are the functions of the Reichstag: decisions concerning the budget, taxation and laws of the Reich; the right of interpellating the Reich Chancellor and to pass resolutions concerning all matters of Reich policy; the election of the Reich Commissioner on the nomination of the Reich Council (*Reichsrat*).

2. The Reich government consists of the Reich Chancellor and the departmental ministers. The Reich Chancellor is appointed by the Reich Commissioner with the approval of the Reichstag. The ministers are appointed by the Reich Commissioner on the nomination of the Reich Chancellor.

The Reich Commissioner can dismiss the Reich Chancellor: such dismissal becomes effective on the appointment of a new Reich Chancellor. A qualified majority of the Reichstag has the right to demand the dismissal of the Reich Chancellor if it submits simultaneously to the Reich Commissioner the name of a new Chancellor.

3. The Reich Council consists of the *Land* Commissioners, the Presidents of the Reichstag and the Reich Chamber of Economics, together with a number of Reich councillors appointed by the Reich Commissioner with the approval of the Reich Government for terms of eight years. The Reich Council will propose to the Reichstag candidates for election to the post of Reich Commissioner: will establish the principles according to which officials are moved from one *Land* to another or transferred from the service of a *Land* to that of the Reich: will make recommendations to the Reichstag: and will exercise disciplinary jurisdiction over the Reich government and the *Land* Commissioners.

4. The Reich Commissioner will be elected by the Reichstag on the nomination of the Reich Council for a twelve years' term of office.

The Reich Commissioner is the supreme commander of the armed forces and presides at meetings of the Reich Council. With the counter-signature of the Reich Chancellor he represents the Reich in external affairs. He executes the laws of the Reich, appoints and dismisses Reich ministers and Reich officials.

ECCLESIASTICAL, CULTURAL AND EDUCATIONAL MATTERS
(see also the more detailed Document C)

The Government of the Reich welcomes the determined co-operation of the two great Churches in the work of shaping public life. Public worship, the cure of souls and the educational activities of the two Christian Churches will not be impeded and are placed under the protection of the Reich government. The publication of religious writings is rendered possible once again. In education and literature, as well as in films and radio, the heritage of Christian thought is once more assigned its rightful role.

The legal relationship between the German Reich on the one hand and the German Evangelical and the Roman Catholic Churches on the other will be settled on a friendly understanding with these two Churches, in accordance with the principles outlined above. The Concordats will not be affected thereby.

The future legal position of other religious and philosophical communities will be regulated after previous discussions with these bodies.

Parents have the right to educate their children according to the principles of Christianity and the dictates of their own conscience. It is the duty of the state to help the family in overcoming internal and external dissension and strife. There will be no compulsory state activities on Sundays.

Family, church and school will together perform the work of educating the young. In so doing the school will safeguard the right of each child to receive an education suitable to that child. The school shall awaken and strengthen his moral powers and will equip him with such knowledge and ability as conform with the educational standards of his age.

Character training creates a decent human being who, on a religious basis, is capable of making his rules of conduct consist of honesty and justice, truth and uprightness, love of his neighbour and loyalty towards his own conscience. A man so brought up will possess the maturity needed to make decisions in the consciousness of responsibility. Learning serves the moral build-up of the personality and also acts as a preparation for practical life.

Vocational and high schools, based upon elementary and infant schools, will carry on the work of the elementary schools and give the scholar a well-knit body of knowledge and ability, and incidentally, impart a growing sense of responsibility.

The state school is a Christian school: religious instruction is a compulsory subject for the adherents of the two Churches. Such instruction will be carried out so far as possible by clergymen acting under instruction of their Churches.

ECONOMY

1. All persons engaged in industry have to perform the same minimum duties. These duties include honest and clean leadership as well as loyalty to, and faithful work within the framework of, contractual obligations.

The security of the living standard of the workers, on which depends their dignity as human beings, is the responsibility of the industrial leadership. At the same time every effort is to be made quickly and broadly to raise the minimum standard of living from the present low level engendered by severe war-damage to industry. The necessary steps to achieve this will be taken by the individual, the factory, the autonomous industrial organizations, the German Trade Union and the state: attention will be paid to ensure also the security of the worker's dependents.

2. The government of the Reich regards, as the basis for the reconstruction of industry, a system of orderly competition, carried out within the framework of an industrial direction by the state and, so far as competitive methods go, under the constant supervision of the state.

In cases where existent agreements and organizations (monopolies, cartels, combines) prevent such competition, it is the duty of the industrial leadership to establish the principles of orderly competition and to safeguard the interests of the general public.

Since the big industrial concerns affect industry as a whole, it is desirable that these branches of industry be subjected to a particularly close control by the state. Key enterprises, that is to say the mining, iron and steel industries, the basic chemical industry and the fuel and power industries, will become public property. Nationalized industries will be run and supervised according to the general principles laid down for industry as a whole.

By means of the influence that it can exercise on markets and on the big industries, industrial control by the Reich will be used to forward the industrial policy of the *Länder* and to ensure that economic life is carried on with minimum friction. The government of the Reich will promote the development of each industrial concern into an economic community of the persons engaged therein. In such communities, called 'Working Unions' ('*Betriebsgewerkschaften*') the owner and representatives of the workers will agree on a system according to which all employees will share in the control and the profits of the concern, particularly in its increment value. This agreement will be subject to the approval of the autonomous industrial corporation of the *Land*.

3. The 'German Trade Union' is a necessary means to the carrying out of the industrial programme outlined above and to the political structure implied. It will fulfil its purpose by completing this programme and then by handing over its responsibilities to the organs of the state and to the autonomous industrial corporation. Should the tasks entrusted to the 'German Trade Union' require its continued existence, then its structure will be adapted to those of State and industry.

4. Industrial, commercial and trading firms will be members of the Chamber of Industry set up within the framework of industrial self-administration on a *Land* basis. Agricultural undertakings will be members of the Chambers of Agriculture. The Chambers of Industry and Agriculture will together form the *Land* Chamber of Economics. Chambers of Industry and Agriculture will consist of an equal number of elected managers and representatives of the workers. The *Land* Chamber of Economics will consist of delegates from the Chambers of Industry and Agriculture.

The Chambers will draw up their own statutes. These will be subject to approval by the *Land* Commissioner. The presidents and deputy presidents of the Chambers will be elected by the Chambers subject to confirmation by the *Land* Commissioner.

The Chambers are responsible for the self-administration of industry. Functions concerning matters of the Reich and the

Land may be imposed upon them by the existent industrial *Land* authorities (the *Land* Industrial Office, etc.). Prominent among the functions of these autonomous bodies is the supervision of the vocational training to follow the nine years' schooling; it is to be adapted to the requirements of industry in general and will normally be organized on a two-year basis. Technical and material facilities for further vocational training are to be made available.

The Reich Chamber of Economics, which is the highest authority of the industrial self-administration, will consist of delegates from the *Land* Chambers of Economics. Economic administration forms part of the general political administration. The Reich Ministry of Economics will deal with the autonomous *Land* organizations of the firms and with the firms themselves, only through the *Land* economic authorities.

Document C

Conclusions of Discussions held between May 22nd and 25th, 1942

I. DECLARATION OF PRINCIPLE

1. *Church and State*

We see in Christianity the most valuable force for the religious and moral renewal of the people, for the overcoming of hatred and falsehood, for the rebuilding of the Western world, for the peaceful co-existence of the nations. We welcome and recognize the existing co-operation of leading men, i.e. two bishops each representing one of the two great Christian denominations, to ensure a uniform regulation of all matters concerning the shaping of public life according to Christian tenets.

Freedom of belief and freedom of conscience will be guaranteed, as will the public practice of the Christian religion. All clergy and laymen arrested for their faith unjustly or on trumped-up charges, are to be released and freedom of movement is restored to all. The freedom of action of the Churches' organizations, such as Youth Clubs, Journeymens' Unions and

241

Vocational Associations, will be restored. The publication of religious writings is rendered possible once again. In the world of education and literature, as well as in films and radio, the heritage of Christian thought is once more assigned its rightful rôle. Parents have the natural right to educate their children according to the principles of Christianity and the dictates of their own conscience. The state will also help the family in overcoming internal and external dissension and strife. There will be no compulsory state activities on Sundays.

Autonomy and self-administration are assured to the German Evangelical Church and the Roman Catholic Church. Building on the basis of historical development and of the existing laws, state supervision, both in factual and personal matters, will be developed in accordance with the changed circumstances.

The future legal position of other religious and philosophical communities will be regulated after previous discussions with these bodies.

2. *Education*

Education, which the school has to perform, in co-operation with the family and the Church, determines the future attitude of the individual towards God and his active participation in the living, natural communities of the family, profession and nation, parish, state and Church. The school shall safeguard the right of each child to an education suitable for that child. It shall awaken and strengthen his moral powers. Creative study forms the child's character in preparation for later life. The child shall be equipped with such knowledge and ability as conform with the educational standards of his age.

Character training creates a decent human being who, on a religious basis, is capable of making his rules of conduct consist of honesty and justice, truth and uprightness, love of his neighbour and loyalty towards his own conscience. A man so brought up will possess the maturity needed to make decisions in the consciousness of responsibility. Learning serves the moral build-up of the personality and also acts as a preparation for practical life. Vocational and high schools, based upon the elementary and infant schools, will actively carry on the work of the elementary schools, and give the scholar a well-knit body of knowledge and ability, and, incidentally, impart a growing sense of responsibility.

The state school is a Christian school in which religious instruction according to the two denominations is a compulsory subject. Such teaching will be carried out so far as possible by clergymen, acting under instruction by the Churches.

The present universities will be classified as high schools or Reich universities. The high schools will cater for technical training for such callings as require a complete secondary education and thorough scholarly training. The Reich universities are centres of research and tuition of a universal character. They are the highest repositories of scholarly education and they will give pride of place to intellectually outstanding personalities, as scholars and teachers, who have proved their capability as undergraduates. The educational task of the universities is the scholarly schooling and training of those who will perform public service, and for whom leadership, and with it the highest sense of responsibility, are therefore necessities.

II. GENERAL DIRECTIVES

Universities and High Schools

The Reich universities are centres of universally directed, scholarly work. They utilize the research work done at high schools and ensure its integration with knowledge as a whole. This task belongs to the teaching body of the university. The teaching body must consist of scholars who combine specialist ability with a universal point of view. Specialization decides the form that all scientific work must take; a general picture of the arts and sciences presupposes the co-operative work of the leading men of the arts faculties.

The arts faculties with their basic branches will form part of every Reich university. Exaggerated specialization would destroy internal unity; that belongs to the high schools. In addition to research work the Reich universities will strive for the highest educational standards.

Since the Reich university is the supreme centre of training and instruction in the arts and sciences, properly trained and tested students are essential and the number to be admitted is therefore limited. Before attending a Reich university the student must have obtained the matriculation certificate of a grammar school and must have completed his studies at a high school.

The way of life at a university, which is a community for research, teaching and study, requires, so far as possible, living conditions in which places of work and of residence adjoin. The medium-sized town offers the most favourable conditions for this. The university town should constitute the centre of a region with a living historic tradition of its own.

The constitution of the Reich university is based upon a large measure of autonomy and self-administration. The first vice-chancellor will be appointed by the State. The first university teachers will be appointed by the State on the recommendation of the vice-chancellor. The Reich university will bestow the degree of master as proof of successful attendance. The possession of a master's degree will as a rule be a pre-requisite to appointment to leading positions in the public service which carry the highest responsibility.

The high schools are responsible for scholarly education for those callings which require a complete secondary school training and a thorough scholarly education. The training of theological students is the responsibility of the Churches. The national high schools comprise the following faculties:

Law, economics, medicine, humanities, science, education, agriculture, veterinary science, forestry, technology, mining.

In order to avoid undue specialist narrowness in research and instruction and in order to ensure the integration of the high schools within the living framework of knowledge as a whole, every high school teacher will be required to possess a master's degree.

III. NOTES

1. The question of whether the training of teachers should be carried out in the high schools or in training colleges remains open. The list of faculties within the high schools may therefore require emendation.

2. Certain guiding principles have been agreed upon in the matter of issuing new school books. A uniform new history

book should be made possible. However, present school books must be banned even before the new ones are made available.

3. The representative of the State with whom the two bishops will deal will be the Reich Chancellor. Further administrative work in this field of relations between Church and State is the responsibility of the Minister of the Interior.

4. The creation of a 'German Christian Union' (*Deutsche Christenschaft*) is proposed. To this union all Christians, regardless of their denomination, would belong. It is to ensure that Christian tenets will be taken into consideration in all matters of public concern, even if of only local importance.

This document, literally corresponding with the corrected drafts, is the original copy. All previous drafts and corrections have been destroyed.

Signed: Moltke.

Kreisau, 27 May, 1942.

Document D

PUNISHMENT OF LAW-DEFILERS

A law-defiler, automatically liable for punishment, is any man who has broken the essential principles of divine or natural law or of international law or of positive laws generally accepted within the community of nations, and who has done so in a fashion which makes it clear that he has wantonly disregarded the binding force of such laws.

A law-defiler is also he who has issued an order which will result in the defilement of the law, he who from a position of responsibility has exhorted others to do so, or who has issued lessons or directives of a nature that will cause defilement of the law.

Accomplices, accessories, and inciters will be judged according to the general criminal code.

The fact that the law has been defiled in consequence of an order received will not be accepted as entitling the defiler to avoid punishment, save only in such cases where the accused was threatened with loss of life or where some other pressure was brought to bear which, on close examination, did not make the carrying out of the order an immoral action at the time. In particular the plea of superior orders is no justification when the performer of the action has shown by his behaviour before, during or after the action that he approved of the order received.

In cases of defilement of the law committed before the publication of this law, the legal process will be terminated with a final judgment stating that the accused is convicted of defiling the law.

Any person against whom there are adequate grounds for suspecting defilement of the law may be declared an outlaw by a public decision of the court or the higher administrative authorities. The outlaw can be arrested by any person. He is to be handed over to the police and forthwith brought before a court. All other safeguards concerning provisional arrest and detention are inapplicable to outlaws. The outlawry ends with the conviction or acquittal of the outlaw or with the quashing of the legal process.

Motivation

1. Many offences have been committed under National-Socialist rule. They are by their nature, extent and intention both grave and abominable. Their punishment is an urgent necessity for the sake of re-establishing the rule of law and thus of internal and external peace. The rule of law can be re-established only through the law itself and not through measures undertaken for political purposes or inspired by passion.

The nature of the law itself and political expediency both require that a morally acceptable and dignified solution be found.

2. In order to condemn the crimes unmistakably and clearly, it is purposed to create a specially punishable offence which carries imprisonment and death penalty for the law-breaker who will be tried, however, according to regular criminal procedure.

In order to facilitate the apprehension of the criminals, the possibility is considered of declaring defilers of the law to be outlaws.

In addition to the measures proposed above, material punishments will be considered applicable to persons who shelter the outlaws, help them evade the officers of the law or fail to denounce them.

3. The retroactive nature of the proposed new law applying

to defilers of the law is contrary to the principle *nulla poena sine lege*. The purely procedural provision regarding outlawry will not be affected by this consideration. Since the eighteenth century the principle of *nulla poena* has been inherent in European criminal law. In historic origin it was a defence against the arbitrary power of the absolute state. It derives from no fundamental moral claim, no matter which system of criminal law be examined. The old penal codes without definite codification of punishment (such as the Bamberg criminal code or the C. C. Carolina) did not contain this principle, even as some of the Swiss cantons do not accept it today. It is also to be noted that the set to which the criminals in question belong, deny and have abolished the principle. A return to a firm application of the law and the re-creation of legal security and trust require, however, that the principle of *nulla poena* be observed even in regard to the defilers of the law: therefore the promulgation of retroactive laws becomes unacceptable. It follows that actions performed before the promulgation of the law cannot be punished on the basis of the new decrees. Punishment can thus only be inflicted in cases when the criminal has committed crimes which are punishable under the laws existing at the time of the offence. The principle of *nulla poena*, however, does not prevent a simple pronouncement on the part of the court that the accused has been found guilty of defilement of the law even though such pronouncement refers to events which took place before the promulgation of the new law. This application of the new law as a *lex imperfecta* is a valuable contribution to the re-awakening of legal consciousness and may be considered a partial atonement. Most defilers of the law under the Third Reich have committed such dastardly crimes, in particular as accessories, that the proper punishment for their crimes can also be obtained in this way.

4. In addition to legal punishment, there is the separate question of restitution towards those who have suffered arbitrary and violent damage whether to life and limb, property, honour, and civic rights and also towards those who have been discriminated against (concentration camps, unjust sentences, deprivations of citizenship, confiscations of property, dismissal of officials). Regulations will be published which will facilitate the taking of legal action against defilers of the law in such cases

and which in general will increase the financial responsibility of the law-defilers.

5. The question of the effect that a pronouncement of law defilement will have upon the civic and political rights of the defilers will be dealt with in a special regulation.

Document E

Directive for the Arrangements to Deal with Defilers of the Law through the Community of Nations

Many legal offences have been committed under National-Socialist rule. They are by their nature, extent and intention both grave and abominable. Their punishment is an urgent necessity for the sake of re-establishing the rule of law and thus of internal and external peace. The rule of law can be established only through the law itself and not through measures undertaken for political purposes or inspired by passion.

The German nation has the greatest interest in ensuring that suitable punishment be imposed for violation of the law. This is an absolutely direct interest of the Germans themselves. It cannot however be contested that the community of nations is justified in demanding that punishment be exacted.

The re-creation of peace based on mutual confidence between the nations was impaired after the 1914–18 war by an inadequate attitude towards, and treatment of, 'war criminals'. In Germany at that time serious dissensions were aroused by the subject, dissensions which contributed to the state of affairs that created the new war. However, it cannot be denied that the problem which existed after the World War of 1914–18 was of an entirely different nature from that which exists today. Nevertheless in view of current demands for a supra-national punishment of 'war criminals' guilty of 'systematic atrocities' it is of interest to recall the relevant clauses of the Treaty of Versailles.

Article 227 accused the Kaiser of 'a supreme offence against international morality and the sanctity of treaties' for which he was to be tried before a court of law consisting of five judges belonging to the major victorious powers. Judgment was to be based on the 'loftiest principles of international politics' with the purpose of 'establishing respect for solemn obligations and international treaties as well as for international morality'. The punishment was left to the discretion of the court.

According to Article 228 the Allied Governments might arraign persons—whom the German government was obliged to extradite—before their military courts on charges of 'offences against the laws and customs of war' and inflict upon them 'the punishments provided by law', regardless of any punishment imposed by a German court.

Article 229 established the competence of the military courts of a victorious power to try persons accused of punishable offences against citizens of that power: in the event of the offences being committed against persons belonging to different victorious powers, military courts would be set up consisting of judges drawn from those powers.

So there was no question of trial before courts representing the community of nations, but rather before organs of the victorious powers. In contradistinction to the wrong solution then advocated, which made the co-operation of the German authorities virtually impossible, a solution of moral value must now be attempted, which derives from the nature of justice. Only such a solution can become a corner-stone of, and not a hazard to, peace.

The demand for the surrender of defilers of the law for punishment by the courts of individual victorious powers or of those powers as a whole is a denial of the natural dignity of the statesmen personally responsible for such surrender and of the nation they represent. But the establishment of standards of personal dignity is the prime condition for any happy future concert of nations.

Punishment by a combined court representing the community of nations and the subjection of defilers of the law to the jurisdiction of such a court does not offend justice or dignity. On the contrary such a procedure could contribute, as foundation and touchstone, to the future mutual co-operation of the comity of nations. Only such a court, drawn from all the nations which took part in the war regardless of the side on which they fought, or even from all the nations of the world, would possess the moral and legal authority necessary to pronounce the great weight of moral and legal condemnation which the defilers of the law have earned. A sham sentence, pronounced by courts whose creation does not correspond to true justice, will not have the effect of re-creating the law but rather a quite contrary one.

In historical and practical terms, the proper court for this purpose would be the Hague Court. Various legal and political considerations concerning the advisability of entrusting the task of criminal jurisdiction to the Court have been ventilated from time to time but no basic argument against this can be effective in present circumstances. Non-membership of the League of Nations does not, according to Article 35 of the Statute of the Court, affect the functions of the Court. For the composition of the Court, however, Article 4 would have to be modified. Benches of six judges (three to be drawn from the victorious powers, two from the neutrals and one from the vanquished) in which, according to Article 55, the presiding judge would have the casting vote would seem to meet the case. According to Article 34 of the Statute prosecution would devolve upon the state whose interests have been damaged by the crime. The appointment of counsel for the defence would be the responsibility of the state to which the accused belongs: the appointment of official defending counsel might also be considered. Details of procedure would be laid down by Court regulations. The factual criteria on which the Court would pass sentence should be the same as are outlined above for use in the trial of defilers of the law in the German national courts. The principle of *nulla poena sine lege* must remain binding for the Court, as it has been found binding in international opinion during recent years with regard to actions of the German government. Thus, even as in cases tried before German national courts, the Hague Court could pronounce the criminal guilty of defilement of the law and could punish him in accordance with the applicable laws which were valid in the country to which he belongs at the time when the action was committed. It can be left to the Court to define the applicability of national criminal laws in cases when offences were committed in occupied territories.

As to the number of persons who should be arraigned before the Court, the experience of English justice before 1689 may be of interest. Macaulay, in his *History of England*, Vol. I, Ch. X., p. 312 (London, 1854), defines this as follows:

'The rule by which a prince ought after a rebellion to be guided in selecting rebels for punishment is perfectly obvious. The ringleaders, the men of rank, fortune and education whose power and whose artifices have led the multitude into error, are the proper objects of severity. The deluded population, when once the slaughter on the field of battle is over, can scarcely be treated too leniently.'

The custody of the accused who are to appear before the Court should, by special arrangement, be provided by the Government of the Netherlands.

Responsibility for the carrying out of sentences would be assigned, by the Court, to various states, excluding the State whose interests have been damaged: the Court would retain the rights of supervision and of control.

Should this attempt succeed in banishing legally the obstacles to peace which are a grievous burden to all the parties concerned, a great step will have been taken towards the realization of the rule of law in international relations, and good will have been born of evil. Should, for practical political reasons, a solution be preferred involving courts which are not recognized as legally constituted, then injustice will have been answered with injustice, and might, which must specifically be abolished as the fount of the law, will once again have resumed its position of final arbiter.

APPENDIX II

DOCUMENTS OF THE *PUTSCH* OF JULY 20TH, 1944

I. GENERAL ORDER TO THE ARMED FORCES OF THE STATE

The Führer Adolf Hitler is dead.   [Omitted from later copies
   sent out]

An irresponsible clique of party leaders, strangers to the front,
have tried to exploit this situation and to stab the hard-struggling
army in the back in order to snatch power for their own selfish
ends.   In this hour of supreme danger the Reich Government,
for the sake of preserving law and order, has proclaimed a state
of military emergency and has entrusted to me both the supreme
command of the armed forces and the executive power in the
Reich.

In this capacity I issue these orders:

1.   I transfer the executive power, with the right of delegation,
to the territorial commanders: in the home territory, to the
Commander-in-Chief of the home army, who has been promoted
to Commander-in-Chief of the home front; in occupied territories to the Commanders-in-Chief.   [Listed by appointment, to
a total of nine.]

2.   To the holders of executive power are subordinated:

(*a*) all army officers within their districts and army units,
including the *Waffen-S.S.*, the Reich Labour Service and the
Todt organization;

(*b*) the entire civil service of the Reich, the Provinces and the
Parishes, the whole security and public order police and police
administration;

(*c*) all officials and branches (*Gliederungen*) of the NSDAP
(National Socialist Workers' Party) and associations belonging
to it;

(d) the lines of communication and supply areas.

3. The holders of executive power are responsible for the maintenance of order and public security. They will in particular ensure:

(a) The security of the signals installations;

(b) The elimination of the *Sicherheitsdienst*;

Any resistance to the military executive power is to be relentlessly suppressed.

4. In this hour of great peril to our country, close unity in the armed forces and the maintenance of discipline is the paramount necessity.

I therefore charge all Commanders-in-Chief in the army, the navy, and the air force to give all the support at their disposal to the holders of executive power in the fulfilment of their important duties, and to secure compliance to their orders from all subordinates. To the German soldier a historic task is entrusted. Whether Germany is to be saved will depend upon his energy and morale.

(Signed) The Commander-in-Chief of the *Wehrmacht*
VON WITZLEBEN, Field-Marshal
Count Stauffenberg.

II. General Order to *WEHRKREIS* Commanders

1. In virtue of the authority given me by the Commander-in-Chief of the armed forces, I invest the Commanding General with executive power in all military districts. The functions of the Reich Defence Commissioners are thereby transferred to the Wehrkreis Commanders.

2. The following immediate measures are to be taken:

(a) *Signals Installations*

Occupation of all transport and communication centres; all radio amplifiers and broadcasting stations; all gas-works, power stations and water-works. [Types of installation listed in detail.]

(b) *Arrests*

To be relieved of office forthwith and placed in especially secure solitary confinement: all *Gauleiter, Reichstatthalter,*

Ministers, Provincial Governors, Police Presidents, all senior S.S. and Police Chiefs, Heads of the Gestapo, of the S.S. Administration, and of the Propaganda Bureaus, and all Nazi District Leaders. Exceptions only by my command.

(c) Concentration Camps

The concentration camps are to be seized at once, the camp commanders arrested, the guards disarmed and confined to barracks. The political prisoners are to be instructed that they should, pending their liberation, abstain from demonstration or independent action.

(d) Waffen-S.S.

If compliance by leaders of the *Waffen-S.S.* appears doubtful, or if they appear unsuitable, they are to be taken into protective custody, and replaced by officers of the Army. Units of the *Waffen-S.S.* whose unconditional obedience appears doubtful are to be ruthlessly disarmed. In so doing energetic action with overwhelming force will prevent greater bloodshed.

(e) Police

All offices of the Gestapo and of the *Sicherheitsdienst* will be occupied. In carrying out this order the public order police will to a large extent replace units of the armed forces. The necessary order is being issued by the Chief of the German Police through police channels.

(f) Navy and Air Force

Contact is to be established with senior naval and air commanders. Unity of action will be ensured.

3. To deal with all political questions arising from the state of emergency, I attach a political officer to every military district commander. Until further notice this political officer will take over the duties of chief of administration. He will advise the *Wehrkreis* commander in all political matters.

4. The effective operational command post of the Commander-in-Chief, Home Area Command, is the Home Command Staff. For purpose of mutual information concerning situation

and intents he will despatch to each *Wehrkreis* Commander a liaison officer.

5. The executive power must tolerate no arbitrary or revengeful acts in the exercise of its authority. The people must be made aware of the difference from the wanton methods of their former rulers.

The Commander-in-Chief of the Home Area
(Signed) FROMM, Colonel-General
Count Stauffenberg.

III. Appeal to the Wehrmacht

German soldiers!

More than four years of the most courageous struggle lie behind you. Millions of your comrades have died on the battlefields of Europe and Asia, in the air and at sea.

Hitler's unscrupulous leadership has sacrificed whole armies made up of the flower of our youth in Russia and in the Mediterranean for his fantastic plans of boundless conquest. The wanton use of the Sixth Army at Stalingrad and its senseless sacrifice throw a harsh light on the grim truth. Capable officers who opposed this insane act were removed, the General Staff pushed aside. In spite of your heroism Hitler's self-imagined military genius is driving us to a fatal end.

At home more and more centres of family life and places of work are being destroyed; already six million Germans are homeless. In the rear, corruption and crime, tolerated from the outset and even ordered by Hitler, are assuming unheard of proportions.

In this hour of extreme trouble and danger German men have done their duty before God and the people; they have taken action and given Germany a leadership of experienced and responsible men.

The man who gave a timely warning, who as (Chief of the General Staff) resolutely opposed this war and for that reason was dismissed by Hitler is (Colonel-General Beck). For the present he has taken over the leadership of the German Reich and the Supreme Command of the *Wehrmacht*. The Government is composed of tried men from all classes of the nation, from all parts of our Fatherland. It has begun its work.

I have been entrusted with the command (*Oberbefehl*) of the whole *Wehrmacht*. The Commanders-in-Chief on all fronts have put themselves under my orders. The German *Wehrmacht* now obeys my command.

Soldiers! We must secure a just peace which will make possible for the German people a life of freedom and honour, and for the nations voluntary and fruitful co-operation. I pledge you my word that from now on you will be called upon to make only those sacrifices necessary to achieve this end. All the strength of the nation will now be thrown in only for this task. The senseless squandering of strength, the half measures and tardy decisions which have cost so much human life are at an end.

Wherever you may be, at the front or in the occupied territories, I call upon you to observe the laws of unconditional obedience, soldierly discipline and honourable, chivalrous conduct. Whoever has not observed these laws in the past or offends against them in the future will be severely called to account. At home too we are fighting for right and freedom, for decency and purity.

I expect each one of you to continue to do your duty loyally and bravely. On that depends the fate of our Fatherland, our own and our children's future.

Soldiers! What is at stake is the continued existence and the honour of our Fatherland, a true community within our own people and with the nations of the world.

(This appeal was to be signed by Field-Marshal von Witzleben.)

IV. APPEAL TO THE GERMAN PEOPLE

Germans!

In recent years terrible things have taken place before our very eyes. Against the advice of experts Hitler has ruthlessly sacrificed whole armies for *his* passion for glory, *his* megalomania, *his* blasphemous delusion that he was the chosen and favoured instrument of 'Providence'.

Not called to power by the German people, but becoming the Head of the Government by intrigues of the worst kind, he has spread confusion by his devilish arts and lies and by tremendous extravagance which on the surface seemed to bring prosperity to all, but which in reality plunged the German people into terrible debt. In order to remain in power, he added to this an unbridled reign of terror, destroyed law, outlawed decency, scorned the divine commands of pure humanity and destroyed the happiness of millions of human beings.

His insane disregard for all mankind could not fail to bring our nation to misfortune with deadly certainty; his self-imagined supremacy could not but bring ruin to our brave sons, fathers, husbands and brothers, and his bloody terror against the defenceless could not but bring shame to the German name. He enthroned lawlessness, oppression of conscience, crime and corruption in our Fatherland which had always been proud of its integrity and honesty. Truthfulness and veracity, virtues which even the simplest people think it their duty to inculcate in their children, are punished and persecuted. Thus public activity and private life are threatened by a deadly poison.

This must not be, this cannot go on. The lives and deaths of our men, women and children must no longer be abused for this purpose. We would not be worthy of our fathers, we would be despised by our children if we had not the courage to do everything, I repeat everything, to ward off this danger from ourselves and to achieve self-respect again.

It is for this purpose that, after searching our conscience before God, we have taken over power. Our brave *Wehrmacht* is a pledge of security and order. The police will do their duty.

Each civil servant shall carry out his duties according to his technical knowledge, following only the law and his own conscience. Let each of you help by discipline and confidence. Carry out your daily work with new hope. Help one another! Your tortured souls shall again find peace and comfort.

Far from all hatred we will strive for inward reconciliation and with dignity for outward reconciliation. Our first task will be to cleanse the war from its degeneration and end the devastating destruction of human life, of cultural and economic values behind the fronts. We all know that we are not masters of peace and war. Firmly relying on our incomparable *Wehrmacht* and in confident belief in the tasks assigned to man by God we will sacrifice everything to defend the Fatherland and to restore a lawful solemn state of order, to live once more for honour and peace with respect for the divine commandments, in purity and truth!

Germans!

Hitler's despotism has been broken.

In recent years terrible things have taken place before our very eyes. Not called to power by the German people, but becoming the head of the Government by intrigues of the worst kind, Hitler has confused the minds and souls of the people by his devilish arts and lies and by his tremendous extravagance, which seemed to bring prosperity to all, but which in reality plunged us into debt and want, and has caused fatal disappointment even outside Germany. In order to remain in power, he set up a reign of terror. There was a time when our people could be proud of its honesty and integrity. But Hitler scorned the divine commandments, destroyed the law, outlawed decency and ruined the happiness of millions. He disregarded honour and dignity, and the freedom and lives of other men. Countless Germans, as well as members of other nations, have for years been languishing in concentration camps, submitted to the most terrible torments and often to frightful torture. Many of them have perished. Our good name has been sullied by cruel mass murders. With blood-stained hands Hitler has pursued his madman's course, leaving tears, sorrow and misery in his train.

With deadly certain his lunatic disregard for all human impulses has brought misfortune to our people, and his self-imagined military genius has brought ruin to our brave soldiers.

In this war the intoxication of power, overweening presumption and the delusion of conquest have reached their epitome. The bravery and devotion of our soldiers have been disgracefully abused. The enormous sacrifices of the whole nation have been senselessly wasted. Against the advice of experts Hitler has sacrificed whole armies to his passion for glory, his megalomania, his blasphemous delusion that he was the chosen and favoured instrument of Providence.

We shall openly state the proofs of the terrible betrayal of the German people and of its soul, of the total suppression of law, of the insult to the noble demand that the good of the community shall come before that of the individual, and the shameless corruption. If anyone still doubts these terrible truths because, as a decent human being, he thinks it impossible that such infamy could be cloaked by high-sounding words, the facts will convert him.

This must not go on! We would not be worthy of our fathers, we would be despised by our children if we had not the courage to do everything, I repeat everything, to ward off this frightful danger from ourselves and to regain our self-respect.

Times without number Hitler has broken the oath he made to the people ten years ago by violating divine and human law. Therefore no soldier, no civil servant, in fact no citizen is any longer bound to him by oath.

At this time of grave emergency I have taken action along with men from all classes of the people and from all parts of the Fatherland. For the time being I have taken over the leadership of the German Reich and have ordered the formation of a Government under the leadership of the Reich Chancellor. It has began its work. (Field-Marshal von Witzleben) is in supreme command of the *Wehrmacht* and the commanders-in-chief on all fronts have placed themselves under his orders.

These men have joined with me to prevent collapse.

We come before you at a grave moment. We are constrained by our responsibility to God, to our people and its history, by the costly sacrifices of two world wars, by the ever increasing misery at home and by the suffering of other nations, by anxiety for the future of our young people.

The principles and aims of the Government will be announced. They will be binding until the opportunity arises of allowing the German people to make its own decision on this. Our aim is the true community of the people, founded on respect, willingness to help and social justice. We wish to replace self-idolatry by the fear of God, force and terror by law and freedom, lies and self-interest by truth and purity. We wish to restore our honour and with it our standing in the community of nations. With the best of our strength we wish to help to heal the wounds which this war has caused to all nations, and to restore confidence among them.

The guilty ones, who have brought disgrace to our good name

and have caused so much misery to us and other nations will be punished.

We wish to end the feeling of hopelessness that this war will go on for ever. We are striving for a just peace which will replace the self-laceration and annihilation of nations by peaceful co-operation. Such a peace can only be based on the respect for the freedom and equal rights of all peoples.

I appeal to all decent Germans, men and women of all families and classes and to the youth of Germany. I rely on the joyous co-operation of the Christian Churches.

Have courage and confidence! The task is a very heavy one. I cannot and I will not make you empty promises. By hard work we will have to struggle in order once more to make our way forwards and upwards. But we will go this way in decency as free men and again find peace of conscience.

Let each one of you do his duty! Let each help to save the Fatherland!

(The appeal was to be signed by Colonel-General Beck.)

V. STATEMENT TO THE PRESS

Germans!

Since this morning, you know what is at stake, you know what our motives and intentions are. The law of extreme self-defence and the duty of self-preservation point the way both to you and to us. Our lot has been not the promised state, firmly and wisely led, but a terrible despotism. The bravery, the courage in dying and the skill of our soldiers have been shamefully abused; and our homeland has been unscrupulously exposed to misery and destruction.

As the final link in an unnecessary chain of oppression and violation of the law, Hitler in his *Reichstag* speech of April 24, 1942, pronounced all Germans to be outlaws, for he claimed for himself the right to overturn every legal judgment as he saw fit. Thus he called into being a depth of lawlessness such as was never before known among civilized peoples and which cannot be surpassed. From the proud Germany of equal rights for all he made a powerless community of slaves, in which the citizen has no longer the opportunity to defend himself against injustice.

The holders of the highest honours, even Adolf Hitler himself, have committed, ordered and tolerated countless crimes against the person and against life, against property and honour. Men in high positions have shamelessly enriched themselves from public funds or from money extorted from others, and chief among these is Field-Marshal Göring! We do not wish to see German honour sullied by such parasites. We do not wish to be led by scoundrels who cannot distinguish between mine and thine, who abuse their positions to lead a sumptuous life in magnificent dwellings even in war-time, when the people are suffering, while abroad sons, husbands and sweethearts are fighting and dying and at home the mad destruction of total war rages.

An opportunist foreign policy, thirsting for power, has brought our people to a situation the seriousness of which can no longer be overlooked. Considerations of war prevent us from calling things by their proper names. But you know or feel to what pitch we have been brought by unscrupulousness and madness. As soon as the situation allows, we will call upon good men from all classes and from all districts and we will tell you their names; they will carefully examine everything that has happened and will give you a detailed report on the situation as we found it.

One thing we can tell you now: the structure of the State which was built up on injustice, tyranny, crimes of all kinds, self-interest and lies will be torn down. The corner-stone of the new State will be the sure principles of human life, right and justice, truth, decency, purity, reason, mutual consideration and respect for the nations created by God and for their vital interests.

If we do not want a repetition of November 1918, this is the last moment at which we can put this plan into action. In the next few days we shall publicly call to account, irrespective of their position, those who are responsible for the ruin of the State and the people.

Hard work in all walks of life lies ahead. There is no magic formula for stopping the frivolous destruction of all the basic principles of life which must gradually be restored. Together we want to save the Fatherland and restore the fabric of duty and community. We cannot promise any alleviation in ordinary life during the war and during the period of reconstruction. Think what is at stake! For what do you want to live and die? What are our soldiers to fight and die for? For justice, freedom, honour and decency, or for crime, terror, shame and disgrace? If you answer these questions rightly, there is hope of ending this war, which has developed into a wretched Second World War, in such a way that Germany's vital interests can be preserved.

But this aim is not the only decisive one. The decisive factor for us is that we will no longer tolerate the dishonouring of our people and the sullying of our good name by insolent criminals and liars. For if they carry on their dirty work, then not even our children and our children's children would be able to restore the Fatherland on a healthy basis.

You shall learn of the criminals and the crimes as soon as possible. You yourselves will be in a position to see that terrible things have happened. But we shall also see to it that only just punishment in accordance with the laws is administered. None of you must allow himself to take precipitate action; for above all feelings of vengeance is the necessity to restore the state of equal rights for all under a just leadership.

Anyone who has an accusation to make on account of some wrong suffered, should make it either himself or through someone he trusts to any authority he thinks fit. It will be the duty of all these agencies to pass on accusations made to them to the new Ministry of Justice, which will see to it that they are dealt with immediately. Each will receive an answer. Only those accusations will be dealt with in which the accuser states his name. All others will go unexamined where they belong: into the waste-paper basket. If the complaint is justified, the proper legal proceedings will be taken; but in the same way anyone who makes an accusation against his better knowledge will be held responsible; for we want the honour of our fellow-men and our own moral sense to be taken seriously again.

No one whose conscience is clear need be afraid or worry. The question is not: Party member or not Party member. Away with these distinctions, which have been artificially grafted on to the German way of life! The question is not: S.S., S.A., or any other organization. The question is: decent or corrupt! Each must continue to do his duty where he is, obeying only the laws and decrees of the new administration. The fate of our soldiers who are fighting a hard battle depends on each one at home giving of his best. We owe everything to them and to our beloved dead. They, the soldiers and the wounded, must come before all other cares.

It is understandable that you must feel extremely excited by what has at long last taken place. From now on, as far as considerations of war allow, you are again free to give unhampered expression to your thoughts and feelings and to follow the dictates of your own conscience. You yourselves will be responsible that our beloved Fatherland does not suffer by this, for the state of war still imposes restrictions on all of us. We will ensure that everything proceeds in a legal and orderly manner, as demanded by the well-being of the Fatherland.

The inner cleansing of Germany from corruption and crime, the restoration of law and decency regardless of the person, but at the same time without prejudice to those who hold other views can be achieved very quickly and very easily in accordance with the proud traditions of our people, if each makes his contribution. That we can expect from all right thinking men and women, for their personal happiness depends on the restoration of these benefits. Even those who previously thought they could or ought to deny this, are aware that it is true.

In war-time no one can loosen the fetters of State control of the economy. For the present we can only introduce simplifications and attack dishonesty for which State control has prepared the ground. But as soon as possible we will restore freedom and self-administration in economy and in family life, in the small community and in the State.

The most serious aspect is that of foreign policy. Here we must take account of the interests and wishes of other nations. We do not yet know what will be the attitude of the outside world to us. We have had to act as our conscience told us. But we will tell you the aims we envisage in foreign policy.

We Germans are no more alone in this world than any other nation. We must therefore reconcile ourselves to the best of our ability with the presence, the qualities and the interests of other nations. We are convinced that this reconciliation will not be achieved by force of arms. The more God has allowed us, through the mental gifts which we owe to Him, to make technical developments, the more destructive has war become. It destroys everything which those mental gifts are intended to build up. In the end it consumes itself.

Therefore we desire a peaceful, just settlement of the conflicting interests in the world at present, conflicting interests which are determined not so much by men as by their environment. We are convinced that such a settlement is possible, because, considered calmly, it is in the interests of all nations. It can take place provided the nations respect each other and grant each nation the right to form and administer a State independently. Nations can best advance their physical and spiritual welfare when they work together and thus bring their various forces into a great harmonious whole, which benefits everyone. Such co-operation will lead to trade which will be as untrammelled as possible. With such trade the large and small States have flourished and thriven since the beginning of the nineteenth century. We must restore it as soon as possible. Every thinking person will realize that this restoration cannot take place overnight or without great disturbance. Thinking men of all nations must study how the surest and shortest way can be found which will allow each to attain his vital interests in the best possible way, in so far as he has the firm intention to work hard and to consider the interests of others.

We therefore think it essential to end as quickly as possible further devastation and the further squandering of the national forces of each nation for the work of destruction. Each nation, whether involved in the war or not, will have a multitude of difficulties to overcome to repair the material losses caused by the war.

Such co-operation is possible only if it is built up on a stable system of acknowledged legal principles. Even a simple game cannot be ended without dispute unless each player observes definite rules of the game. How much more impossible is it if nations, living under the most widely differing conditions, will not co-operate in the greatest task of all, namely, the harmonious fusion of all forces. We believe that God wishes this. We therefore regard as the best bulwark to ensure these rules of the game in the life of nations: purity of mind; that moral sense which springs only from religious conviction. We do not forget that these rules need to be formulated and that man's imperfection makes it necessary to entrust them in addition to a protecting power. Recognizing the independence of all States as it has developed in the course of history we are prepared to co-operate in this way in small as well as in big matters.

The quickest possible restoration of an ordered public economy in all countries is essential; for, without this, stable currencies cannot exist and without them the orderly and regular exchange of goods and services is impossible.

We shall not hesitate to transform these necessities into reality. In doing so we must take into account the facts of this terrible war. But we shall see to it that, where foreign territory must still remain occupied, it will be made possible for the countries affected to be self-governing, and the presence of German troops as little of a burden as possible. We know from painful experience how deeply it enters into the soul of every nation to see the soldiers of another power on the sacred soil of their country.

So, not knowing what the attitude of the outside world towards us will be, we must continue the struggle. All of us have bitter experiences behind us. We are men who were accustomed to do our duty even in the most repugnant circumstances. We are men who took over an evil inheritance without complaining about the previous faithless arbiters of our fate. We do not want to lessen our own responsibility or to put ourselves in a better light by putting the blame on others and by slandering them. We wish to return to the language of civilized decency such as was the custom in every self-respecting German family.

We call upon you to practise active self-searching and trust and to be ready to make sacrifices. Do not hate, help rather! Accomplish the highest good: find the soul of our nation again. Thus you will gain strength to achieve more and help even more effectively our brave soldiers on land, at sea and in the air. Let us unite with you, knowing in our hearts that no more German blood will be sacrificed to the thirst for power of an incompetent leadership, but only for the defence of our vital interests.

With God for right and freedom and the security of peaceful work!

(This appeal was to be signed by Goerdeler as Chancellor on behalf of the Reich Government.)

VI. RADIO GOVERNMENTAL STATEMENT No. 2
(3rd Version)

The principles on which the Government will be conducted and the aims which we are pursuing have been announced. We make the following statement on this:

1. The first task is the restoration of the full majesty of the law. The Government itself must be careful to avoid any arbitrary action, it must therefore submit itself to orderly control by the people. During the war this control can only be organized provisionally. For the time being upright and experienced men from all classes and from every *Gau* will be called to form a Reich Council; we will be accountable to this Reich Council and will seek its advice.

There was a time when we were proud of the integrity and honesty of our people, of the security and excellence of German administration of justice. Our grief at seeing it destroyed must be all the greater.

No human society can exist without law, no one, not even those who think they can despise it, can live without it. For each man there comes the moment when he calls upon the law. In His ordering of the universe, in His creation and in His commandments God has given us the need for the law. He gave us insight and power to ensure human institutions within the framework of the law. Therefore the independence, irremovability and security of office of the judges must be restored. We know quite well that many of them acted as they did only under the pressure of extreme terrorization; but apart from that a strict investigation will take place to find out whether judges committed the crime of misapplying the law. Those guilty will be removed. In order to restore public confidence in the administration of the law, laymen will take part in passing sentence in penal cases. This will also apply to the courts-martial which have been established temporarily.

Justice will be restored. It is not the business of the judge to make new laws. His duty is to apply the law and to do so in

266

the most scrupulous manner. The law shall not be a rigid written code, but it must be definite and clear. It was a crime against the people and against the judge to give the latter vague ideas and so-called ideology as a guiding principle. It is intolerable that men should be condemned when they could not know that what they had done was punishable. In cases where the State has by law declared actions of its own bodies to be exempt from punishment, when in fact these actions were punishable, these exemptions will be cancelled as being incompatible with the nature of the law and those responsible will be called to account.

The law will be applied to all those who have offended against it. The punishment deserved will be meted out to the offenders.

Security of person and property will again be protected against arbitrary action. According to the law only the judge can interfere in these personal rights of the individual which are essential for the existence of the State and for the happiness of men and women.

The concentration camps will be abolished as soon as possible, the innocent released and the guilty brought to justice.

But in the same way we do not expect anyone to carry out lynch justice. If we are to restore the majesty of the law we must energetically oppose personal vengeance which, in view of the injustices suffered and the wounding of the souls of men, is only understandable. If anyone has a grudge, let him lodge an accusation with whatever public authority he likes. His accusation will be forwarded to the proper quarter. The guilty will be pitilessly punished. But the accusation must be genuine. False accusations will be punished, anonymous accusations will find their way into the waste-paper basket.

2. We wish to restore the principles of morality in all spheres of private and public life.

Among our people who were once so upright, corruption has been practised by high, and even by the highest, officials of the Nazi Party to an extent never known before. While our soldiers were fighting, bleeding and dying on the battlefields, men like Göring, Goebbels, Ley and company were leading a life of luxury, plundering, filling their cellars and attics, urging the people to endure, and, cowards as they were, avoiding the sacrifice going on around them, both they and their entourage.

All evil-doers will be called to account before the full severity of the law, their ill-gotten gains will be taken from them and restored to those from whom they were stolen. But the chief culprits shall pay with their lives and property. All their property and that which they have assigned to their relatives will be taken from them.

The reserved occupations established for political pretexts are abolished. Every man who is fit to fight can prove his worth and his will to endure at the front. We will tolerate no more fireside heroes.

An essential part of the safeguarding of law and decency is decent treatment of all human beings. The persecution of Jews which has been carried out by the most inhuman, merciless and degrading methods and for which there can be no compensation is to cease forthwith. Anyone who thought that he could enrich himself with the assets of a Jew will learn that it is a disgrace for any German to strive for such ill-gotten possessions. The German people truly wants to have nothing more to do with pillagers and hyenas among the creatures made by God.

We feel it as a deep dishonour to the German name that crimes of all kinds have been committed in the occupied countries behind the backs of the fighting soldiers and abusing their protection. The honour of our dead is thereby sullied. There, too, we will see that restitution is made.

Anyone who has taken advantage of the war in these countries to fill his pockets or has departed from the rules of honour will be severely punished.

One of our noblest tasks is to restore the family as the nucleus of the community. For this we need the influence of the home, the power of religion, the co-operation of the Churches. Pure and healthy family life can only be built upon a serious and responsible conception of marriage. Immorality must be attacked if our children are not to be demoralized; for how can parents expect their children to be pure if they themselves do not exercise self-control and show their children the best example? The life of our nation will only recover when there is once more healthy family life.

We want no split in the nation. We know that many entered the Party out of idealism, out of bitterness against the Versailles dictate and its results and against the many national degradations caused by economic or other pressure. The nation must not be divided in this way. All Germans, who feel and act as Germans, belong together. The only distinction which is to be made is between crime and unscrupulousness on the one hand and decency and integrity on the other. On this basis we will strive with all our might for the inner reconciliation of the people. For only if we remain united on the basis of justice and decency can we survive the fateful struggle into which God has plunged our nation.

3. We declare war on falsehood. The sun of truth shall dispel the thick fog of untruth. Our nation has been most shamelessly deceived about its economic and financial position and about military and political events. The facts will be ascertained and made public, so that everyone can examine them. It is a great mistake to assume that it is permissible for a Government to win over the people for its own purposes by lies. In His order of things God admits no double morality. Even the lies of Governments are short-lived and are always born of cowardice. Successful assertion of the nation's position, the happiness of the people and the tranquillity of the individual can only be based on truth. The truth is often hard; but a people which cannot bear the truth is lost·in any case. The individual can only summon up true strength if he sees things as they are. The climber who underestimates the height of the peak to be scaled, the swimmer who misjudges the distance to be covered, will exhaust his energy too soon. All untrue propaganda shall therefore stop; that applies first and foremost to the Reich Ministry of Propaganda. Then abuse of the propaganda agencies of the *Wehrmacht* must also cease. The living and dying of our soldiers needs no propaganda. It is deeply engraven in the heart of every German wife and mother, in the heart of every German at home.

4. The freedom of mind, conscience and faith which has been destroyed will be restored.

The Churches will again have the right freely to work for their faith. In future they will be completely separated from the State, because only by being independent and by remaining aloof from all political activity can they fulfil their task. The life of the State will be inspired by Christian thinking in word and deed. For we owe to Christianity the rise of the white races, and also the ability to combat the evil impulses within us. No community, whether based on race or on the State, can renounce this combat. But true Christianity also demands tolerance towards those of other faiths or free-thinkers. The State will again give the Churches the opportunity to engage in truly Christian activities, particularly in the sphere of welfare and education.

The Press will again be free. In war-time it must accept the restrictions necessary for a country in any war. Everyone who reads a newspaper shall know who is behind that paper. The Press will not again be allowed to publish lies either deliberately or through carelessness.

By strict jurisdiction the editors will ensure that the rules of decency and of duty towards the welfare of the Fatherland are also observed in the Press.

5. It is, above all, German youth which calls out for truth. If proof of the divine nature of man is needed, here it is. Even the children with their instinctive knowledge of what is true and what is false turn away ashamed and angry from the falseness of the thoughts and words expected of them. It was probably the greatest crime of all to disregard and abuse the sense of truth and with it the idealism of our young people. We will therefore protect it and strengthen it.

Youth and the education of youth is one of our main cares. First and foremost this education will be placed in the hands of the parents and the schools. All schools must implant elementary principles simply, clearly and firmly in the child. Training must again be general, embracing the emotions and the understanding. It must have its roots in the people, and there must be no gulf between the educated and uneducated.

Education must again be placed deliberately on the Christian-religious basis, and the Christian laws of the utmost tolerance towards those of other faiths must not be broken. On this basis the educational and training system must again be conducted calmly and steadfastly, and must be protected against constant changes and disturbances.

6. The administration must be reorganized. Nothing which

has proved its value will be abolished. But it is essential to restore at once clear responsibility and the freedom to make independent decisions. Our once so proud administration has become a collection of machines and smaller machines working to no purpose. No one dares to make an independent and true decision. We will demand just the opposite from the civil servants. They will do right with the greatest simplicity and with little red tape.

The civil servant must again become an example in his whole way of life, official and private; for the people have entrusted him with public sovereign power. This power may only be exercised by those who are upright, who have acquired the technical knowledge, steeled their character and proved their ability. We will put an end to the civil servants who followed the Party rules. The civil servant shall once again obey only the law and his conscience. He must show himself conscious and worthy of the distinction of being assured of a secure livelihood by the community, while others must struggle for the barest necessities. Secure in his authority and in his rights he must proceed in the ideal endeavour to be worthy of his special position by special devotion to duty.

In order to make it possible for the civil servant to carry out his duties in this loyal way, and to spare the people from having public power exercised by unworthy persons, all appointments and promotions made since January 1st, 1933, are declared to be temporary. Every individual civil servant will in the very near future be examined to find out whether he has offended against the law, against discipline or against the behaviour expected of every civil servant. If this is found to be the case the proper measures will be taken, either by punishment, dismissal or transfer. The Civil Service tribunals will co-operate in this. Temporary civil servants, whose performance does not fulfil the demands of their office, will be transferred to positions for which they are fitted, or if this is not possible, they will be dismissed.

Luxury is out of place in Government offices, but there must be comfort in the home of the individual. Heads of departments are instructed to take the necessary measures at once. Superfluous articles of furniture will be handed over to those who have suffered damage by bombing.

7. The arrangement of the administration, the proper distribution and fulfilment of public duties are only possible on the basis of a Constitution. A final Constitution can only be drawn up with the agreement of the people after the end of the war, for the front-line soldiers have the right to have a special say in this. So for the time being we must all content ourselves with a temporary Constitution, which will be announced at once. We too are bound by this.

Prussia will be dissolved. The Prussian provinces, as well as the other German *Länder*, will be amalgamated into new *Reichsgaue*. The *Reichsgaue* will in law again be given a life of its own. To a large extent they will be self-governing. Public duties, so far as this is compatible with the unity of the Reich and the systematic conduct of the Reich, will be handed over to the self-administration of these *Reichsgaue*, *Kreise* and *Gemeinden*.

In all *Reichsgaue* authority will be exercised on behalf of the Reich by *Reichsstatthalter*, who are to be appointed at once. As far as possible they will grant freedom of activity to the organs of self-government, but at the same time will preserve the unity of the Reich. Elected corporations in the self-governing body will guarantee liaison with the people.

8. In war-time economy can only be conducted in the form of State control and of control of prices. As long as there is a shortage of essential goods, a freer economy is, as everyone will realize, impossible, unless we want to ignore cold-bloodedly the vital interests of those with smaller incomes. We know quite well how distasteful this economy is, the abuses it fosters and that it does not, as is so often maintained, serve the true interests of the small consumer. For the time being, we can only simplify it, and free it from obscurities and from the confusion of different authorities and from the lack of a sense of responsibility. We will cancel all measures which have interfered too much with the freedom of the individual and which have destroyed livelihood in trade, handicraft, business, industry and agriculture without due consideration or where this was not absolutely necessary.

Furthermore, economy may not be unnecessarily disturbed by State interference nor may the joy of production or the possibilities of creation be stifled (economic freedom shall only be held in check by law, by the safeguarding of the integrity of competition and by decent intentions). In view of our country's poverty in raw materials and the fact that we cannot grow enough to feed ourselves, autarchy is a cowardly denial of the possibility of participating in the goods and services of the whole world by an exchange of services.

The aim of our conduct of economy is that every worker, every employee and every employer shall have a share in the benefits of our economy. It is not a question of establishing free enterprise for the employer and forcing him to struggle in competition. No, the German worker too must and will have the opportunity to take part in a creative capacity in the responsibility of the economy; only we cannot free him from the effect of the natural laws governing the economy.

Property is the basis of all economic and cultural progress; otherwise man gradually sinks to the level of the animal. It will therefore be protected not only in the hands of the large, but also in the hands of the small, property owner, who can only call his household goods his own. The abuse of property will be combated just as will the accumulation of capital which is unhealthy and only increases men's dependence.

The organization of the economy will be based on self-administration. The system so far employed of administration from above must cease. What must be done is to restore the beneficial functioning of independent decision and thus the responsibility of the individual. As far as possible the confidence of all, including the workers, in the justice of the organization of the economy must be restored.

9. From this arises the essence of State policy directed towards equality—social policy. Those who through no fault of their own have fallen upon evil days or who are weak must be protected and given the opportunity of securing themselves against the accidents of this life. The State must also intervene where the interest in acquiring savings (capital) conflicts with the interests of assuring work for those now living. (Such conflicts of interests can arise in times of great political and economic tension. It would be very foolish to overcome them in such a way that only capital, i.e. savings, was destroyed. It would please the small saver just as little as it would serve the interests of the people as a whole, if, for example, all farms and factories were suddenly

without machinery. On the other hand, all these capital goods have no value unless they can be made to serve men living now.) Thus conscientiously and with a sense of responsibility we must find a just compromise, in which each individual knows from the outset that sacrifices must be made by him as well as by others.

In cases where the powers and responsibility of the individual branches of business and industry are not sufficient to make such compromises, all those citizens engaged in business must co-operate and in the last resort a just compromise, laid on the shoulders of the people as a whole, must be assured by the State. In so far as social institutions affect the worker, they will have the right to full self-administration.

But we must realise that the State does not have inexhaustible means. Even the State can only exist on what its citizens do and give to it. It cannot give to the individual citizens more than it receives from the efforts of its citizens. We therefore clearly and definitely refuse to make promises of economic well-being. Each of us knows that those who have wasted their savings must work specially hard to regain their accustomed standard of life. Thus it is in the family, in every company and also in the State. Any other idea is foolish. Cheap promises that the State can do everything are irresponsible demagogy. You with your resources are the State. We and the organs of the State are only your trustees. Each of you must put his back into his work. It is obvious that after the enormous devastation of this war we must all make special efforts to work hard to create replacements for clothing, for bombed homes and factories and for destroyed household goods. And finally we want to give our children the possibility of a better life. But we are convinced that we are all capable of doing this if we can again work in justice, decency and freedom.

10. The basic condition for a sound economy is the organization of public funds. Expenditure must be kept within the real income which the State, the *Gau* and the *Kreis* and the *Gemeinde* can draw from their citizens. Effort, character, renunciation and struggle will be required to restore this order; but it is the most important and essential basis of an assured currency and of all economic life. The value of all savings depends on it. Without

it, foreign trade, on which we have depended for more than a hundred years, is impossible.

Taxes will be considerable; but we will watch over their careful use all the more strictly. It is more important that the citizen should have the necessities of life than that the administration should provide itself with magnificent establishments and take upon itself duties which are in contradiction to the simple way of life of the individual.

We will also demand the same care from industry, which must again realize that expenditure in the administration only serves the comfort and the needs of the individual but must be borne by all in the shape of higher prices and by workers in the form of lower wages. The cessation of the enormous expenditure of the Party is a beginning of the remedy.

Since 1933 the principle of orderly State economy was forsaken by constant and unscrupulous wasting of funds by increasing debts. It was inconvenient to pretend to the people that the general welfare had been successfully increased by extravagance. This method was in reality contemptible, for it consisted in piling up debts. Therefore even in war-time when each State is forced to spend enormous sums, we will restore the utmost simplicity and economy in all public services. A real levelling out generally can only take place when the war is over.

We regard the mounting debts of all belligerent and neutral States as an extremely great danger. They threaten currency. After this war every State will be faced with an extremely difficult task. We hope to be able to find ways of paying off the debts if we succeed in restoring confidence and co-operation between the nations.

11. But we are still at war. We owe all our work, sacrifice and love to the men who are defending our country at the front. We must give them all the moral and material resources which we can summon. We are with them in rank and file, but now we know that only those sacrifices will be demanded which are necessary for the defence of the Fatherland and the well-being of the people, and not those which served the lust for conquest and the need for prestige of a madman; we know too that we will carry on this war until we obtain a just peace, fighting with clean hands, in decency and with that honour which distinguishes

every brave soldier. We must all give our care to those who have already suffered in this war.

In our anxiety about the front we must reconcile the necessities with clarity and simplicity. There must be an end of the welter of bombastic orders which are incapable of fulfilment and which today demand from industry impossible numbers of tanks, tomorrow aircraft and the next day weapons and equipment. We shall only demand what is necessary and expedient. In contrast to the former despotic tyranny we expect from each who is called upon to carry out an order that he will on his own account point out mistakes and discrepancies.

12. We gave a warning against this war which has brought so much misery to mankind, and therefore we can speak boldly. If national dignity at present prevents us from making bitter accusations, we will call those responsible to account. Necessary as this is, it is more important to strive for an early peace. We know that we alone are not masters of peace or war; in this we depend on other nations. We must stand firm. But at last we will raise the voice of the true Germany.

We are deeply conscious of the fact that the world is faced with one of the most vital decisions which have ever confronted the peoples and their leaders. God himself puts the question to us whether we wish to live in accordance with the order of justice imposed by Him and whether we wish to follow His commandments to respect freedom and human dignity and help each other or not. We know that this order and these commandments have been gravely violated ever since, in 1914, the nations forsook the blessed path of peace. Now we are faced with the question whether we are willing to turn to good use the bitter experiences we have had to undergo and to turn to reconciliation, the just settlement of interests and the healing of the terrible wounds by working together.

In this hour we must tell our people that it is our highest duty bravely and patiently to cleanse the much dishonoured German name. Only we Germans can and will fulfil this task. Our future, no matter what material form it takes, depends on our doing this pitilessly, seriously and honestly. For God is not there to be appealed to as Providence on each petty occasion, but He demands and ensures that His order and His commandments are not violated. It was a fatal mistake, the origins of which can be traced to the unhappy Versailles dictate, to assume that the future can be built up on the misfortune of other nations, on suppression and disregard of human dignity.

None of us wishes to malign the honour of other nations. What we demand for ourselves we must and will grant to all others. We believe that it is in the interests of all peoples that peace should be lasting. For this international confidence in the new Germany is necessary.

Confidence cannot be won by force or by talking. But whatever the future may bring, we hate the cowardly vilification of our opponents, and we are convinced that the leaders of all States want not only the victory for their own peoples but a fruitful end to this struggle, and that they are ready to alleviate at once with us the inhuman hardships, which affect all peoples, caused by this total war which was so thoughtlessly started.

(Here would follow an insertion depending on the situation.)

With this consciousness and relying on the inner strength of our people we shall unwaveringly take those steps which we can take towards peace without harm to our people. We know that the German people wants this.

Let us once again tread the path of justice, decency and mutual respect! In this spirit each of us will do his duty. Let us follow earnestly and in everything we do the commands of God which are engraved on our conscience even when they seem hard to us, let us do everything to heal wounded souls and to alleviate suffering. Only then can we create the basis for a sure future for our people within a family of nations filled with confidence, sound work and peaceful feelings. We owe it to our dead to do this with all our might and with sacred earnestness—those dead whose patriotism and courage in sacrifice have been criminally abused. To how many of you who have realized this did the fulfilment of your duty become the most bitter grief of your conscience? How much beautiful human happiness has been destroyed in the world?

May God grant us the insight and the strength to transform these terrible sacrifices into a blessing for generations.

BIBLIOGRAPHICAL NOTE

A great deal on the subject of July 20th has been published in German, much of it in newspapers and periodicals. For a full bibliography, the reader is referred to Eberhard Zeller's *Geist der Freiheit* (see below).

The following is a selection of those books which have appeared in English, and which in the author's opinion are of interest.

Germany's Underground, by Allen Welsh Dulles. Macmillan, New York, 1947.
> Mr. Dulles was the principal United States secret service agent in Switzerland from 1942 to 1945. His book casts a very clear light on relations between the Western Allies and the conspirators, as seen from his vantage point. However, when describing events within Germany he relies largely on Gisevius, who is not always trustworthy.

To the Bitter End, by Hans Bernd Gisevius. Cape, London, 1948.
> A somewhat disingenuous picture of the German resistance as seen by a man who was in it and is intent on justifying himself. It is not always accurate, and the author's judgments should be treated with caution.

The German General Staff, by Walter Goerlitz. Hollis and Carter, London, 1953.
> A long passage of this history is devoted to July 20th and the events leading up to it, in the context of the German General Staff.

The Von Hassell Diaries, 1938–44. Doubleday, New York, 1947.
> Very valuable first-hand material, describing both the political aspirations of the conspirators and the psychological climate in which they lived.

A German of the Resistance. Oxford University Press, London, 1948.
> The last letters of Count Helmuth von Moltke, together with a

biographical note. A very clear portrait of the leader of the Kreisau Circle.

The German Opposition to Hitler, by Hans Rothfels. Henry Regenry, Hinsdale, Illinois, 1948.
A general treatment of the subject rather than a detailed history.

Revolt Against Hitler, by Fabian von Schlabrendorff. Eyre & Spottiswoode, London, 1948.
The most authoritative first-hand account to be written by a central figure of the German resistance. The events of 1943 are described in great detail.

The Nemesis of Power, by John Wheeler-Bennett. Macmillan, London, 1953.
Some sixty pages are devoted to the events of July 20th, many more to the developments within the army that led up to it. In particular the attempts of the conspirators to establish contact with the Allies are dealt with in considerable detail.

The two most important books so far to have appeared on the subject in German are:

Goerdeler und die deutsche Widerstandsbewegung, by Gerhard Ritter. Deutsche Verlags-Anstalt, 1954.
This scholarly and definitive work examines the subject from the point of view of the political figures involved and therefore complements . . . .

Geist der Freiheit, by Eberhard Zeller. 2nd Edition. Hermann Rinn Verlag, Munich, 1954.
This is undoubtedly the most detailed study so far published of July 20th and its background, as seen primarily from the point of view of the military figures involved, particularly Claus von Stauffenberg.

Other recommended books on the subject—though this is not an exhaustive list—are:

Abshagen, K. H.: *Canaris.* Union Deutsche Verlagsgesellschaft, Stuttgart, 1949.

Budde, Eugen and Lütches, Peter: *Die Wahrheit über den 20. Juli.* Düsseldorf, 1952.

Foerster, Wolfgang: *General-Oberst Ludwig Beck.* Isar Verlag, Munich, 1953.

Halder, Franz: *Hitler als Feldherr*, Münchener Domverlag, Munich, 1950.

Kiesel, Georg: *S.S.-Bericht über den 20. Juli*. 'Nordwestdeutsche Hefte', Vol. 2, No. 2, February, 1947.

Kraus, Herbert: *Der Remerprozess*. Girardet, Hamburg, 1953.

Krause, Friedrich: *Carl Goerdelers Politisches Testament*, New York, 1945.

Leber, Annedore: *Das Gewissen steht auf*, Mosaik Verlag, Berlin, 1954.

Leber, Julius: *Ein Mann geht seinen Weg*, Mosaik Verlag, Berlin, 1952.

Lonsdale Bryans, J.: *Blind Victory*, Skeffington & Son, London, 1951.

Das Parlament, Bonn, Special numbers of July 20th, 1952, and of January 19th and 26th, 1955.

Pechel, Rudolf: *Deutscher Widerstand*. Rentsch Verlag, Zurich, 1947.

Poelchau, Harald: *Die Letzten Stunden*. Verlag Volk und Welt, Berlin, 1949.

Schramm, Wilhelm von: *Der 20. Juli in Paris*. Kindler und Schiermeyer Verlag, Bad Wörishofen, 1953.

Speidel, Hans: *Invasion 1944*. Wunderlich Verlag, Tübingen, 1949.

Steltzer, Theodor: *Von Deutscher Politik*. Frankfurt am Main, 1949.

Weisenborn, Gunter: *Der lautlose Aufstand*. Rowohlt Verlag, Hamburg, 1954.

ACKNOWLEDGEMENTS

The author and publishers wish to acknowledge their debt to the following:

Lionel Curtis and the Oxford University Press for permission to quote from *A German of the Resistance* by Count von Moltke.

Macmillan & Co. Ltd., and J. W. Wheeler-Bennett for permission to quote from his *Nemesis of Power*, his translation of documents III–VI in Appendix II.

Jonathan Cape Ltd., and Hans Bernd Gisevius for permission to quote from his *To the Bitter End*.

Allen W. Dulles, for permission to quote from his *Germany's Underground*.

Hollis & Carter Ltd., for permission to quote from *The German General Staff* by Walter Goerlitz.

Eyre & Spottiswoode (Publishers) Ltd., for permission to quote from *Officers Against Hitler* by Fabian von Schlabrendorff.

Michael Joseph Ltd., for permission to quote from *Panzer Leader* by Heinz Guderian.

Professor Gerhard Ritter for permission to quote from his *Goerdeler und die deutsche Widerstandsbewegung*.

Dr. Rudolf Pechel for permission to quote from his *Deutscher Widerstand*.

Verlag Hermann Rinn and Dr. Eberhard Zeller for permission to quote from his *Geist der Freiheit—Der Zwanzigste Juli 1944*.

Isar Verlag and Wolfgang Foerster for permission to quote from his *General-Oberst Ludwig Beck*.

Verlag Josef Knecht and Dr. Theodor Steltzer for permission to quote from his *Von Deutscher Politik*.

Christ und Welt Verlag for permission to quote from Dr. Gerstenmaier's article in their issue of July 20th, 1950.

Frau Leber for permission to quote from *Ein Mann geht seinen Weg* by Julius Leber.

The author would also like to express his gratitude to the following persons who have kindly read part or all of this book, and who have helped him with their advice: Mr. Eric Birley, Herr Herwarth von Bittenfeld, Mr. Lionel Curtis, Mr. Hans Jaeger, Frau Leber, Countess Lehndorff, Captain B. H. Liddell Hart, Dr. Fabian Freiherr von Schlabrendorff and Countess Stauffenberg: to Mr. Nigel Dennis, who read the proofs: and finally to Mrs. Wolff and the assistant librarians of the Wiener Library whose help has been invaluable.

INDEX